HUMANITY AT

This interdisciplinary study engages law, history, and political theory in a first attempt to crystallize the lessons the global "refugee crisis" can teach us about the nature of international law. It connects the dots between the actions of Jewish migrants to Palestine after World War II, Vietnamese "boat people," Haitian refugees seeking to reach Florida, Middle Eastern migrants and refugees bound for Australia, and Syrian refugees currently crossing the Mediterranean, and then legal responses by states and international organizations to these movements. Through its account of maritime migration, the book proposes a theory of human rights modeled around an encounter between individuals in which one of the parties is at great risk. It weaves together primary sources, insights from the work of twentieth-century thinkers such as Hannah Arendt and Emmanuel Levinas, and other legal materials to form a rich account of an issue of increasing global concern.

ITAMAR MANN is a member of the Faculty of Law at the University of Haifa, Israel. Before moving to Haifa, he was a research fellow at Georgetown University Law Center, and completed his dissertation at Yale Law School. He has published in the areas of human rights, refugee and migration law, political theory, and international criminal law. In 2009–2010, he held a Bernstein Fellowship during which he reported for Human Rights Watch from Greece and Turkey.

CAMBRIDGE STUDIES IN INTERNATIONAL AND COMPARATIVE LAW

Established in 1946, this series produces high-quality, reflective, and innovative scholarship in the field of public international law. It publishes works on international law that are of a theoretical, historical, cross-disciplinary, or doctrinal nature. The series also welcomes books providing insights into private international law, comparative law, and transnational studies which inform international legal thought and practice more generally.

The series seeks to publish views from diverse legal traditions and perspectives, and of any geographical origin. In this respect it invites studies offering regional perspectives on core problématiques of international law, and in the same vein, it appreciates contrasts and debates between diverging approaches. Accordingly, books offering new or less orthodox perspectives are very much welcome. Works of a generalist character are greatly valued and the series is also open to studies on specific areas, institutions, or problems. Translations of the most outstanding works published in other languages are also considered.

After 70 years, *Cambridge Studies in International and Comparative Law* remains the standard-setter for international legal scholarship and will continue to define the discipline as it evolves in the years to come.

General Editors

Larissa van den Herik
Professor of Public International Law, Law School Leiden University

Jean D'Aspremont
Professor of Public International Law, Manchester International Law Centre, University of Manchester

A list of books in the series can be found at the end of this volume.

HUMANITY AT SEA

Maritime Migration and the Foundations of International Law

ITAMAR MANN

University of Haifa Faculty of Law, Israel

CAMBRIDGE
UNIVERSITY PRESS

CAMBRIDGE
UNIVERSITY PRESS

University Printing House, Cambridge CB2 8BS, United Kingdom

One Liberty Plaza, 20th Floor, New York, NY 10006, USA

477 Williamstown Road, Port Melbourne, VIC 3207, Australia

4843/24, 2nd Floor, Ansari Road, Daryaganj, Delhi - 110002, India

79 Anson Road, #06-04/06, Singapore 079906

Cambridge University Press is part of the University of Cambridge.

It furthers the University's mission by disseminating knowledge in the pursuit of education, learning and research at the highest international levels of excellence.

www.cambridge.org
Information on this title: www.cambridge.org/9781316602652

First published 2016
First paperback edition 2017

A catalogue record for this publication is available from the British Library

Library of Congress Cataloging in Publication data
Mann, Itamar, author.
Humanity at sea : maritime migration and the foundations of international law / Itamar Mann, Georgetown University School of Law.
New York NY : Cambridge University Press, 2016. | Series: Cambridge studies in international and comparative law | Includes bibliographical references and index.
LCCN 2016026283 (print) | LCCN 2016026603 (ebook) | ISBN 9781107148765
LCSH: Refugees – Legal status, laws, etc. | Boat people – Legal status, laws, etc. | International law and human rights.
LCC KZ6530 .M326 2016 (print) | LCC KZ6530 (ebook) | DDC 341.4/86–dc23
LC record available at https://lccn.loc.gov/2016026283

ISBN 978-1-107-14876-5 Hardback
ISBN 978-1-316-60265-2 Paperback

In loving memory of my grandfather, Kurt Kanowitz

[...] it is easier for the world to express concern and outrage for the unknown refugee who drowns, or otherwise perishes, for he makes no demand on any nation. It is far more difficult to be reconciled to resolving the problems of those who live.

– *Kurt Waldheim, United Nations Secretary General (1979)*

CONTENTS

FIGURES

ACKNOWLEDGMENTS

At Tel Aviv University I studied under Adi Ophir, whose moral and political thought left an enduring mark on my own ideas. A number of fantastic law professors, most importantly Aeyal Gross, Leora Bilsky, and Shai Lavi, introduced me to the history and theory of international law. Anat Ben-Dor, Tally Kritzman-Amir, and Ora Bloom at the law school's Refugee Rights Clinic helped spark my interest in refugee law.

Soon afterwards, with two friends, we started an organization that provided pro bono representation to refugees. We named the organization after "We Refugees," an essay by Hannah Arendt that also features in this book. Omer Shatz and Iftach Cohen, who led that project, remain an inspiration. Ahmad Musa and a number of other members of the Sudanese community in Tel Aviv shared with me their experiences of what it means to be a refugee.

Paul Kahn, my advisor at Yale Law School, has been the single most important influence on my work. The many hours we spent talking in his office taught me how to think about law philosophically and historically. This book is a reflection of some of Paul's own profound insights and methodological commitments, and is also an attempt to argue with some of his positions. Owen Fiss has also been a mentor over the course of my studies. I am humbled by the opportunity to be in ongoing conversation with both of them.

I am grateful to several others at Yale who have shaped my thinking. Seyla Benhabib has been helpful far beyond what I could expect or hope for, particularly in terms of revisions to the work. Patrick Weil provided invaluable advice and guidance, alongside emotional support and friendship. James Whitman read the dissertation and provided insightful comments. David Singh Grewal assisted me immensely in my research at the early stages. Jim Silk offered helpful comments on several occasions, and allowed me to present my work at the Schell Center's Human Rights Workshop and at a workshop he conducted with Michael

Reisman. Anthony Kronman helped more than he knows with a few razor-sharp insights and suggestions.

Samuel Moyn, who I also initially met at Yale, read multiple early drafts and has provided copious intellectual support of various kinds. Perhaps most importantly, he responded to my presentation at the Modern Jewish Worlds Workshop at Harvard University, organized by Adam Stern and my dear friend Ofer Dynes. Sam's often biting and always incisive critique was a kind gift that encouraged me to sharpen my arguments. Guy Goodwin-Gill and Hagar Kotef gave me a number of invaluable comments briefly before publication.

I'm thankful for the Robert L. Bernstein International Human Rights Fellowship, which allowed me in 2010–2011 to work with Human Rights Watch and the Open Society Justice Initiative on a project concerning refugee rights in Europe. During this period I worked closely with Bill Frelick, Rupert Skilbeck, Yiota Massouridou, and Simone Troller. Yiota's commitment to the rights of asylum seekers in Greece was particularly powerful to behold. I will always feel indebted to the many resilient refugees and migrants who agreed to speak with us.

Thanks to Tendayi Achiume and Jeffrey Kahn for co-organizing "The Globalization of High Seas Interdiction" with me. Harold Koh, a protagonist of Chapter 3, deserves particular thanks for his support of this conference. I'm thankful to Thomas Gammeltoft-Hansen not only for joining us but also for remaining a supporter of my work.

I'd like to thank the Institute for Global Law and Policy (IGLP) for fantastic opportunities to present my work. Heidi Matthews convened a workshop in which Ioannis Kalpouzos responded to my work. They both became two of my most cherished academic and intellectual fellow travelers. Andrew Lang also provided fantastic feedback. A workshop Rose Sydney Parfitt convened gave me an opportunity to hear responses by Manuel Iturralde and Ernesto Mieles.

Gearóid Ó Cuinn, who I also met at the 2014 IGLP Workshop, is a central presence in my closest group of colleagues. Through his work as Director of the Global Legal Action Network (GLAN), he is currently helping me put together an advocacy agenda that stems to some extent from my work on this book.

Naor Ben-Yehoyda supported me tremendously over many years. Apart from reading and discussing drafts, Naor helped putting together the John Harvard Colloquium at Cambridge University's Centre for Research in the Arts, Social Sciences and Humanities (CRASSH). I'm grateful for Simon Goldhill's lead of our conversations there, and for

Mezna Qato's thoughtful and critical response to a short paper that came out of my ideas in Chapter 2.

I've benefitted from conversations with Jaya Ramji-Nogales and Peter Spiro, who recently founded an interest group on International Migration Law at the American Society of International Law. Among the people affiliated with that group, I have an especially big debt to Moria Paz. No one has shown a quicker, deeper, and more sympathetic reaction to what I have to say in this book.

I'd like to thank the Max Planck Institute for the Study of Religious and Ethnic Diversity, which hosted a workshop, and especially my kind host Ayelet Shachar.

Ariella Azoulay co-organized a conference at Brown University – "What is a Refugee Crisis?" – that was enormously beneficial. At the conference I met Charles Heller and Lorenzo Pezzani, who have proven to be critical interlocutors, as one would expect based on their important work.

At the Center on National Security and the Law at Georgetown Law Center, I would like to thank Laura Donohue and Nadia Asanchayev for making this supportive environment possible. I also benefitted greatly from conversations with David Luban and David Koplow. During my time at Georgetown, Robin West and Greg Klass were especially helpful, as were Rabia Belt, Allegra McLeod, Sherally Munshi, and Julia Tomassetti.

Carmi Lecker offered research advice throughout my work.

Thanks also to the team at Cambridge University Press for their efficient and precise work on the book.

Many thanks to my friends who helped by reading or talking about the work, including Dov Alfon, Tomer Barak, Omri Boehm, Kiel Brennan-Marquez, Tom Dannenbaum, Ido Gideon, Florian Grisel, Kevin Jon Heller, Tatsushiko Inantani, Hassan Jabareen, Yoav Kenny, Zvika Lachman, Lilach Lachman, Nitzan Lebovic, Lital Levin, Darryl Li, Paul Linden-Retek, Claudia Medina-Aguilar, Liron Mor, Dina Omar, Mehrdad Payandeh, Kalyani Ramnath, Yaman Salahi, Diala Shamas, Pioter Shmugliakov, Assaf Tamari, Isaias Tesfalidet, and Reuven Ziegler.

Oded Na'aman and Dan-Avi Landau helped shape my arguments during special time we spent together in Cambridge, Massachusetts.

My family, Daniel, Eytan, Gabriella, and Kenneth Mann, have each had a distinct mark on what I wrote. I clearly identify each of you in specific parts of this book, and will tell you more about that when we meet. Above all

I'm thankful for your love. I'm grateful to Dalia and Moti Shmu'ely for always standing beside us. Shira Shmu'ely is my most critical and valued of readers. Nitai Mann-Shmu'ely slept on me during much of the early writing. He's now becoming quite a big boy, and is the joy of my life.

Washington DC, May 2016

~

Introduction

Humanity Washed Ashore

Unauthorized migration has become one of the most visible and contentious political issues everywhere. As the catastrophe in Syria unfolds, the more ordinary atrocity of abject poverty continues to uproot populations.[1] Perhaps the most alarming images related to this phenomenon are those of unauthorized migrants crossing the sea in insecure vessels. For years newspapers have been publishing photos of migrants' boats from locations as far from each other as the Canaries and Indonesia. These rickety vessels are overloaded with men, women, and children, drifting upon vast expanses of water. The spectacle has reached a new extreme in two areas of the Mediterranean – the Aegean Sea and the Waterway between Sicily and North Africa. Sunbathers confront exhausted survivors pulling themselves out of the water.[2] Fishermen fear they might lift dead bodies with every fresh net pulled aboard.[3] The most iconic of these images is the widely circulated photograph of a Syrian toddler lying face down on the beach in the Turkish resort town of Budrum. This macabre shot immediately went viral and within hours the hashtag #KiyiyaVuranInsanlik – "humanity washed ashore" – became the top trending topic on Twitter. A few days later, the image of the boy – his name became a matter of some dispute – was cast as a

---

[1] Alice Su, "How Do You Rank Refugees," *The Atlantic*, November 22, 2013, available at www.theatlantic.com/international/archive/2013/11/how-do-you-rank-refugees/281771/ (last accessed January 5, 2016) (discussing the difficulties East African migrants and refugees are facing in Jordan, with the country facing an enormous influx of Syrian nationals fleeing the civil war).

[2] Jonathan Samuels, "Emotional Scenes As Sunbathers Help Refugees," *Sky News*, available at http://news.sky.com/story/1549651/emotional-scenes-as-sunbathers-help-refugees (last accessed January 5, 2016).

[3] Nick Squires, "Mediterranean Migrant Tragedy: Fishermen and Naval Officers Describe Horror and Despair," available at www.telegraph.co.uk/news/worldnews/europe/italy/11549236/Mediterranean-migrant-tragedy-fishermen-and-naval-officers-describe-horror-and-despair.html (last accessed January 5, 2016).

symbol of our times.[4] This book aims to give an answer to one question: What can the phenomenon these images capture tell us about the nature of legality?

It will come as no surprise that the contemporary migration crisis and its maritime aspects are a matter of some significance to legal theory, particularly international legal theory. As Hilary Charlesworth wryly observed, "International lawyers revel in a good crisis." Crisis becomes a focal point particularly in a genre of international law characterized by a desire for "a counterweight to the formalism of the study of rules."[5] Indeed, it has been suggested that for the international lawyer crisis plays the role precedents play in the case method.[6] As a so-called discipline of crisis, international law has often been exposed to a number of recurring pitfalls that seem to come with this fraught territory. These might be characterized as a certain penchant for drama.[7] Yet critical engagement with an ongoing crisis that has for too long fallen below the radar of

[4] Before the end of the day, this article appeared: Ishaan Tharoor, "A Dead Baby Becomes the Most Tragic Symbol Yet of the Mediterranean Refugee Crisis," *The Washington Post*, September 2, 2015, available at www.washingtonpost.com/news/worldviews/wp/2015/09/02/a-dead-baby-becomes-the-most-tragic-symbol-yet-of-the-mediterranean-refugee-crisis/ (last accessed September 22, 2015). On the dispute over the boy's name, see "What's in the Name of a Dead Syrian Child?" *Al Jazeera America*, available at http://america.aljazeera.com/opinions/2015/9/whats-in-the-name-of-a-dead-syrian-child.html (last accessed February 5, 2016).

[5] Hilary Charlesworth, "International Law: A Discipline of Crisis," *The Modern Law Review* 65 (2002): 377. See also Josef L. Kunz, "Natural-Law Thinking in the Modern Science of International Law," *The American Journal of International Law* 55, no. 4 (1961): 954 (observing that "periods of profound crisis foster a flight into natural law as ideas and values on which man can rely, as a barrier against the misuse of law").

[6] This was Michael Reisman and Andrew Willard's proposal, which Charlesworth rejects. Michael Reisman and Andrew Willard (eds.), *International Incidents: The Law That Counts in World Politics* (Princeton: Princeton University Press, 1988), 15. See also Martti Koskenniemi's foreword to Fleur Johns, Richard Joyce, and Sundhya Pahuja, *Events: The Force of International Law* (Oxfordshire: Routledge, 2011), xviii (recalling his work at Finland's Foreign Office: "for the political decision makers, every situation is always new, unprecedented, and very often . . . a crisis. It then became the legal advisers task to calm down that decision-maker by explaining that . . . far from being singular or unprecedented . . . the situation . . . was in fact a recurrent pattern and could therefore be treated in the same way 'we' had done with those previous cases").

[7] See Martti Koskenniemi, "International Law in Europe: Between Tradition and Renewal," *European Journal of International Law* 16, no. 1 (2005): 113–124 (on international law and kitsch); Karen Knop and Susan Marks, "The War against Cliché: Dispatches from the International Legal Front," in Christine Chinkin and Freya Baetens (eds.), *Sovereignty, Statehood and State Responsibiilty: Essays in Honour of James Crawford* (Cambridge: Cambridge University Press, 2015), 3–22; Gerry Simpson, "The Sentimental Life of International Law," *London Review of International Law* 1 (2014): 1–27.

international attention can be revealing.[8] Events of momentous historical importance are unfolding.[9] In confronting these events, I will argue, the formalism of rules, indeed, does not give us sufficient guidance.

The question what are the appropriate policy responses to the migration crisis has become an obsession of sorts, not only in Europe, but also in other parts of the so-called developed world. The many calls for action are as contradictory as they are dramatic. Juxtapose, for example, two statements by two very different politicians in Europe. Jean-Claude Juncker, president of the European Commission, proclaimed in a resounding speech: "Europe is the baker in Kos who gives away his bread to hungry and weary souls." He referred to the seventy-six-year-old Dionysis Arvanitakis – an unlikely celebrity who had become famous for distributing his oven's bread among the island's newcomers.[10] In contrast, Laszlo Toroczkai, a Hungarian mayor of the far right, characterized Brussels' ostensible message of welcome: "If one jumps from the 20th floor, one could view this as an expression of freedom from a liberal point of view, while in fact it looks more like suicide."[11]

These, of course, are expressions of political sentiment rather than pronouncements of law. But the legal terrain is just as rich with contradiction. The European Court of Human Rights (ECtHR), an often-lauded human rights tribunal, has in its jurisprudence on unauthorized migration developed some of its most fundamental tenets of human rights law. In celebrated decisions it has meted out judgments recognizing the prohibition on inhuman and degrading treatment, the right to asylum, the prohibition on collective expulsion,

---

[8] Of course, not entirely; indeed the "crisis" has invoked for quite a long time. See, e.g., Deborah Anker and Michael L. Posner, "The Forty Year Crisis: A Legislative History of the Refugee Act of 1980," *San Diego Law Review* 19 (1981–1982): 9–90; Gil Loescher, *Beyond Charity: International Cooperation and the Global Refugee Crisis* (Oxford: Oxford University Press, 1996); Aristide R. Zolberg, Astri Suhrke, and Sergio Aguayo, *Escape from Violence: Conflict and the Refugee Crisis in the Developing World* (Oxford: Oxford University Press, 1992), 37–39.

[9] Johns, Joyce, and Pahuja, *Events*, 1 (noting that "international lawyers listen, above all, for the screech accompanying an event").

[10] European Commission, Press release, "State of the Union 2015: Time for Honesty, Unity and Solidarity," available at http://europa.eu/rapid/press-release_SPEECH-15-5614_en .htm (last accessed February 5, 2016). I will spend some time interpreting this image below, in Chapter 6.

[11] Dan McLaughlin, "'Borderless' Europe in Peril Amid Refugee Crisis," *Al Jazeera America*, available at http://america.aljazeera.com/articles/2015/9/19/borderless-europe-in-peril-as-hungarys-fence-brings-calm-and-chaos.html (last accessed January 5, 2016).

and the right to effective remedy.[12] In the context of maritime migration in particular, it expounded its doctrine of extraterritorial personal jurisdiction. The latter is central to contemporary understandings of human rights law.[13] Yet it would be misleading to focus on these decisions without putting them in the context of legal instruments formulated by executive agencies to *prevent* migrants and refugees from seeking human rights remedies.[14] Good examples are bilateral and multilateral agreements that outsource border-enforcement activities to developing countries.[15] Developed countries have sought to frustrate the access of refugees to asylum before these people enter their jurisdiction, while seemingly following the letter of the law.[16] They have harnessed international law in efforts to exclude people from human rights remedies.[17]

The policies of the various actors participating in the transnational management of migration may seem like different moving parts of one system. But their rationales and their consequences do not fit together comfortably. Many affluent states, in Europe and around the world, make public legal commitments to protecting the world's most vulnerable populations. At the same time they seek to prevent such protections from stimulating demand for access and employ various measures designed to "deter" unauthorized migration. The latter is a polite term for the idea that some migrants must suffer to prevent other migrants

---

[12] See, e.g., *Khlaifia and others v. Italy*, Application no. 16483/12; *Hirsi Jamaa and Others v. Italy*, Application no. 27765/09; *M.S.S. v. Belgium and Greece*, Application no. 30696/09.

[13] *Hirsi*; See generally, Marko Milanovic, *Extraterritorial Application of Human Rights Treaties* (Oxford: Oxford University Press, 2011); Cedric Ryngaert, *Jurisdiction in International Law* (Oxford: Oxford University Press, 2015), 22–27.

[14] For a good compilation of the particular role of the executive branch, see Thomas Gammeltoft-Hansen and Jens Vedsted-Hansen (eds.), *Transnational Law Enforcement and Human Rights: The Dark Side of Globalisation* (London: Routledge, forthcoming).

[15] See, e.g., James Hathaway, "The False Panacea of Offshore Deterrence," *Forced Migration Review* 26 (2006): 56–57; Thomas Gammeltoft-Hansen, *Access to Asylum: International Refugee Law and the Globalisation of Migration Control* (Cambridge: Cambridge University Press, 2013), 63.

[16] James Hathaway and Thomas Gammeltoft-Hansen, "Non-Refoulement in a World of Cooperative Deterrence," *Columbia Journal of Transnational Law* 53 (2015): 235–284 (arguing against this tendency).

[17] I have argued elsewhere that positive human rights law and particularly human rights tribunals have at times played a role in this process. Itamar Mann, "Dialectic of Transnationalism: Unauthorized Migration and Human Rights, 1993–2013," *Harvard International Law Journal* 54, no. 2 (2013): 315–391.

from seeking remedies.[18] Moreover, their executive, judicial, and legislative bodies speak in different technical vocabularies and often express different normative commitments. The international legal environment of "migration management" is thus fragmented and confusing (even in comparison with other subfields of international law).[19] James Hathaway and Thomas Gammeltoft-Hansen have gone so far as saying that the prevailing attitude is "schizophrenic."[20] "Human rights law" is rhetorically invoked, but there is no "basic norm" that is agreed upon or otherwise available.[21] It is thus hard to escape the conclusion that underlying this universe of law and policy there are enormous unresolved tensions (and, as explained in this book, an existential embarrassment).[22] Everyone understands that migrants clamoring on the doorsteps of one's country demand a legal response. It is even clear enough that migrants deliver a basic message about the very *nature* of international law.[23] But what is that message?

---

[18] A textbook violation of the Kantian categorical imperative to "Act in such a way that you treat humanity, whether in your own person or in the person of any other, never merely as a means to an end, but always at the same time as an end." The imperative has enjoyed some recognition within extant understandings of human rights law, in the context of the principle of human dignity. See Jürgen Habermas, "The Concept of Human Dignity and the Realistic Utopia of Human Rights," in Claudio Corradetti (ed.), *Philosophical Dimensions of Human Rights: Some Contemporary Views* (Dordrecht, Heidelberg, NY: Springer, 2012), 63–79.

[19] This is of course not true only about migration and is a much commented feature of international law more generally. See *Fragmentation of International Law: Difficulties Arising from the Diversification and Expansion of International Law*, Report of the Study Group of the International Law Commission, Finalized by Martti Koskeniemmi A/CN.4/L.682 (2006); Vincent Chetail, "Sources of International Migration Law," in Brian Opeskin, Richard Perruchoud, and Jillyanne Redpath-Cross (eds.), *Foundations of International Migration Law* (Cambridge: Campridge University Press, 2012).

[20] Hathaway and Gammeltoft-Hansen, "Non-Refoulement in a World of Cooperative Deterrence."

[21] The idea that all of international law ultimately leans on one basic norm ("*grundnorm*") was advanced by German jurist Hans Kelsen in the 1930s and became central to discussions in international law ever since. For an excellent study of Kelsen's work, see Mónica Garcia-Salmones Rovira, *The Project of Positivism in International Law* (Oxford: Oxford University Press, 2013).

[22] Compare with Samuel Moyn, "The Embarrassment of Human Rights," *Texas Journal of International Law: The Forum* 50, no. 1 (2015): 1–7 (criticizing my position).

[23] For an alternative conceptualization of the significance of this crisis to the basic understanding of international law, see Jaya Ramji-Nogales, "Migration Emergencies," *draft on file with the author*; Jaya Ramji-Nogales, "Undocumented Migrants and the Failures of Universal Individualism," *Vanderbilt Journal of Transnational Law* 477 (2014): 699–763. For a good analysis of the significance of unauthorized migration for a critique of human rights, see Moria Paz, "Between the Kingdom and the Desert Sun: Human Rights,

The current global migration and refugee crisis, we are told time and time again, is "a global exodus unlike any in modern times."[24] Yet viewing it as historically exceptional serves to conceal rather than to expose the most important lessons this crisis can teach.[25] This book will look to the history of unauthorized maritime migration since the mid-twentieth century in order to articulate a new theory of human rights. This theory will be explained against the backdrop of the argument that the "refugee crisis" is far from being as exceptional as it may seem.[26]

Human Rights and Bare Life

When bodies are washed ashore, we are made keenly aware of the fragility and indeed the false promises of human rights law. From a historical perspective, the dynamic is a familiar one. The plight of migrants today recalls Hannah Arendt's insight about the interwar refugee crisis.[27] The problem Arendt pointed to, in more powerful terms than anyone before her, was the problem of the relationship between the "citizen" and "human."

In the political tradition that began with the French Revolution, the rights of humans were to be legally secured through their membership in political communities, imagined as particular social contracts. Article 1 of the 1789 *Declaration of the Rights of Man* reads: "Men are born and remain free and equal in rights." The natural equality of human beings was to be protected by citizenship. The social contract tradition reflected

Immigration, and Border Walls," *Stanford Public Law Working Paper No. 2526521* (2014), available at http://papers.ssrn.com/sol3/papers.cfm?abstract_id=2526521 (last accessed May 3, 2016).

[24] Griff Witte, "New U.N. Report Says World's Refugee Crisis Is Worse than Anyone Expected," *The Washington Post*, June 18, 2015, available at www.washingtonpost.com/world/europe/new-un-report-says-worlds-refugee-crisis-is-worse-than-anyone-expected/2015/06/17/a49c3fc0-14ff-11e5-8457-4b431bf7ed4c_story.html (last accessed September 22, 2015).

[25] Historicizing the crisis is one way of avoiding the lure of crisis, which international lawyers have often taken as an opportunity for simplified, de-contextualized, and ultimately counter-productive focus on "great men." See Charlesworth, "International Law: A Discipline of Crisis," 388.

[26] On the regularization of emergencies in the contemporary stage of globalization, see Giorgio Agamben, *Homo Sacer: Sovereign Power and Bare Life*, trans. Daniel Heller-Roazen, 1st edition (Stanford: Stanford University Press, 1998), 38.

[27] Hannah Arendt, *The Origins of Totalitarianism*, New edition (New York: Harcourt, Brace, Jovanovich, 1973); Ayten Gündogdu, *Rightlessness in an Age of Rights: Hannah Arendt and the Contemporary Struggles of Migrants* (New York: Oxford University Press, 2015).

in these documents had an enormous influence on contemporary legal theory, both on the domestic and on the international spheres. The imagination of the social contract provides the normative justification for contemporary liberal conceptions of sovereignty.[28] For legal theorists of diverse political orientations, domestic law derives its legitimacy from the social contract. This domestic legitimacy in turn allows the state to grant consent to positive international law. The state can accede to treaties. Its behavior – when coupled with a belief that it is carried out under legal obligation (*opinio juris*) – constitutes customary international law. To use Louis Henkin's often-quoted words, international law forms a social contract among states.[29]

But in her essay "The Decline of the Nation State and the End of the Rights of Man," Arendt famously demonstrated the failures of this model of political life. When massive populations in Europe became de facto stateless, the legal regimes of states granted them no protective remedy. When states confronted foreigners and had to choose between protecting their citizens and protecting all humans, the rights of citizens prevailed. *The Rights of the Man* – crown jewel of the French Revolution and of the social contract tradition – proved illusory. As long as human rights were grounded in social contract, there could be no structural commitment to humans per se. As Arendt wrote, humans with no effective citizenship had no "place in the world."[30] In this situation, the fate of "bare life" – human life stripped of membership in a particular political community – is at best that of animals.[31] Charitable organizations might choose to feed

---

[28] Fernando R. Tesón, "The Kantian Theory of International Law," *Columbia Law Review* 92, no. 1 (1992): 53–102, doi:10.2307/1123025; Luke Glanville, "The Antecedents of 'sovereignty as Responsibility'," *European Journal of International Relations* XX, no. X (2010): 1–23 (on the roots of contemporary views in classical social contract theory); for a critique, see Martti Koskenniemi, "What Use for Sovereignty Today?," *Asian Journal of International Law* 1, no. 01 (2011): 61–70, doi:10.1017/S2044251310000044. For a critique, see Paul W. Kahn, *Putting Liberalism in Its Place* (Princeton: Princeton University Press, 2008).

[29] See Louis Henkin, "That 'S' Word: Sovereignty, Globalization, and Human Rights, Et Cetra," *Fordham Law Review* 68, no. 1 (1999): 12; Anne Marie Slaughter and Jose E. Alvarez, "A Liberal Theory of International Law," *Proceeding of the Annual Meeting (American Society of International Law)* 94 (2000): 24 (explaining the relationship between liberalism in international law and international relations); Thomas M. Franck, *Fairness in International Law and Institutions* (Oxford: Oxford University Press, 1998), 28; Hedley Bull, *The Anarchical Society: A Study of Order in World Politics* (New York: Columbia University Press), 253 (explaining the idea of a social contract among states in the context of classical social contract theory).

[30] Arendt, *The Origins of Totalitarianism*, 296.

[31] Arendt, *Origins of Totalitarianism*, 302. Compare with Agamben, *Homo Sacer*.

refugees or the stateless and extend some compassion to them. But law does not give them enforceable rights. This is precisely what seems to be happening today, on a wider, global, scale:[32] Humanity washed ashore.

Arendt's critique inflicted a devastating blow on the entire tradition of human rights. For critically inclined scholars at the intersections between law, politics, and the humanities, the debt to Arendt is often explicit and well articulated.[33] Related insights about the lack of enforcement of international human rights generate a persistent concern among scholars that international law is really not "law" at all.[34] For some scholars, "human rights law" appears as an urge to wish moral prescription into legal obligation, misleading at best, destructive at worse.[35]

The post-World War II period – which *Origins of Totalitarianism* does not address – is sometimes regarded as a kind of "international constitutional moment."[36] The emergence of human rights treaties takes up the central part in this celebratory rhetoric. During this period the emphasis of human rights law shifted from constituent assemblies and their declarations and constitutions to public interstate agreements. Treaties, some suggest, have allowed human rights to come of age and recognize the rights of the "person," independent of the legal regime of any particular state.[37] Special emphasis is given to the United Nations

[32] This has been reiterated in contemporary scholarship. See, e.g., Jacques Rancière, "Who Is the Subject of the Rights of Man?" *The South Atlantic Quarterly* 103 (2004): 299 (commenting that Arendt's "analysis, articulated more than fifty years ago, seems tailor-made, fifty years later, to fit the new 'perplexities' of the Rights of Man on the 'humanitarian' stage"); Gündogdu, *Rightlessness in an Age of Rights*; Alison Kesby, *The Right to Have Rights: Citizenship, Humanity, and International Law* (New York: Oxford University Press, 2012).

[33] See, e.g., Samuel Moyn, *The Last Utopia: Human Rights in History*, Reprint edition (Cambridge, MA: Belknap Press, 2012); Didier Fassin, *Humanitarian Reason: A Moral History of the Present* (Berkeley: University of California Press, 2011); Miriam I. Ticktin, *Casualties of Care: Immigration and the Politics of Humanitarianism in France* (Berkeley: University of California Press, 2011); Nicola Perugini and Neve Gordon, *The Human Right to Dominate*, 1st edition (New York: Oxford University Press, 2015).

[34] See, e.g., Jack L. Goldsmith and Eric A. Posner, *The Limits of International Law*, 1st edition (Oxford and New York: Oxford University Press, 2006); Anthony D'Amato, "Is International Law Really Law," *Northwestern University Law Review* 79 (1985–1984): 1293.

[35] See, e.g., Joseph Raz, "Human Rights without Foundations," in Samantha Besson and John Tasioulas (eds.), *The Philosophy of International Law* (Oxford: Oxford University Press, 2010), 321–338.

[36] See, e.g., Anne-Marie Slaughter and William Burke-White, "An International Constitutional Moment," *Harvard International Law Journal* 43 (2002).

[37] Article 3 of the UN Charter provides that "Everyone has the right to life, liberty and security of person."

Charter (1945), the Charter of the International Military Tribunal at Nuremberg (1945), the Universal Declaration of Human Rights (1948), and the Geneva Conventions (1949).[38] Particularly notable in this context are specialized treaties that protect refugees and stateless people. These two categories were interchangeable for Arendt, but came to be understood as distinct. The Refugee Convention defines refugees as those who suffer from a "well-founded fear" of being persecuted for reasons of political opinion race, religion, nationality, or membership of particular social groups. The preference for these groups was shaped largely by the experience of World War II.[39] The two major human rights treaties, the International Covenant on Civil and Political Rights and the International Covenant on Social, Economic, and Cultural Rights (both from 1966), are viewed as extensions of this postwar project. The International Criminal Court, established by the Rome Statute (1998), ostensibly reflects the way the international community has incrementally expanded a framework protecting persons the world over.[40] Taken together, these documents provide the basis for what Ruti Teitel has called "humanity's law."[41]

But the basis for all these instruments is state consent. The postwar international legal order did not solve the principal problem of the refugee – the one Arendt identified. This was the problem of legal protections *independent* of citizenship or of state consent. Using a formulation that has both inspired and baffled theorists and lawyers ever since, Arendt called this the problem of "the right to have rights."

Within the terrain of international law the doctrine that most clearly reflects the recognition of rights independent of state consent is *jus cogens*: law deemed binding upon all international actors regardless of their agreement. *Jus cogens* is defined in the Vienna Convention on the Law of Treaties as law that is accepted and recognized by the

---

[38] The creation myth around these legal instruments is one about a world rising "from the ashes of war." See Barry Carter and Allen Weiner, *International Law*, 6th edition (New York: Wolters Kluwer, 2011), 746.

[39] James C. Hathaway, "Reconsideration of the Underlying Premise of Refugee Law, A," *Harvard International Law Journal* 31 (1990): 129.

[40] This incrementalist sensibility pervades international law from its enlightenment origins. See Immanuel Kant, Idea for a Universal History from a Comparative Perspective; Martti Koskenniemi, "Constitutionalism as Mindset: Reflections on Kantian Themes about International Law and Globalization," *Theoretical Inquiries in Law* 8, no. 1 (2007): 9–36.

[41] Ruti G. Teitel, *Humanity's Law* (New York: Oxford University Press, 2011).

international community of states as a whole, and from which no derogation is permitted.[42] The most common examples are the norms against slavery, genocide, crimes against humanity, and torture.[43] Any person must be protected from these regardless of whether she finds herself within the jurisdiction of a state that agreed to that or not. But of course, the normative bite of *jus cogens* stems precisely from the fact that it is *not* in fact universally adhered to.[44] Can such norms nevertheless be defined as "law," rather than moral prescription or political interest?[45]

Whatever one's answer, it is relevant to the question if rights can exist regardless of a state's consent. If no such rights exist, the idea that some rights are granted to all persons will need to be discarded. The conclusion, in other words, would be that, as Arendt observed at her time, the "bare life" of humans continues to be "rightless."[46] Through the history I examine below, I argue that as long as some people feel bound by human rights, humans are never rightless. I do this based on one particular context, only controversially included in the list of *jus cogens* norms: this is the duty of *non-refoulement*, which prohibits the deportation of a person to where he or she may be subject to torture or cruel, inhuman, or degrading treatment.[47] When interpreted correctly, this duty can shed light on the moral and legal structure of the entire normative universe of human rights.

[42] Article 53 of the Vienna Convention.

[43] The International Law Commission, the United Nations' authoritative body for the interpretation of international law, also adds the prohibition on aggression, racial discrimination, and the right to self-determination as "preemptory norms that are clearly accepted and recognized." See para. 5 of the Commentary to Draft Article 26 on state responsibility.

[44] Georges Abi-Saab put this point elegantly, saying that even if the normative category of *jus cogens* were to be an "empty box, the category was still useful; for without the box, it cannot be filled." Georges Abi Saab, "The Third World and the Future of the International Legal Order," *Revue Egyptienne de Droit International* 29 (1973): 53.

[45] On the temptations and the perils of the language of *jus cogens*, see Koskenniemi, "International Law in Europe," 122.

[46] Gündogdu, *Rightlessness in an Age of Rights*.

[47] For a discussion, see Guy S. Goodwin-Gill, "The Right to Seek Asylum: Interception at Sea and the Principle of Non-Refoulement," *International Journal of Refugee Law* 23, no. 3 (2011): 443–457, doi:10.1093/ijrl/eer018 (discussing *non-refoulement* and torture, and suggesting that the former is "sharing perhaps in some of the latter's *jus cogens* character"); Aoife Duffy, "Expulsion to Face Torture? Non-Refoulement in International Law," *International Journal of Refugee Law* 20, no. 3 (2008): 373–390; Alice Farmer, "Non-Refoulment and Jus Cogens: Limiting Anti-Terror Measures That Threaten Refugee Protection," *Georgetown Immigration Law Journal* 23 (2008): 1.

The Rights of Encounter

Looking at the history of unauthorized migration at sea, I will argue, demonstrates that human rights are a part of international law that extends beyond sovereign consent (and beyond its normative basis in social contract). To explain this, however, the notion of "law" itself must be reconsidered. The following exploration of the notion of law responds to Arendt's extraordinarily powerful challenge. I will marshal some of Arendt's own insights in order to read her against the grain. Some scholars, like Seyla Benhabib and, more recently, Ayten Gündogdu, have offered interpretations of Arendt in which her critique is consonant with particular understandings of human rights.[48] Though I'm much indebted to their work, my own purpose is not to offer an interpretation of Arendt's work. I aim, rather, to contribute to international legal theory by offering a new theory of human rights law. Arendt's devastating critique of human rights is a useful challenge to start from.

Turning to the history of migration at sea reveals that precisely *because* some people are protected by no government, they are able to confront state agents with an existential dilemma: either save a stranger's life, or let the stranger die. For governments with ostensible human rights commitments, the dilemma has ultimately been between treating people as humans and risking changing who "we" are (in terms of the composition of our population), or giving up human rights and risking changing who "we" are (in terms of our constitutive commitments). With an ever-growing number of migrants and refugees crossing the Mediterranean, both drowned and saved, this challenge has turned into a catastrophe. Whether that catastrophe will ultimately lead to the closing of borders is yet to be seen as I write these words. The theory of human rights this book advances is also meant to provide a comprehensive and foundational argument against such closure.

The multiple legal self-contradictions and the consequent collective embarrassment in confronting the current refugee crisis are not something that can be eliminated or disregarded. Considering this embarrassment is a first step in proposing a new theory about the foundations of human rights. Migration at sea starkly poses the question as to what protections accrue to all humans. Actors in the name of developed states find themselves pressed to give their own answers. No appeal to

---

[48] Compare Seyla Benhabib, *The Rights of Others: Aliens, Residents, and Citizens* (Cambridge: Cambridge University Press, 2012); Gündogdu, *Rightlessness in an Age of Rights.*

positive or natural law can provide an answer. In such circumstances, international legal actors, states as well as individuals, may experience a command of the conscience triggered by defenseless human presence.[49] This command, I will argue, is at the core of human rights law, properly conceived.

That human rights law has an origin beyond state consent to human rights treaties is by no means a novel position among theorists of human rights. In the classical international legal thought of seventeenth-century European jurists, this origin was the religiously based notion of natural rights. More recently, authors like Martha Nussbaum, James Griffin, and John Tasioulas (among others) have aimed to establish natural rights on moral grounds.[50] Like the older religiously based projects, such arguments too require metaphysical bases. My own argument aims to bracket metaphysical questions.[51] It remains agnostic on whether or not moral imperatives can flow from "human nature," and indeed on whether there is such a thing as "human nature." Instead, it starts from a phenomenological account of experience. This methodological starting point will allow me to observe that being bound by human rights means experiencing the presence of other persons as projecting a certain kind of imperative.[52] And while this experience may not be universal, it remains robust and can grip one's self regardless of its purported metaphysical

---

[49] The political and philosophical tradition of non-violent civil disobedience, which I have chosen not to engage with in any sustained way in this context, is surely in the background (especially in Chapter 4). See Martin Luther King Jr, "Letter from Birmingham Jail," *U.C. Davis Law Review* 26 (1993): 835; Hannah Arendt, *Crises of the Republic: Lying in Politics; Civil Disobedience; on Violence; Thoughts on Politics and Revolution* (San Diego, New York, and London: A Harvest Book, Harcourt Brace & Company, 1972); Chibli Mallat, *Philosophy of Nonviolence: Revolution, Constitutionalism, and Justice beyond the Middle East*, 1st edition (Oxford and New York: Oxford University Press, 2015).

[50] James Griffin, *On Human Rights*, 1st edition (Oxford: Oxford University Press, 2009); John Tasioulas, "Taking Rights Out of Human Rights," *Ethics* 120, no. 4 (2010): 647–678 (reviewing Griffin's book); Martha C. Nussbaum, *Creating Capabilities: The Human Development Approach*, Reprint edition (Cambridge: Belknap Press, 2013).

[51] Such bracketing is a central move of much liberal political theory. See, e.g., John Rawls, "Justice as Fairness: Political Not Metaphysical," *Philosophy & Public Affairs* 14, no. 3 (1985): 223–251. It is also (if a different way) a basic technique of phenomenology, which Edmund Husserl termed "epoché." See Edmund Husserl, *Cartesian Meditations: An Introduction to Phenomenology* (Dordrecht: Martinus Nijhoff Pub., 1977).

[52] This position is associated with the work of Emmanuel Levinas. See, e.g., Emmanuel Lévinas, *Totality and Infinity: An Essay on Exteriority* (Pittsburgh: Duquesne University Press, 1969). As Richard Cohen has explained in an introduction to Levinas's writing, for Lévinas "Significance originally emerges from the face-to-face encounter as ethical event, that is, from the other person as moral command and the self

justification. Human rights are imperatives that we experience as extra-political *albeit with the knowledge we have that they are, certainly, political.* Indeed, they reflect a commitment to paradoxically and counter-factually regard some form of imperative as extra-political.

Today, conceptualizing human rights is not only a matter for high-minded international lawyers drafting treaties and declarations.[53] It is firstly a task of careful description and phenomenological characterization of the actions of those who have no state protection and the experience of being confronted by their claims. The historical materials this book marshals and engages with will provide a fuller account of the two faces of this experience and its significance for international law. "The rights of encounter" are those rights that stem not from inclusion in particular political communities but from the bare life of humans as such, as experienced by those of us who are bound by human rights law. These rights arise when refugees make demands in the name of their own humanity and authorities are pressed to respond. I will use the term "the universal boatperson" to refer to such refugees who make demands collectively and generally – a figure of the imagination as much as a group of particular people.[54] Departing from the basic tenets of contemporary doctrine, human rights law is revealed as a thin but firm modicum of legal responsibility individuals may experience toward all other individuals upon encounter.[55] By potentially opening the social contract and letting new members in, this sense of responsibility implicates sovereignty: the most fundamental political structure that positive international law recognizes. What I will call the "human rights encounter" should be juxtaposed with sovereignty and its normative basis in the social contract. Together, these are the two foundations of international law.[56]

---

as moral response." See Emmanuel Lévinas, *Humanism of the Other*, trans. Nidra Poller (Champaign: University of Illinois Press, 2003).

[53] Compare Balakrishnan Rajagopal, *International Law from below: Development, Social Movements and Third World Resistance* (Cambridge and New York: Cambridge University Press, 2003); Arnulf Becker Lorca, *Mestizo International Law: A Global Intellectual History 1842–1933* (Cambridge: Cambridge University Press, 2015).

[54] On imagination and the law, see Paul W. Kahn, *The Cultural Study of Law: Reconstructing Legal Scholarship* (Chicago: University of Chicago Press, 2000).

[55] Compare with Stephanie Jones and Stewart Motha, "A New Nomos Offshore and Bodies as Their Own Signs," *Law & Literature* 27, no. 2 (2015): 253–278, doi:10.1080/1535685X.2015.1034479.

[56] I developed a related thesis in the context of international criminal adjudication here: Itamar Mann, "The Dual Foundation of Universal Jurisdiction: Towards a Jurisprudence for the 'Court of Critique'," *Transnational Legal Theory* 1, no. 4 (2010): 485–521.

Law of the Land and Law of the Sea

The case studies in this book all occur at sea – often in the maritime space international law designates as "the high seas." But my attention to maritime space is not only inspired by the recent images in the news, powerful as they may be. This focus allows access to aspects of our experience that may otherwise remain concealed.

In common law countries, one of the first things law students learn is that, save for few exceptions, law imposes no duties of rescue. Law professors often use this point to illustrate a basic tenet of legal positivism: the distinction between legal and moral prescription (or "the separation thesis"). According to the most rudimentary view of legal positivism, associated with the work of John Austin, law is defined as the sovereign's command, backed by a sanction.[57] Rescuing the drowning stranger, students may be comforted, is *morally* required. But law does not always follow moral prescription. More rarely acknowledged in basic law school courses is the fact that travelers on the earth's oceans and seas are bound by a duty of rescue. This joins a number of other rules that distinguish between the high seas and territorial waters. Importantly, the high seas are considered the territory of no sovereign. Save for several important exceptions, the movement of vessels traveling at sea cannot be restricted.[58]

Common explanations for these peculiarities of the law of the sea hark back to the importance of maritime space as conduit for commerce. The seventeenth century in particular was crucial for the emergence of this doctrine. In 1608, Dutch jurist Hugo Grotius first published his *Mare Liberum*, the most influential, if not the first, articulation of the freedom of the high seas.[59] The book spelled the beginning of a process whereby the freedom of the high seas secured "unimpeded international trade for both established and emerging maritime powers, with the dual main goals of maximizing profits for their economies and increasing strategic dominance over new territories."[60] The high-seas commons are still today believed to be

---

[57] John Austin, *The Province of Jurisprudence Determined* (Cambridge: Cambridge University Press, 1995).

[58] Hugo Grotius, *The Freedom of the Seas: Or, the Right Which Belongs to the Dutch to Take Part in the East Indian Trade* (New York: Oxford University Press, 1916).

[59] Hugo Grotius, *Mare Liberum* (Indianapolis: Liberty Fund, 2004).

[60] Davor Vidas, "The Anthropocene and the International Law of the Sea," *Philosophical Transactions of the Royal Society* 369 (2011): 913.

economically beneficial for all seafaring nations engaged in international trade.[61] The duty of rescue, respectively, is imagined as
a reciprocal duty among seafarer-peers, acting according to self-
interest. These adventurers often embarked on dangerous journeys
and commonly faced the threat of an omnipotent nature. If any asymmetry of power was involved, it wasn't between vessels or their crews.[62]

But how might reference to the sea help in an experience-based
account of human rights law? The key is an implicit division of responsibility between sovereign rule and maritime space.[63] From the perspective of a social contract-based theory of sovereignty, there are sound
reasons for the different ways in which law allocates rescue duties at land
and at sea. Relinquishing their capacity to inflict private violence, and
granting the sovereign a monopoly over its legitimate use, members of
the social contract also require the sovereign to protect its citizens.
Within this context, it is the sovereign and not the fellow person that
I must look to when I expect my most basic rights to be enforced.[64] Only
by establishing a public body, a private space opens up in which I'm *freed*
of responsibility toward strangers. The social contract and the consequent rule of law somehow suspend duties we may or may not have
toward each other, *qua individuals*.[65]

But stepping out of sovereignty and into the high-sea commons, the
balancing of relations between individuals shifts. Law defines differently
the ways in which we are implicated by each other's claim upon life.
The absence of sovereign control leaves open the possibility of mutual

---

[61] Eric Posner and Alan O. Skyes, "Economic Foundations of the Law of the Sea," *American Journal of International Law* 104, no. 4 (2010): 569–596. For the classical articulation of the underlying economic rationale for common property, see Carol Rose, "The Comedy of the Commons: Custom, Commerce, and Inherently Public Property," *The University of Chicago Law Review* 53, no. 3 (1986): 711–781 (while Rose does not discuss the high seas, she does discuss the preservation of navigable rivers as public property for the purposes of transportation of people and goods).

[62] This reality was famously depicted, e.g., by Herman Melville. Herman Melville, *Moby Dick* (Lexington, KY: CreateSpace Independent Publishing Platform, 2014).

[63] See generally, Carl Schmitt, *The Nomos of the Earth in the International Law of Jus Publicum Europaeum* (New York: Telos Press Publishing, 2006).

[64] This may of course be easier to grasp in the context of a well-funded welfare state with a tangible "safety net." But, in fact, it remains true as long as we assume that citizens somehow participate in choosing the state protections they want and that they are free to rescind their implied consent to the social contract, by engaging in revolt or in disobedience.

[65] Arthur Ripstein, "Tort, the Division of Responsibility and the Law of Tort," *Fordham Law Review* 72, no. 5 (2004): 1811.

responsibility among individuals.[66] It is this possibility that the book interrogates.

Outline

The narrative arc of this book begins immediately after World War II. This point of departure is not a necessary one, and indeed others could have been chosen. For international lawyers, however, World War II remains a crisis par excellence.[67] If, according to the familiar narrative, the war shocked the "conscience of mankind," the migration and refugee crisis we are now witnessing is comparably transformational. Even while choosing the standard point of departure, I aim to show that these events establish a wholly different understanding of the binding nature of human rights.

In the late 1940s and early 1950s, the question as to what legal protections should be afforded to refugees and stateless persons was a burning one. Not unlike today, European societies were clamoring for an answer: What should be done with the uprooted populations? This question prompted an exchange between two remarkable lawyers: Hersch Lauterpacht and Paul Weis. On the pages of professional journals the two debated then-emerging international law protecting refugees, including the Universal Declaration of Human Rights, and the 1951 Refugee Convention. The debate centered on an even-more basic question: What are the necessary and sufficient conditions for human rights to be called "law"?

Each of the interlocutors had an interesting answer, foreshadowing a more general orientation toward the discipline of international law in the second half of the twentieth century. Yet limiting the discussion to one account or another, without regard to what displaced people did to ensure their futures, is a symptomatic mistake of international legal method. This book is an attempt to reclaim these refugees' agency as participants in the shaping of international law.

To exemplify this point, I start by focusing on one such action: a journey in which Jewish displaced people traveled on a boat set for

---

[66] Compare with Jones and Motha on the construction of the Indian Ocean in the common law as a place where human bodies can be ousted from normative consideration. Jones and Motha, "A New Nomos Offshore and Bodies as Their Own Signs."

[67] David Kennedy, "My Talk at the ASIL: What Is New Thinking in International Law?," *Proceedings of the Annual Meeting (American Society of International Law)* 94 (2000): 116–117 (describing the disciplinary crisis in international law following the War).

Palestine, which was then under the British Mandate. The *Exodus*, at the center of Chapter 1, was operated by Jewish paramilitaries who sought to establish a Jewish state in Palestine. This national impulse may be familiar to readers: the ship quickly garnered international fame, complete with a 1960 Hollywood rendition starring Paul Newman. Yet the chapter returns to a period prior to such celebrity. It suggests that this national narrative has somehow distracted us from another aspect of the journey, which may renew its relevance today. The national liberation story must be coupled with a yet-untold account of the journey as a struggle for human rights. I thus highlight the ways in which the journey was employed to make a claim of membership in humanity. We, said the passengers, must be granted some basic protections. In the course of doing so, several passengers of the *Exodus* conducted a legal battle in a British court, the documentary record of which allows us to reconstruct their claims. And they confronted a British navy vessel face-to-face, a positioning that will allow me to draw a detailed outline of the human rights encounter.[68]

On its own, the *Exodus* story might mistakenly lead us to think that there are no human rights outside the context of collective nation building. For better or worse, the journey did become part of a state-building project. One point I make, however, is that human rights norms are analytically antecedent to any such institutional arrangement. This is shown in Chapter 2, which recounts the Southeast Asian "boat people" crisis starting from the United States' withdrawal from Vietnam in 1975. Rather than establishing a new state of their own, the "boat people" were distributed across many other countries, first among them the United States. Rather than concluding a new social contract, they were granted access into multiple existing ones.

While the aim of Chapter 1 is to give an account of the human rights encounter as a whole, Chapter 2 focuses particularly on one side of this encounter. The chapter addresses the following question: What is a human right *claim*? Revisiting narrative materials produced by former boat people clarifies the gap between the human rights claim and Western countries' responses to it. The former sought to make membership claims that are beyond mere survival. The latter often attempted to extinguish any obligation, beyond making sure that the boat people would not face persecution in Vietnam or drown while leaving. This

---

[68] For a critique of an earlier version of this chapter, see Moyn, "The Embarrassment of Human Rights."

tension provides an important lesson about the potential cruelty of human rights law. By building camps, for example, developed states have continuously sought to avoid killing people, but to grant them nothing more than mere life. But this tension also frames perhaps the most optimistic chapter of this book: The boat people's efforts resulted in the 1979 Orderly Departure Program, thanks to which many got new citizenships. Despite all its difficulties, this remains an important precedent. The Orderly Departure Program was the most successful large-scale refugee resettlement program ever to be implemented.

Chapter 3 moves the focus to the powerful party in the encounter – the addressee of the human rights claim. What does it mean to have a human rights *commitment*? Focusing on the United States' response to Haitian refugees and migrants in the 1980s and 1990s, the chapter examines a particular kind of constitutionalism. This constitutionalism is characterized by a political imagination affirming that all government actors have obligations toward members of humanity as a whole. Harold Koh, a prominent US international lawyer, took this view of constitutionalism in oral argument before the United States Supreme Court, which rejected it in an 8–1 decision.[69] Responding to this landmark case, I argue that human rights commitments cannot be merged with constitutional commitments. The former are obligations that stem from dislocation in our own pasts and remind us that we too were not always parties to a social contract. An early essay by Arendt, "We Refugees," is an oblique yet nuanced articulation of the view that there are such obligations toward non-members.[70] This foundational debt to the uprooted has proven resilient and has most recently figured prominently in public debate on the refugee crisis in Europe.

Taking its cue from the precedent set by the United States Supreme Court, Australia tried to seal its maritime borders completely in the early 2000s, with the "Pacific solution." It thus attempted to establish a social contract with no potential opening for non-members. This amounts to renouncing human rights obligations, as defined here. Chapter 4 focuses on the ensuing dynamic. During the Australian attempt to enforce this resolution, refugees and migrants engaged in last-resort attempts to

---

[69] *Sale* v. *Haitian Refugees Council*, 113 S. Ct. 2549, 113 S. Ct. 2549, 125 L. (92–344), 509 U.S. 155 (1993).

[70] Hannah Arendt, "We Refugees," in Marc Robinson (ed.), *Altogether Elsewhere: Writers on Exile* (London and Boston: Harvest, 1996), 110. Originally published in *The Menorah Journal* 31 (1943).

address individual members of the navy with human rights claims. These included riots and self-inflicted harm and often verged upon violence. The Australian parliamentary report about the events reflects how navy boats monitored asylum-seeker vessels from beyond the line of the horizon in order to avoid encountering them. From afar, the Australian navy discovered that migrants often prepared to meet them with life-jackets. Jumping into the water or destroying their own boats, they had a chance to trigger rescue obligations even when faced by reluctant authorities. When all else fails, a "humanitarian duty" to save lives at sea is not easy to eradicate. As it turn out, any "humanitarian" duty also opens possibilities for political action.

The dynamic is redoubled by the case analyzed in Chapter 5, which came to be known as the "left to die" boat. Multiple actors in the Mediterranean knew about a refugee vessel that left Libya in 2011, thanks to surveillance technologies covering the maritime space. But the overlapping responsibility that surveillance established created a collective action problem. The migrants could not successfully address any individual person or authority exclusively. The case study is used in order to raise a question about how the binding force of human presence may or may not remain possible in a time of all-encompassing surveillance.

Unlike its preceding chapters, Chapter 6 no longer focuses on a physical encounter between state agents or other seafarers and refugees at risk. Here I analyze the human rights encounter as a trope of the political imagination. The main part of the chapter is a reading of Juncker's State of the Union speech (mentioned above). At the center of this speech is an encounter between Europe – symbolically represented by Arvanitakis – and the migrant and refugee populations that attempted entry in the summer of 2015. The figurative positioning is not aimed to refer to any particular individuals literally, but it is supposed to capture a certain understanding of politics beyond the bounds of membership. Though ultimately, in my view, Juncker's figurative positioning rings hollow, it does suggest a prescriptive edge that the human rights encounter may have. We must *imagine* our polities not only in terms of our obligations toward fellow members but also in terms of how obligations toward non-members can be institutionalized. We must establish porous social contracts, which are open to changes in the lineages of population, as they are to amending their basic terms through the democratic process.

In the conclusion I contextualize "the rights of encounter" within the larger conceptual terrain of international law. More work will be necessary in order to fully generalize the theory and apply it to other legal subfields. But if this book proves successful, the argument will suffice in order to clarify that law rests on two foundational sources: one is sovereignty, which should be understood in social contractarian terms and generates positive law; the other is the human rights encounter, which should be understood as independent of sovereign decree, and generates human rights law, properly conceived. A concise postscript offers an interpretation of the biblical story of Moses in the ark of bulrushes, in light of the figure of the universal boatperson.

Needless to say, much of human rights law, as ordinarily invoked both in scholarly and in professional contexts, is positive law (inscribed in treaties, constitutions, or whatever legal instruments). Clearly, for all practical purposes, we will continue to speak that way. But the way this book is written – and the sounder one conceptually – is to reserve the term "human rights law" to the non-positive law originating from the human rights encounter.

The first chapter of this book takes a page out of modern Jewish history, and the postscript returns to a Jewish cultural source (the bible). Some readers may find this objectionable. But this is not to say that Jewish experience – if there is such a collective category apart from the experience of individuals – has an exceptional status. It is a reflection of my own felt identity rather than one of any objective truth. If this book is successful, anyone who feels committed to human rights can make an analogous argument based on their own felt identity. What will remain important in any such case is that the commitment to value the claims of all human beings will remain rooted in embodied experience. A commonplace perception ascribes national affiliation to identity, while human rights are believed to be the product of a disembodied exercise of reason. But this is not the case. Human rights commitments are never exclusively derived from the exercise of reason and are always also rooted in who we are.

Flagless Vessel

"For the lawyer," wrote Paul Weis in a 1954 article titled "The International Protection of Refugees," "the status of a person who is deprived of national protection is 'anomalous.' A stateless person – and this applies equally to refugees – has been compared to a vessel on the open sea, not sailing under any flag."[1] By invoking this image, the legal advisor to the newly established United Nations High Commissioner for Refugees (UNHCR) posed a seemingly technical dilemma.[2] "The lawyer" is not sure where jurisdiction over such persons lies, or who is to be held accountable for their plight. She may consult her books, but what she'll find is a missing page.[3]

Weis's answer to this dilemma was his life's work. One of the major participants in formulating the 1951 Refugee Convention, he directed UNHCR's legal division up to his retirement in 1967.[4] The treaty,

---

[1] Paul Weis, "The International Protection of Refugees," *American Journal of International Law* 48, no. 2 (1954): 193–221. See the same assertion in Erwin Loewenfeld, "Status of Stateless Persons," *Transactions of the Grotius Society* 27 (1941): 59–112.

[2] See, e.g., in this passage, presenting the puzzle:
> While in the common law countries the personal status of an individual is governed by the law of his country of domicile, the countries of Europe and several countries of Latin America apply the law of the country of nationality. In both cases difficult questions of conflict of laws may arise for refugees; it may be doubtful whether a refugee has acquired a domicile of choice; that nationality of refugees is often difficult to determine, and the status of stateless refugee gives rise to difficulties in countries which apply the law of the country of nationality and which lack provisions covering the status of stateless persons.

> Weis, "The International Protection of Refugees," 202, *supra* note 1.

[3] Jurisdiction over boats has been compared to "personal" jurisdiction over an individual's body. Edwin D. Dickinson, "Jurisdiction at the Maritime Frontier," *Harvard Law Review* 40, no. 1 (1926): 1.

[4] This is how the agency described Weis, upon awarding him the Nansen Refugee Award: "Paul Weis, a survivor of the Nazi concentration camps, shared the award posthumously. He escaped from Dachau and found asylum in Britain. As UNHCR's first Protection Director, he was called the 'founding father of protection.' The Vienna-born Weis was a strong advocate for refugees and worked constantly to remind the world of its responsibility towards them." Available at www.unhcr.org/pages/49c3646c467-page4.html (last accessed May 3, 2016).

alongside a host of other international legal instruments, sought to fill a gap in international law and grant a remedy to those who lost their ties to community or citizenship. Responding to events from the interwar period and during WWII, it culminated an attempt to solve the "refugee problem" through treaty law. Human rights would become a discipline that identified more than any other with a number of postwar treaties. A host of international governments, international organizations, and private actors would become entrusted with the task of administering treaty obligations in what came to be known as "transnational governance."[5]

Introducing the analogy of the flagless vessel – and the dilemma it represented – Weis probably did not have in mind a widely publicized chain of events that took place only a few years earlier.[6] But when about 4,500 displaced Jews left Marseilles for Palestine on a boat that came to be known as the *Exodus*, they literally enacted his analogy. Though only one of many boats of Jews that aimed to reach Palestine clandestinely, the *Exodus* came to be the most famous of them all.[7]

By literally enacting Weis's hypothetical, these migrants put it to a test. But the answer to his dilemma that their actions represented was a far cry from his efforts to advance treaty law as the foundation for human rights protection. Their answer relied on the actions the refugees took for themselves, aiming to realize their own rights, as well as on the actions (and inactions) of the authorities that confronted them. Their answer provided an alternative to the developing patchwork of international organizations that fashioned human rights to advance state interests by disseminating a modicum of relief.

The story of the *Exodus* is often told within the framework of a Jewish liberation narrative leading from bondage to sovereignty. The often-tragic stories of the Jewish unauthorized migrants leaving Europe for

---

[5] The word "transnational" is used somewhat anachronistically to indicate that its contemporary use fruitfully described the period this chapter considers as well. The word is credited to Phillip Jessup, who in his 1955 Storrs Lectures at Yale Law School defined "transnational law" as "all law which regulates actions or events that transcend national frontiers." The analytic bite of the term is the way in which it demands collapsing the distinction of public and private law, as well as public legal entities. See Phillip Jessup, *Transnational Law* (New Haven: Yale University Press, 1956), 2.

[6] On the importance of analogy in legal argument, see Paul Kahn, *The Cultural Study of Law* (Chicago and London: University of Chicago Press, 1999), 51.

[7] See, e.g., Ruth Gruber, *Exodus 1947: The Ship that Launched a Nation* (New York: Union Square Press, 2007). The Hollywood epic *Exodus* staring Paul Newman established the boat's iconic status. *Exodus* (Alpha and Carlyle Productions, 1960).

Palestine remain a symbol of Israel's independence. Driving out of Tel Aviv to the north, one can see one of the smaller boats, beached as a monument on a sandstone mound overlooking the highway. In this story, those who had no place in the international legal order organized around the idea of sovereignty by an act of founding. From now on, the Israeli social contract, and Israeli law, would protect Jewish refugees by granting them the rights to citizenship in a community. This enforcement of rights, as Hannah Arendt noted early on, also came at the expense of violence against those who were not included in the new social contract. The uprooting of about 750,000 Arab Palestinians recreated the "the refugee problem."

However, a closer look at the relevant history shows that the *Exodus* affair is not reducible to a positivist picture according to which rights are protected either by international organizations – as Weis thought – or by state sovereignty. Both these paradigms failed to secure universal human rights. Both proved in practice to secure the rights of some while reproducing violations of the rights of others. Indeed, they both occlude human rights as *the rights of encounter*, the normative source the *Exodus* passengers appealed to.[8] But before clarifying what are "the rights of encounter," the basic idea this book seeks to introduce, I provide some context. I do this by exploring the possibilities and limitations of rights protected by transnational governance and by sovereignty.

The Rights of Transnational Governance

Weis's dilemma was not a theoretical one. For him, as for other actors at his time, refugees and stateless people presented pressing moral and political concerns.[9] The two groups – often conceived of as one – exposed a lacuna in international law that had to be filled with new

---

[8] This idea has been introduced into political thought by the momentous and much-celebrated work of Emmanuel Lévinas, both in his two main philosophical works, *Totality and Infinity* and *Otherwise than Being*, and in several modest but indicative essays he wrote about human rights, or the Rights of Man. See Emmanuel Lévinas, *Totality and Infinity: An Essay on Exteriority* (Dordecht: Kluwer Academic Publishers, 1991); Emmanuel Lévinas, *Otherwise than Being or Beyond Essence* (Dordecht: Kluwer Academic Publishers, 1991); Emmanuel Lévinas, *Alterity and Transcendence* (New York: Columbia University Press, 1999), 121–130, 145–148.

[9] Gerald Daniel Cohen, *In War's Wake: Europe's Displaced Persons in the Postwar Order* (Oxford: Oxford University Press, 2011), 35–57.

international legal instruments. As a participant both in the framing of the Convention and in the international organization that was to implement it, Weis was particularly sensitive to practical problems. He is representative of a broader orientation toward human rights, in which human rights became first and foremost a matter of treaty law. Treaties, drafted and signed by state parties, then provided the basis for varying degrees of international administration, including implementation and oversight bodies, reporting mechanisms, and advisory functions.

Taken together, these international legal processes, which developed around treaty law, later came to be known as the basic processes of transnational governance. Transnational governance is the basis for a dominant understanding of human rights today. Transnational governance associates human rights with a network that cooperates in a partially disaggregated fashion across borders, often through private–public partnerships.[10] It advances a mode of governance that uses "soft power" to encourage voluntary international institutional arrangements that are supposed to quell the more violent politics of sovereignty.[11] Through such soft power it facilitates compliance with treaties, which might not otherwise be enforced.

The legal lacuna of refugees and stateless people first appeared in an unprecedented way during the interwar period.[12] Tides of refugees were triggered primarily by the disintegration of the Ottoman Empire and the Austro-Hungarian Empire.[13] Among the displaced were Russians, who fled during the 1917 Revolution or who were forced to leave their homes during the war. There were also Poles, Germans, Armenians, Greeks, Turks, and Hungarians – more than a million of each group.[14] This mass displacement caused an international state of

---

[10] This orientation was represented, e.g., by the work of Harold Koh during the 1990s. See Harold Hongju Koh, "How is International Human Rights Law Enforced?," *Indiana Law Journal* 74 (1999): 1085. On the "disaggregation" of sovereignty, see Anne-Marie Slaughter, *A New World Order* (Princeton: Princeton University Press, 2004).

[11] Today, this often means the displacement or shifting of political violence to authorities and locations that are not part of these transnational networks, rather than putting an end to them. See Itamar Mann, "Dialectic of Transnationalism: Unauthorized Migration and Human Rights, 1993–2013," *Harvard International Law Journal* 54, no. 2 (2013): 315. See especially discussion on "disaggregated violence," at 346–355.

[12] Hannah Arendt, *The Origins of Totalitarianism* (New York: Harcourt, 1973), 267.

[13] On Ottoman disintegration and resulting displacement, see Umut Özsu, *Formalizing Displacement: International Law and Population Transfers*, 1st edition (Oxford; New York, NY: Oxford University Press, 2015).

[14] Nevzat Soguk, *States and Strangers: Refugees and the Displacement of Statecraft* (Minneapolis: University of Minnesota Press, 1999), 57.

emergency of sorts.[15] One journalist depicted the refugees from Belgium as a procession that included humans alongside animals, all of which were in need of food.[16] He reported even more striking events from Eastern Europe, where the displaced are compared to a cloud or a swarm of locusts, consuming produce and vegetation as they move.[17] Such accounts are consistent with Hannah Arendt's descriptions of the refugees as *bare life*.[18] This European emergency endured, though in differing intensities, until the end of WWII. Though Arendt under-emphasizes its legal aspects, this period was also generative of a considerable body of international law: treaties and arrangements of varying degrees of formality for refugee protection.[19] These were initial experiments that led to the emergence of the postwar legal arrange-ments governing the plight of refugees, still very much in place today.

The transformation of the refugee problem into one of transnational governance started as early as the 1920s. This happened in several institutions, most of which were organs of the League of Nations or its satellite organizations. The first was the High Commissioner for Refugees, established as part of the League of Nations. The High Commissioner was not regulated by rules that could be applied univer-sally. The League's mandate was applied discriminately to different groups – ostensibly according to the intensity of the catastrophe they suffered. Russian expatriates were the first to be declared refugees after

---

[15] The phrase is adopted from Kim Lane Scheppele's work on post-9/11 international law. See Kim Lane Scheppele, "The International State of Emergency: Challenges to Constitutionalism After September 11," *Version prepared for the Yale Legal Theory Workshop* (September 21, 2006) available at http://digitalcommons.law.umaryland.edu /cgi/viewcontent.cgi?article=1048&context=schmooze_papers (Scheppele's analysis is useful in illustrating the way international responses to emergency are often also oppor-tunities for global superpowers to advance far-reaching transnational policy interventions).

[16] Arthur Ruhl, *White Nights and Other Russian Impressions* (New York: Charles Scribner's Sons, 1917), 92.

[17] Arthur Ruhl, *Antwerp to Gallipoli: A Year on the War on Many Fronts* (New York: Charles Scribner's Sons, 1916), 109.

[18] Arendt, *Origins of Totalitarianism*, 267 (the chapter on "The Decline of the Nation-State and the End of the Rights of Man," in which refugees and stateless people are discussed, begins with the description of an explosion. Refugees are those objects that the explosion releases to every direction). The problem of *bare life* and its relation to the classical metaphysical problem of free will and natural necessity are the focus of Chapter 2.

[19] The other extremely generative body of international law at the time were the minority treaties; see Nethaniel Berman, "'But the Alternative Is Despair': European Nationalism and the Modernist Renewal of International Law," *Harvard Law Review* 106, no. 8 (1993): 1792–1903.

Lenin revoked their citizenship in 1921. They received the Nansen pass-ports, named after Fridtjof Nansen, the League of Nations' High Commissioner for Refugees. In 1928, this arrangement was broadened to include Armenian, Assyrian, Chaldean, and Turkish refugees, based on either de jure or de facto statelessness. During the 1930s and 1940s, definitions identifying a particular group for relief were reapplied when people lost their citizenships or fled from different regions, including from the Nazi regime in Germany.[20] International organizations deter-mined refugee status for large groups collectively and more or less ad hoc – without reference to individual asylum seekers. The idea was that relevant groups could be placed under the direct authority of an inter-national organization, which would replace the state.[21]

The deficiencies in this patchwork system were rampant. Gaps con-sistently emerged between de jure recognition of a person as a refugee and de facto statelessness. In her descriptions of the interwar period, Arendt stresses the refugees' awful circumstances: shunted away from any political community, many of the refugees and stateless people were reduced to mere survival, or to *bare life*, as she calls it. As Arendt explains, when some people prefer to commit petty crimes in order to benefit from food and shelter in detention, the Rights of Man lose their meaning: "The best criterion by which to decide whether someone has been forced outside the pale of the law is to ask if he would benefit by committing a crime. If a small burglary is likely to improve his legal position, at least temporarily, one may be sure he has been deprived of human rights."[22]

Paradigmatic of the failures of transnational governance at the time was the Évian Conference, which Franklin D. Roosevelt convened at Évian-les-Bains, France, in July 1938. With much fanfare, Roosevelt brought together thirty-two countries and thirty-nine private organiza-tions.[23] Twenty-four "voluntary organizations" also participated, many of

[20] James Hathaway, "The Evolution of Refugee Status in International Law: 1920–1950," *International and Comparative Law Quarterly* 33, no. 2 (1984).

[21] At work was an underlying principle of complementarity: the international organization steps in to grant a remedy where a sovereign state has failed. Compare with the idea of complementarity in international criminal law, in which an international body is expected to replace a state that has not fulfilled its most fundamental obligations. Robert Cryer, Hakan Friman, Darryl Robinson, and Elizabeth Wilmhurst, *An Introduction to International Criminal Law and Procedure* (Cambridge: Cambridge University Press, 2007), 127.

[22] Arendt, *Origins of Totalitarianism*, 286.

[23] This contemporary vocabulary aims to indicate that the underlying features were in many respects similar to other processes that were later celebrated, in the post-Cold War

which provided testimony. The Jews of Austria and Germany were hopeful, believing that this international conference would provide them a safe haven. Hitler famously responded to the news of the conference by saying that he would help the Jews leave.[24]

But both the United States and Britain refused to take in substantial numbers of Jews. Most of the countries at the conference followed suit, and the Jews were ultimately subject to "The Final Solution." The rhetorical commitment to rescue met with a political reality in which no actor would agree to pay rescue's price. Later critics accused the major powers, especially the United States and the United Kingdom, of some responsibility for the extermination of Jews. For example, Democrat Senator Claiborne Pell, while Chairman of the United States Committee on Foreign Relations, wrote a dramatic foreword for the provocatively titled *The Holocaust Conspiracy: An International Crime of Genocide*: "In my view, just about every Jew who was killed could have been saved if the governments of the Allied powers had provided timely refuge to European Jews who lived in countries coming under the control of Hitler's forces."[25] The transnational governance of human rights seemed to be but a wishful thought. Would things be fundamentally different in the postwar period?

The Universal Declaration of Human Rights (UDHR) was concluded in 1948, in conjunction with the UN Charter and the establishment of the United Nations. It was the first among a series of postwar documents that sought to provide universal protection for refugees. Article 14 UDHR thus provided that "Everyone has the right to seek and to enjoy in other countries asylum from persecution." The language, it would seem, referred to human beings as such, wherever their location may be, and whatever their nationality (or lack thereof).

moment. The contemporary use, generated primarily by Harold Hongju Koh, celebrated public–private participation to solve "transnational" problems. See Harold Hongju Koh, "Transnational Legal Process," *Nebraska Law Review* 75 (1996): 181–207.

[24] "I can only hope and expect that the other world, which has such deep sympathy for these criminals [Jews], will at least be generous enough to convert this sympathy into practical aid. We, on our part, are ready to put all these criminals at the disposal of these countries, for all I care, even on luxury ships." Quoted in Ronnie S. Landau, *The Nazi Holocaust* (London and New York: I.B. Tauris, 2006), 137.

[25] William R. Perl, *The Holocaust Conspiracy: An International Policy of Genocide* (New York: Shapolsky Publishers), 37. Perl was the lawyer who prosecuted the Malmedy Massacre, in which members of the Waffen SS were charged for the murder of American prisoners of war at Malmedy, Belgium, in December 1944. He later became the leader of the Washington branch of the far-right movement the Jewish Defense League. The league was designated as a terrorist organization in 2001.

On January 1, 1951, the UNHCR was established. This new institution was to provide individual assistance to refugees based on uniform criteria.[26] UNHCR's mandate was initially granted only temporarily – for three years. Six months later, in July 1951, the Refugee Convention was signed, and yet another definition of the term "refugee" was included in it. This formal definition would later come to be understood as globally applicable.[27] Its principal part appears in Article 1(2) of the Convention, according to which the term "refugee" would apply to any person who

> owing to well founded fear of being persecuted for reasons of race, religion, nationality, membership of a particular social group or political opinion, is outside the country of his nationality and is unable or, owing to such fear, is unwilling to avail himself of the protection of that country; or who, not having a nationality and being outside the country of his former habitual residence, is unable or, owing to such fear, is unwilling to return to it.

The most important right provided by the convention is *non-refoulement* – the right not to be returned to the state the refugee came from. The five bases for refugee claims – religion, ethnicity, nation, particular social group, or political opinion – were directly influenced by the events of the time.[28] Famine, disease, natural disasters, and wars were not included as bases for refugee claims. The categories of ethnicity, religion, and nationality were all fashioned around the "archetypical" example of the persecution of Jews by the Nazis.[29] Developing Cold War tensions influenced the fifth category – political opinion. The Soviet government criticized the protections for political dissenters and declared them to be a Western conspiracy designed to provide incentives for treason. The Soviets

[26] Soguk, *States and Strangers*, 166.

[27] In his much-discussed *Homo Sacer*, Agamben makes the argument that during the twentieth century, states of emergency have had the tendency to persist and transform into the norm. In the later *State of Exception*, he makes the same argument with regard to the legal norm in the post-9/11 United States, and especially the Patriot Act. Most readers of Agamben therefore tend to emphasize the ways in which states of exception render rights violations intractable. The emphasis here is different, reflecting the entrenchment of an emergency legal mechanism that aimed (successfully or not) to alleviate rights abuses. See Giorgio Agamben, *Homo Sacer: Sovereign Power and Bare Life* (Stanford: Stanford University Press, 1998), 38; Giorgio Agamben, *State of Exception* (Chicago: University of Chicago Press, 2005).

[28] Hathaway, "The Evolution of Refugee Status in International Law." See also Daniel J. Steinbock, "Interpreting the Refugee Definition," *UCLA Law Review* 45 (1997–1998): 733; and Christina Boswell, "European Values and the Asylum Crisis", *International Affairs* 76, no. 3 (2000): 537–557.

[29] Steinbock, "Interpreting the Refugee Definition," 766.

therefore boycotted the Convention negotiations.[30] Some celebrated the Convention and its Protocol as the culmination of a gradual process of individualization and universalization of human rights. But the idea that international law could provide enforceable human rights for the "flagless vessels" remained questionable. Importantly, unlike the UDHR, the Refugee Convention was also geographically limited. It applied only to refugees from Europe, and it was not until the 1967 Protocol that it would be applied to non-European refugees. Did the postwar declaration and treaty fill in the legal lacuna that Arendt described in her writing about the interwar period?

In an article published in 1948, British international lawyer Hersch Lauterpacht explained the starkest failure of UDHR was its attempt to provide refugees and stateless people with remedies.[31] Contrary to the rhetoric of some international lawyers who began discussing the status of individuals under international law, the crux of Lauterpacht's argument was that individuals were not the objects of international law at all. International law was and remained the law between states. For him, the UDHR was misleading in pretending otherwise. Such a shift would require changes in the fundamental privileges afforded by international law to sovereignty, and no such changes had occurred. Sovereignty remained the exclusive source of rights. As Lauterpacht wrote,

> few persons – and perhaps few lawyers – reading Article 14 of the declaration relating to asylum will appreciate the fact that there was no intention to assume even a moral obligation to grant asylum ... That article provides, in its first paragraph, that "everyone has the right to seek and enjoy in other countries asylum from persecution". The Committee rejected the proposal that there shall be a right to be granted asylum. According to the article as adopted there is a right "to seek" asylum, without any assurance that the seeking will be successful. It is perhaps a matter for regret that in a Declaration purporting to be an instrument of moral authority an ambiguous play of words, in a matter of this

---

[30] See Hathaway, "Reconsideration of the Underlying Premise of Refugee Law," *Harvard International Law Journal* 31 (1990): 129. The countries that partook in the formulation of the convention were Belgium, Brazil, Canada, China, Denmark, France, Great Britain, Israel, Sweden, Turkey, the United States, and Venezuela. For background on the development of a political East–West rift on international refugee law, see Georg Schwarzenberger, "The Impact of the East–West Rift on International Law," *Transactions of the Grotius Society* 36 Problems of Private and Public International Law, Transactions for the Year 1950 (1950): 243.

[31] Hersch Lauterpacht, "The Universal Declaration of Human Rights," *British Yearbook of International Law* 25 (1948): 354.

description, should have been attempted. Clearly, no declaration would be necessary to give an individual the right to seek asylum without an assurance of receiving it. The right "to enjoy asylum" was interpreted by the British delegation, which introduced the amendment containing these words, "as the right of every state to offer refuge and to resist all demands for extradition". But this, with regard to political offences and persecution generally, is the right which every state indisputably possesses under international law.[32]

In other words, the UDHR declares that it gives people something they already have – which happens to be nothing at all. The paragraph is "couched in language which is calculated to mislead and which is vividly reminiscent of international instruments in which an ingenious and deceptive form of words serves the purpose of concealing the determination of states to retain full freedom of action."[33] Lauterpacht reiterated the same critique in similarly caustic terms in the context of the UDHR provision on statelessness.[34]

Weis's essay, opening with the image of the flagless vessel, *The International Protection of Refugees*, was a direct response to Lauterpacht's. The legal advisor to the newly established UNHCR sought to challenge Lauterpacht's central point that individuals were not subjects of international law. Just as Lauterpacht took refugees and the stateless as paradigmatic examples of the lack of individual legal status, Weis returned to these groups to show that individuals do have status under international law. But Weis believed the UDHR was the wrong instrument to examine. The landmark shift in recognizing the status of the individual under international law was the Refugee Convention and the establishment of the UNHCR.

---

[32] Lauterpacht, "The Universal Declaration of Human Rights," 373.   [33] Id.

[34] The same purely nominal – and, in effect, deceptive – solution was adopted in the matter of nationality. After stating, in the first part of Article 15, that "everyone has the right to a nationality," the Declaration proceeds to lay down that "no one shall be arbitrarily deprived of his nationality." The natural implication of the principle that everyone is entitled to a nationality would be the prohibition of deprivation – whether arbitrary or otherwise – of nationality in a way resulting in statelessness. None of the states which in the period between the two world wars resorted to deprivation of nationality en masse for political or racial reasons would have admitted that such measures were arbitrary. They were, in their view, dictated by the highest necessities of the state. In a pronouncement claiming primarily moral authority there should have been no room for the institution of statelessness, which is a stigma upon international law and a challenge to human dignity in an international legal system in which nationality is the main link between the individual and international law.

Reading Weis, however, does not alleviate Lauterpacht's concerns. The poverty of international human rights law within the transnational governance paradigm is reproduced even in this self-conscious attempt to deny it. Lauterpacht and Weis were not thinking about the same thing when they were talking about "law." While Lauterpacht thought the possibility of enforcement was a necessary condition for a rule to be held "legal," Weis did not. "Universality and enforcement are two moot points of international law," he admitted. "Although the international agencies created for the protection of refugees have no means of enforcement at their disposal, their establishment marks a new method of international supervision of the rights and interests of individuals."[35] In its practical implementation, says Weis, the Convention requires the cooperation of particular state authorities, which at best can progress *incrementally.* Human rights in the transnational governance paradigm thus decouple the turn to the individual from the enforcement of rights. The universalist message in Weis's "method" is not in applying equal standards to all humans, conjoining rights with remedies. Rather, it is a promise that may happen in some projected future. While not providing reliable legal remedies for human rights claims, this type of regulation may still seem theoretically satisfying. Yet it is necessary to consider how it worked in practice. What would the adoption of incremental multilateralism mean for those suffering from the most urgent human rights violations?

The dark side of transnational governance is perhaps best illustrated by the allied forces' treatment of the many displaced persons (DPs) during and after WWII. This late chapter in the war's history demonstrates that there was no underlying agreement – neither theoretical nor practical – on what "human rights" entailed. In the face of the enormous emergency, humanitarian relief came dangerously close to the violence it promised to alleviate.[36] Some of the most well-intentioned transnational governance proposals were marred by racism.[37]

---

[35] Weis, "The International Protection of Refugees," 195.

[36] This tension will later be replayed in numerous contexts. See David Kennedy, "The International Protection of Refugees," in *The Dark Side of Virtue* (Princeton: Princeton University Press, 2004), 199–233.

[37] One author grounds his suggestion to relocate DPs to "the tropics," in a quasi-Darwinian idea that certain people are more adaptive to warm weather. Let us begin by defining the terms 'white,' 'settlement' and 'tropics' from the viewpoint of refugee and other white colonization. All the European refugees will be white in the popular sense, but there may be many ethnic (properly 'racial') differences . . . we have no scientific information as to the reasons, but they probably lie in the climatic experience of peoples who live in warm

The allies cooperated immediately after WWII in order to find solutions for the countless DPs. This massive operation involved the military management of camps.[38] In the context of this management, disagreements about the legal foundations of the protection of the war's victims grew between the allies. British authorities felt that creating camps specifically for Jews would amount to a particularly heinous form of racial segregation: "it is undesirable to accept the Nazi theory that the Jews are a separate race. Jews, in common with all other religious sects, should be treated according to their nationality, rather than as a race or a religious sect."[39]

It is too easy to respond that this position was disingenuous. According to such a response, the British were motivated by their complicated relationship to the developing Jewish national movement. Such a dismissal mistakenly assumes that politics is independent of genuine normative convictions regarding the entitlements of human beings. In fact, the view that all those in need should be treated equally, regardless of distinctions of race or religion, is more familiar to human rights advocates today than the view the United States advanced, of maintaining separate groups.[40]

On September 29, 1945, Harry Truman sent Dwight Eisenhower, then his Chief of Staff, a report that reflected just how deep the differences of fundamental normative convictions within transnational networks were. The report, authored by American lawyer Earl Harrison, representative to the Intergovernmental Commission on Refugees (and Dean of Pennsylvania Law School), was the fruit of a "Mission to Europe to inquire into the conditions and needs of those among the displaced persons in the liberated countries of Western Europe and in the

---

climates of Southern Europe, and in the fact that ethnic groups such as those just mentioned possess an historic mixture of Moorish and other 'colored' bloods. The Jews appear to do fairly well in the moderate tropics, such as Curacao in the Dutch West Indies; and this matter should be investigated more closely, for the Jews are the chief people likely to figure in refugee immigration." A. Grenfell Price, "Refugee Settlement in the Tropics," *Foreign Affairs* 8 (1940): 660.

[38] Liisa Malkki, "From 'Refugee Studies' to the National Order of Things," *Annual Review of Anthropology* 24 (1995): 495–523, 499.

[39] Quoted in Aviva Halamish, *The Exodus Affair: Holocaust Survivors and the Struggle for Palestine* (Syracuse: Syracuse University Press, 1998), 2.

[40] The British view is unsurprising within the context described above of transnational governance networks gravitating toward a teleological narrative of ever-increasing universality and individuality.

SHAEF area of Germany – with particular reference to the Jewish refugees – who may possibly be stateless or non-repatriable."[41]

From a contemporary perspective, this document reads like a prototypical human rights report – one that might be authored by a government, an international organization, or even an NGO like Human Rights Watch or Amnesty International. Like the contemporary genre of human rights reporting, it seamlessly weaves together law, fact, and policy. Like that genre, it relies heavily on interviews, focusing on such issues as detention conditions, nutrition, and accommodation. Substantively, however, its recommendations seem to be taken from a universe far removed.

Harrison responds to the British emphasis on color blindness and the resulting treatment of the Jews according to their differing nationalities. "While admittedly it is not normally desirable to set aside particular racial or religious groups from their nationality categories," he writes, "the plain truth is that this was done for so long by the Nazis that a group has been created which has special needs." Jews, he writes, should be treated as Jews.[42]

> In this connection, I wish to emphasize that it is not a case of singling out a particular group for special privileges. It is a matter of raising to a more normal level the position of a group which has been depressed to the lowest depths conceivable by years of organized and inhuman oppression.

This opinion too can easily be reduced to politics: the American interest in supporting Zionist national aspirations. But it too may have been informed by the normative convictions that someone like Harrison expressed in his report. The British and American positions point to two distinct potentials that human rights had in the twentieth century – one focusing on the defense of individuals and the other focusing on the defense of groups.[43] The distinct policies they entailed in terms of the

---

[41] Available at www.ushmm.org/exhibition/displaced-persons/resourc1.htm (last accessed May 3, 2016). Hereinafter "Harrison Report."

[42] The question about what was the role of the Jews as a group in meting out justice remained alive at least until the Eichmann trial, as reflected in Arendt's *Eichmann in Jerusalem*. Compare the British position expressed here with that of the Israeli prosecution, as described in her book. See Hannah Arendt, *Eichmann in Jerusalem* (New York: Penguin Classics, 2006), 6.

[43] This debate played out in the influential "antisubordination" approaches to equality in the United States. See generally, Owen Fiss, "Groups and the Equal Protection Clause," *Philosophy and Public Affairs* 15 (1976): 107; Derrick Bell, *And We Are Not Saved: The Elusive Quest for Racial Justice* (New York: Basic Books, 1987); Reva B. Siegel and Jack M. Balkin, "The American Civil Rights Tradition: Anticlassification of

administration of the DPs reflect how these potentials were not only different but also contradictory.[44]

More important than these philosophical considerations, however, Harrison emphasizes conditions on the ground, which indicated the depth of the failure of transnational networks to protect refugees and stateless people. Three months after the war ended, "many Jewish displaced persons and other possibly non-repatriables" were living behind barbed wire, in some of the camps where the Nazis had interned them. Their sanitary conditions were deplorable, and they lived "in complete idleness, with no opportunity, except surreptitiously, to communicate with the outside world, waiting, hoping for some word of encouragement and action on their behalf." Harrison documents a lack of medical supplies, as well as "pathetic malnutrition cases both among the hospitalized and in general population of the camps." The daily caloric intake per person was determined at 2,000 calories, which "included 1,250 calories of a black, wet and extremely unappetizing bread." Many still wore their concentration camp garb, "a rather hideous striped pajama," while others had to wear SS uniforms. As Harrison adds, "[I]t is questionable which clothing they hate more."

Harrison's most startling observation, however, is one that appears also as a quote in Truman's letter to Eisenhower: "As matters now stand, we appear to be treating the Jews as the Nazis treated them except that we do not exterminate them." The Jews, in other words, were reduced to mere survival. It is in this context that Harrison makes two recommendations that would be inconceivable in a contemporary human rights context. One was to ensure avenues of legal immigration for displaced Jews from Europe to colonial Palestine. Another was to evacuate German civilians from their homes, in order to make room for the DPs. Evacuating Germans from their homes would likely be thought of today as a war crime, but it was carried out in staggering numbers, as

Antisubordination?" *University of Miami Law Review* 58 (2003–2004): 9; Reva B. Siegel, "Equality Talk: Antisubordination and Anticlassification Values in Constitutional Struggles Over Brown," *Harvard Law Review* 117, no. 5 (2004): 1470. For a recent application in the context of refugee law and policy, see Tendayi Achiume, "Beyond Prejudice: Structural Xenophobic Discrimination Against Refugees," *Georgetown Journal of International Law* 45, no. 3 (2014).

[44] It is significant that both opposing positions in this quasi-legal dispute frame their ideas on the same backdrop of distinguishing themselves from Nazi policies. See Kahn, *The Cultural Study of Law*, 115 (arguing that "[t]o investigate the history of belief in the rule of law, we need to focus on what unites the opposing sides in a legal dispute").

historian R.M. Douglas has shown.[45] As Douglas explains, such operations occurred while the allies were prosecuting Germans in Nuremberg for comparable activities. In Harrison's legal imagination, it was possible to harness such operations for the cause of justice, precisely because the German civilian population was thought of as *accountable* for their government's atrocities. As he says quite plainly, they deserved it.[46]

The DP crisis became, along with Évian, one of the most glaring examples of the failures of human rights as transnational governance. In their attempt to produce policies independently of the aspirations of the subjects of rights, human rights were inconsistent and self-contradictory. In their transnational governance instantiation, human rights at times increased rather than alleviated violence against brutalized populations. Harrison's coupling of seemingly apolitical humanitarianism with particular remedies may sound quite peculiar to a contemporary reader. "For some of the European Jews, there is no acceptable or even decent solution for their future other than Palestine. This is said on a purely humanitarian basis with no reference to ideological or political considerations so far as Palestine is considered." How can a position that effectively came to side with the Jewish national movement over the Palestinian Arab one be regarded as "humanitarian," or free of politics?

Harrison's comparison between the administration of DP camps and Nazi atrocities suggested that transnational networks mandated with enforcing rights came dangerously close to repeating the German violations.[47] Such unreliable international conditions left the victims with no choice but to act for themselves. In order to defend Jewish DPs' rights, Harrison tells Truman, one must choose between being their friend today – or their enemy tomorrow:

> Unless this and other action, about to be suggested, is taken, substantial unofficial and unauthorized movements of people must be expected, and

---

[45] R.M. Douglas, *Orderly and Humane: The Expulsion of the Germans after the Second World War* (New Haven: Yale University Press), 512.

[46] Compare with Karl Jaspers' famous 1952 discussion of the German "political guilt" in Karl Jaspers, *The Question of German Guilt* (New York: Fordham University Press, 2001).

[47] As political scientist and Jewish émigré Otto Kirsheimer opined years later, the Refugee Convention could not guarantee anything, if another international emergency were to occur. Otto Kirscheimer, "Asylum," *American Political Science Review* 53, no. 4 (1959): 994 (arguing that "Experiences of some European nations which date back to the 1930's and 1940's suggest, however, that countries adjacent to areas of cataclysmic social and political upheavals will not guarantee refuge nor even be likely to grant as much as temporary asylum to huge numbers of escapees from revolutionary turmoil").

these will require considerable force to prevent, for the patience of many
of the persons involved is, and in my opinion with justification, nearing
the breaking point. It cannot be overemphasized that many of these
people are now desperate, that they have become accustomed under
German rule to employ every possible means to reach their end, and
that the fear of death does not restrain them.[48]

The Rights of Sovereignty

Not long before Weis wrote his defense of the transnational governance
of refugees, a group of displaced Jews and Jewish paramilitaries literally
enacted his metaphor: a flagless vessel on the high seas. But the understanding of human rights the *Exodus* demonstrated differed greatly from
any idea of human rights as transnational governance. While the latter
relied essentially on the cooperation between world superpowers to solve
the "Refugee Problem," the former relied upon the efforts of the stateless
to vindicate their own rights by establishing a state.

The assumption that human rights can only be granted by a sovereign
state has been extremely influential and is still shared by many.[49] In the
Israeli case, such human rights commitments were presumably
enshrined first in the Israeli Declaration of Independence; later in
Israel's Basic Laws; and finally in the judiciary's pronouncements.
The movement from migration to constitution is seamlessly translated
into the more familiar movement from revolution to constitution.[50]
The latter is of course a foundational narrative in the legal traditions of
the West. Instead of the stateless falling into a lacuna in international law,
managed by the incoherent networks of transnational governance, the
Exodus ostensibly demonstrated that those relegated to *bare life* could
abandon lawlessness and establish sovereignty. Only by doing so could
they secure their own rights – those rights that Lauterpacht found lacking
from the UDHR.

In this narrative, the *Exodus* affair is indivisible from various state-
building policies – diplomatic, military, and administrative – that could

---

[48] Harrison Report.

[49] Louis Henkin wrote in 1994 that "[e]ven for the daring international lawyer, human
rights remain national rights, rights to be enjoyed in a state's domestic legal order." See
Louis Henkin, "A Post-Cold War Human Rights Agenda," *Yale Journal of International
Law* 19 (1994): 249; Louis Henkin, "International Human Rights as 'Rights'," *Cardozo
Law Review* 1 (1979): 425.

[50] This movement is exemplified, e.g., in Michael Walzer, *Exodus and Revolution*
(New York: Basic Books, 1986).

only have one intelligible result: the establishment of Israel as an independent state. The state, accordingly, vindicates the rights of the rightless by its very founding and facilitates their enforcement by solidifying them within an institutional framework. To understand what human rights might be if framed exclusively through the prism of sovereignty, it is useful to reexamine the historical *Exodus* affair in some detail.

Steamer *President Warfield* was formerly operated by the Baltimore Steam Packet Co. and ran between Baltimore, Maryland, and Norfolk, Virginia. During World War II it was put to use by the British Navy and sent to Europe. There, the *Haganah*, a Jewish paramilitary group that sought to establish an independent Jewish state in Mandatory Palestine, purchased the boat. On July 11, 1947, *President Warfield* embarked on a journey that would gain international acclaim: Leaving from the South of France, it set sail to Palestine with around 4,500 European Jews on board. A few days later – while on the high seas – passengers of the *President Warfield* organized a ceremony in which the ship was renamed *Exodus*.[51] A blue-and-white flag with a Star of David was hoisted. This flag signaled particular political aspirations and later became Israel's flag. From the point of view of international law, however, it was still no flag at all.[52]

The British Navy intercepted the ship, which had intended to enter Mandatory Palestine illegally. As a British judge hearing a case regarding the *Exodus* later explained, "The question of the immigration of Jews into Palestine had for many years been the subject of acute controversy, and his Majesty's Government and the Government of Palestine have found it necessary to impose certain restrictions on immigration."[53] Many of the Jews, he exclaimed, "strenuously objected" to those restrictions, "and it has become the common practice for the champions of unrestricted immigration to organize parties of Jews from Europe and to send them to enter Palestine, if they can, in defiance of the regulations restricting immigration."[54] Violence erupted in the interception operation, and three of the *Exodus*'s passengers, among them a fifteen-year-old boy, were killed. While Zionists thought of the journey as one of national

---

[51] Some wanted to call it "Jewish resistance," signaling how close were the conceptual ties between their action and the idea of establishing what came to be known as a "Jewish state." This name was rejected, preferring the more abstract and possibly more universal one.

[52] For the purposes of the international law of the sea, a flag can only be a flag of a state.

[53] *R v. Sec of State for Foreign Affairs, ex Parte Greenberg* [1947] 2 All ER 550.

[54] *R v. Sec of State for Foreign Affairs, ex Parte Greenberg* [1947] 2 All ER 550, para 2.

liberation, British sources described it as criminal. The British Foreign
Office even declared that Zionists abducted 200 Jewish children from
Hungary and sent them out to sea.[55] In some of the Zionist accounts, the
very same children are considered among the most important actors
behind the fatal decisions on how the voyage would be carried out.[56]

After landing in the port of Haifa, the British Navy deported the
passengers from Palestine in three ships. The ships arrived at Port de
Bouc in the south of France on July 29, but the deportees would not
disembark. The ships therefore continued toward their final destination,
which was Hamburg. On September 9, *The New York Times* reported:
"after a two-hour token struggle against British military police, 1,406
Jews turned back from Palestine debarked this morning on German
soil."[57] When the deportees once again refused to step off the ship, they
were hosed and tear-gassed to compliance. The rest of the deportees, who
arrived later on the two other ships, didn't resist the landing.

Though the Jews of the *Exodus* were deported to Germany, the story
acquired iconic status in Israel's official history.[58] In this narrative, it
remains one of great courage and indeed a story of political success.[59] It is
commonly understood as a watershed in the responses of international
superpowers to the Jewish refugee problem after Jewish extermination
during World War II: "Slowly, despite everything, the story seeped into
the conscience of people all over the world. The name *Exodus* acquired
a face."[60] Most of the *Exodus* refugees, we are told, found their ways back
to Palestine, either legally or equipped with forged documents.
In Palestine, and then in Israel, they built their own homes.[61]

The Exodus affair is thus recounted as one of national self-
determination. It is only one phase among several: the initial Zionist
colonization of Palestine in the late nineteenth century; the establishment
of civilian institutions and Jewish paramilitary forces under British rule

[55] "Zionist Abduction of Jews Alleged," *New York Times*, September 6, 1947.
[56] Compare with the discussion of children in Chapters 2, 4, 5, and in the Conclusion.
[57] Edward Morrow, "Token Fight Waged as Jews of Exodus Begin Debarkation," *New York Times*, September 9, 1947.
[58] Halamish, *The Exodus Affair*. See also Didi Herman, *An Unfortunate Coincidence: Jews, Jewishness and English Law* (New York: Oxford, 2011), 105.
[59] See Halamish, *The Exodus Affair*, xxi.
[60] Yoram Kaniuk, *Commander of the Exodus* (New York: Grove Press, 2001), 149. From the perspective of the rights of encounter expounded below, the reference to "a face" may not be arbitrary, and may relate to the very nature of human rights. See "Ethics and the Face" inside Lévinas, *Totality and Infinity: An Essay on Exteriority*, 194–219.
[61] Kaniuk, *Commander of the Exodus*, 149.

in Palestine; the resettlement of Holocaust refugees; the war of the disempowered Jews against multiple Arab forces bent on their annihilation, and against a hostile Palestinian population; and finally, the Declaration of Independence. This story emphasizes that even though the refugees of the *Exodus* were sent back to German soil, their message was heard the world over. In this political imagination, the *Exodus* signals one important chapter in a story running from the ancient Israelites' forty-year journey in the Sinai desert to the European ghetto.[62] Instead of a teleological narrative of increasing individuality and universality (as transnational governance provided in the postwar moment), we find a narrative of a solidifying collectivity and particularity (which Harrison already hinted at). But both stories echo the same basic problem of the flagless vessel.

One of the most articulate narrators of the role of the *Exodus* in this story of collective self-determination is Israeli author Yoram Kaniuk. Kaniuk (1930–2013) was a novelist who in his late teens participated as a paramilitary soldier in Israel's war of independence, and among other roles served on a Jewish migrant boat. He unfolds this story in *Commander of the Exodus* (1999). The work is centered on the ship's legendary Captain Yossi Harel.[63] Harel, who grew up on a kibbutz in Palestine, joined the Jewish paramilitary when he was fourteen. He is described as the true salt of the earth, a partisan with a code of honor and silence passed to him by his brothers in arms. Before he joined the immigration operations, Harel trained in covert action. He studied the hidden pathways of his home country's rocky deserts, and he started participating in deterrence and revenge operations geared toward civilian casualties among the Palestinian Arabs.

For Kaniuk, who based his book on conversations with Harel, the *Exodus* affair was not merely one of the stages through which Israeli

---

[62] Kaniuk, *Commander of the Exodus*, 150.

[63] This is, in Hegel's terms, "original history": The author's spirit, and that of the actions he narrates, is one and the same. He describes scenes in which he himself has been an actor, or at any rate an interested spectator. It is short periods of time, individual shapes of persons and occurrences, single unreflected traits, of which he makes his picture. And his aim is nothing more than the presentation to posterity of an image of events as clear as that which he himself possessed in virtue of personal observation, or life-like descriptions. Reflections are none of his business, for he lives in the spirit of his subject; he has not attained an elevation above it. If, as in Caesar's case, he belongs to the exalted rank of generals or statesmen, it is the prosecution of *his own aims* that constitutes the history. See G.W.F. Hegel, *The Philosophy of History* (Mineola: Dover Publishing, 2004), 2.

independence was realized but rather the decisive one. He declares this immediately in the book's first paragraph:

> The State of Israel was not established on May 15, 1948, when the official declaration was made at Tel Aviv Museum. It was born nearly a year earlier on July 18, 1947, when a battered and stricken American ship called *President Warfield*, whose name was changed to *Exodus*, entered the port of Haifa with its loud-speakers blaring the strains of "Hatikva".[64]

Kaniuk's message – the message carried by this boat – is abundantly clear. It is not only that an act of unauthorized migration becomes an act of founding. It is also that this founding finds its necessary expression in sovereignty. Shifting independence temporally from declaration to migration suggests that there is no gap between de facto action and its de jure realization within the institutional structure of the state. If the *Exodus* was a literal embodiment of Weis's dilemma of the stateless, it suggests an answer to this dilemma that lies a far cry away from his reliance on transnational governance. The stateless enforced their rights not by appeal to the UDHR. The internationally issued Nansen passport and identity card surely could not grant them *identity*. Their own power made this transformation. If there is anything "transnational" about this power, it is the idea of heroic sacrifice in the face of omnipotent imperial armies.[65]

Unauthorized migration is thus no longer relegated to the sphere of *bare life* but is part and parcel of a revolutionary liberation struggle. It is imagined as collective and public action: an expression and at the same time a foundation of a community. The Jewish refugees and stateless made a resolute determination to guarantee their own rights.

In his retelling of the *Exodus* story, Kaniuk emphasizes the continuity between migration, the act of founding, and the war Jews fought for their independence in Palestine. As he describes at length elsewhere in his work, this war entailed the forceful displacement of the local Palestinian population. Harel personally partook in assassination operations, and as

---

[64] Kaniuk, *Commander of the Exodus*, ix. *Hatikva* later became Israel's national anthem.

[65] Harel constantly returns to a classic novel he read in his boyhood about the Armenian genocide and its resistance – *The Forty Days of Mousa Dagh* by Franz Werfel. For Kaniuk, this becomes an opportunity for a word play: Mousa Dagh is juxtaposed with Masadah, the mythic site where members of the Jewish resistance to Roman rule collectively committed suicide. See Kaniuk, *Commander of the Exodus*, 5, 49, 86. See also Franz Werfel, *The Forty Days of Musa Dagh* (Jaffrey, New Hampshire: Verba Mundi, 2012).

Kaniuk tells us, one of the tragic figures who arrived on the *Exodus* from Europe ends up finding work as a teacher in "an Arab dwelling whose inhabitants had fled under duress."[66] Those who deny this violence in the name of a purported international rule of law, says the author elsewhere, are deceiving themselves and their listeners.[67] Implicitly echoing Lauterpacht's critique of a certain style of international law, Kaniuk dismisses human rights as the hypocrisy of the privileged.

Though they were no doubt familiar to her, in Arendt's cursory remarks on the subject in "The Decline of the Nation State and the End of the Rights of Man" she doesn't explore the specific phenomenon of the *ma'apilim* (or "ascendants") – the Jewish unauthorized migrants who arrived in Palestine through the Mediterranean Sea. She does, however, consider the role of Israeli sovereignty within the more general context of a question about the source of rights. For Arendt, the displacement that resulted from the establishment of Israel shows that sovereignty and bare life are irrevocably bound up together:

> After the war it turned out that the Jewish question, which was considered the only insoluble one, was indeed solved – namely, by means of a colonized and then conquered territory – but this solved neither the problem of the minorities nor the stateless. On the contrary, like virtually all other events of our century, the solution of the Jewish question merely produced a new category of refugees, the Arabs, thereby increasing the number of the stateless and rightless people by another 700,000 to 800,000 people. And what happened in Palestine within the smallest territory and in terms of hundreds of thousands was then repeated in India on a large scale involving many millions of people. Since the Peace Treaties of 1919 and 1920 the refugees and the stateless have attached themselves like a curse to all the newly established states on earth which were created in the image of the nation-state.[68]

When refugees assert themselves within the framework of sovereignty, they are likely to end up reproducing displacement, as if in a vicious circle. As in the context of transnational governance, the protection of rights becomes continuous with and indistinguishable from their violation. The dialectic movement tying the enforcement of human rights to their violation is irrevocable in both these teleological narratives: one in which salvation is supposed to express itself in universal and individual

---

[66] Kaniuk, *Commander of the Exodus*, 146.
[67] See, e.g., Yoram Kaniuk, *Eṭim u-nevelot* (Tel-Aviv: Yedi'ot aharonot, 2006); Yoram Kaniuk, 1948 (New York: New York Review Books, 2012).
[68] Arendt, *Origins of Totalitarianism*, 290.

terms and one in which it is supposed to be concretized within state institutions. But the story of the *Exodus* encapsulates yet another theory of human rights, which does not fall within either paradigm.

The Rights of Encounter

To consider this third option, return yet again to this chapter's beginning: Weis's analogy to a flagless vessel on the high seas. This analogy merits more attention than Weis granted it. It should be approached as an embodied, physical, encounter. It serves as a kind of hypothetical, asking the reader to put herself in the position it describes.

The author chose to stage this dilemma on the "open sea" for evident reasons. The sea was traditionally thought of as outside of all sovereign territories and free for the navigation of all.[69] It thus simulates a global, ever-present state of nature.[70] For international lawyers, it historically presented a problem of dividing jurisdictions and responsibilities. Dutch Jurist Cornelius Van Bynkershoek famously formulated the eighteenth-century "cannonball rule," according to which a strip of water measured by the reach of a shot would count as part of a state's sovereign territory. This, however, did not change the basic principle asserted by his predecessor Hugo Grotius: The sea remained outside the reach of sovereignty.

The law applicable on the high seas historically was composed of customary norms that developed among merchants from European seafaring empires. These travelers showed a solidarity that did not always exist on the continent. This solidarity often united them against "savage" non-Europeans, who presented both danger and economic opportunity. Sailing without a flag would violate custom, placing the flagless vessel

---

[69] Carl Schmitt puts this in a characteristically ominous light when he writes that "The peaceful fisherman has the right to fish peacefully precisely where the belligerent sea power is allowed to lay its mines, and the neutral party is allowed to sail freely in the area where the warring parties have the right to annihilate each other with mines, submarines, and aircraft." Carl Schmitt, *The Nomos of the Earth in the International Law of Jus Publicum Europaem* (New York: Telos Free Press Publishing, 2006), 43.

[70] Think of Herman Melville's Benito Cereno. A merchant vessel is attacked off the Argentinean shoreline by a mutinied slave ship. As long as the ship is at sea, the events on board remain unintelligible. When Captain Cereno docks at shore, both law and comprehension are restored. As an admiralty tribunal recounts the whole story, the chain of events is for the first time coherently exposed. Herman Melville, *Benito Cereno* (New York: Bedford / St. Martin's, 2012).

literally beyond the pale of law. It was precisely in order to benefit from being outside law that pirates carried no recognized state flag.[71]

Arendt, in her essay "The Decline of the Nation State and the End of the Rights of Man," makes the same point as the flagless vessel analogy does, but with a different analogy: the stateless person (*apatride*) was a "legal freak."[72] The two images – Weis's and Arendt's – are very different from one another. To think of the refugee as a "freak" casts her condition as exceptional to the extreme. To think of the refugee as a flagless vessel on the high seas is to imagine an encounter. The image of a flagless vessel suggests questions like "Who are the refugees?" To which legal authority do they belong? If one imagines oneself on the high seas sailing under one's own national flag, one must also ask: What do I have to do with this person? How am I implicated in a refugee's life? And perhaps most importantly, how should I respond?[73]

The common law recognizes no duty of rescue apart from the exceptional context of the high sea commons.[74] Law is accordingly thought to draw a sharp line between killing someone and simply letting one die.[75] But Weis identified a context in which this line is blurred. In the flagless vessel analogy, someone *must* decide what rule to apply: whether to allow someone to board a deck or to cross a border.[76]

The authority from which Weis borrowed his little illustration of a flagless vessel on the high seas was no other than the father of international legal positivism, German-British Jurist Lassa Oppenheim.[77] In his

---

[71] Jenny Martinez, "Antislavery Courts and the Dawn of International Human Rights Law," *Yale Law Journal* 117 (2008): 551–641, 609.

[72] Arendt, *Origins of Totalitarianism*, 278.

[73] This way of posing the question inevitably implicates law with an ethical question, one in which responsibility for the other is always directed at an individual *personally*. See Lévinas, *Totality and Infinity: An Essay on Exteriority*, 215.

[74] For a challenge of this tradition, see Hanoch Dagan, "In Defense of the Good Samaritan," *Michigan Law Review* 97 (1998–1999): 1152.

[75] This has sometimes been thought of as simply a "fact": "if I conceptualize what happens to you as 'caused by my action' I will, as a matter of empirically demonstrable fact, feel much worse about your suffering than if I conceptualize it as something that I might have, but did not, intervene to prevent." See Duncan Kennedy, "Cost-Benefit Analysis of Entitlement Problems: A Critique," *Stanford Law Review* 33, no. 3 (1981): 401.

[76] This interrogation of rescue remedies is complementary to a foundational interrogation of the violence of law, and it is not by chance that both appear on the frontier of formalized jurisdiction. On violence and the border, see Kahn, *The Cultural Study of Law*, 94.

[77] For a discussion of Oppenheim's positivism, see Mathias Schmoeckel, "The Internationalist as Scientist and Herald: Lassa Oppenheim," *European Journal of International Law* 11 (2000): 699; Benedict Kingsbury, "Legal Positivism and Normative Politics: International

classic 1905 treatise, *International Law*, the London professor imagined the person-of-no-flag quite differently than did Weis. For Oppenheim, the image did not present a lawyer's dilemma (or any other dilemma, for that matter): "The position of such individuals destitute of nationality may be compared to vessels on the Open Sea not sailing under the flag of a state, *which likewise do not enjoy any protection whatever.*"[78] Indeed, continues Oppenheim, to say that refugees and the stateless are protected under international law is wrong: "In practice, stateless individuals are in most States treated more or less as though they were subjects of foreign States, but as a point of international legality there is *no restriction whatever* upon a State's *maltreating them to any extent*" (italics added).[79] Oppenheim's articulation of this idea had significant traction in mainstream international law literature.[80] But was it really the case that the refugee could simply be done away with?

A part of the *Exodus* story that remains less known is the short (and failed) legal battle that the Jewish deportees waged against their order of deportation from Palestine. This battle sheds a different light on Weis's dilemma. It demonstrates how in certain circumstances humans can

Society, Balance of Power and Lassa Oppenheim's Positive International Law," *European Journal of International Law* 13, no. 2 (2002): 401–436.

[78] Lassa Oppenheim, *International Law* (New York and Bombay: Longman, Green, and Co., 1905), 366.

[79] Oppenheim, *International Law*. Giorgio Agamben often refers to a class of people (each person labeled by the Roman legal term "homo sacer") who can be "killed with impunity." See Agamben, *Homo Sacer*, 47.

[80] During World War II, international lawyers cited these words approvingly. On October 7, 1942, W.R. Bisschop delivered introductory remarks to a conference on "Nationality in International Law," at the British Grotius Society, saying that: Individuals are objects of the Law of the Nations. It is only through the medium of their nationality, that is to say their being members of a State, that individuals can enjoy benefits from the Law of the Nations. Such individuals as do not posses any nationality enjoy no protection whatever and if they are aggrieved by a State they have no way to redress since there is no State which would be competent to take their case in hand. W.R. Bisschop, "Nationalty in International Law," *Transactions of the Grotius Society 28 Problems of Peace and War, Papers Read before the Society in the Year 1942* 28 (1942): 151–152. Loewenfeld too cites Oppenheim, and continues to say that "what cannot be denied at the background of this opinion is the fact that certain ethical ideas based on Christian morals have, and will again require, the help of International Law. Yet a guarantee of the so-called Rights of Mankind cannot be found in such facts." Erwin Loewenfeld, "Status of Stateless Persons," *Transactions of the Grotius Society* 28 Problems of Peace and War, Papers Read before the Society in the Year 1941 (1941), 59. Georg Schwarzenberger, a German–Jewish jurist who fled the Nazis, put forth the same idea in another variation: the refugee is a res nullius – ownerless property, free to be acquired by anyone. Quoted in Paul Weis, "Human Rights and Refugees," *International Migration* 10, nos. 1–2 (1972): 20.

impose duties on authorities, which arise neither from governments nor transnational organizations. Through such action, they can gain rights that would not otherwise be afforded to them.

As the *Exodus* sailed North from France to Germany, six members of the group granted power of attorney to a team of two lawyers, D.N. Pritt and S.N. Bernstein, who filed an application for a writ of *habeas corpus* on their behalf. Pritt and Bernstein argued before the Court of Appeals of England and Wales that the passengers were held illegally and should therefore be immediately released. Pritt, the senior of the two, was a communist who took on numerous political cases and especially labor disputes. Neither transnational governance nor Jewish sovereignty drew Pritt to the case. For him, the case was more about making a political point than about winning in court:

> The idea that hundreds of Jews who had left the country where they had been subjected to all the horrors of Nazism from 1933 to 1945 should be forcibly returned to that country by orders of the British Labour Government shocked a great many Jews – and a great many non-Jews, in Britain, and one of the Jewish organizations consulted me professionally as to what could be done. I advised them that there were an arguable if not very strong case for the propositions: (1) that, from the moment the ships sailed westwards from Palestine for anywhere but Cyprus, the Jews were illegally detained, since the order of the High Commissioner for Palestine deporting them could have no effect beyond Palestine territorial waters, and in any case could not empower the British Government or anybody else to tip them out into a country to which they did not want to go; and, (2) that the remedy of Habeas Corpus could be invoked against the Foreign Secretary.[81]

There was some controversy whether *President Warfield* was intercepted on the high seas or in Palestine's territorial waters (the opinion uses the vessel's official name, rather than *Exodus*). This was apparently a crucial issue even as the boat was intercepted. As Kaniuk described the event, "'The British Assault,' said Yossi [Harel] on the loudspeaker so that all the British officers on the ships would hear, 'is taking place in international waters. We are not responsible if soldiers are killed. If any do get killed, you are to blame, not us!'"[82]

The British court, however, did not really believe the attack was on the high seas. "On the whole," writes Justice Jenkins, "I think that the better

---

[81] D.N. Pritt, *The Autobiography of D. N. Pritt Part Two: Brasshats and Bureaucrats* (1966), 267.
[82] Kaniuk, *Commander of the Exodus*, 137.

view is that it took place inside territorial waters, but, be that as it may, the ship was escorted into territorial waters, and while it was within the jurisdiction of Palestine a deportation order was made in respect of the immigrants in the ship."[83] With this determination, the Court of Appeals attempted to avoid Weis's dilemma. Judgment in de-territorialized and legally under-determined circumstances was replaced by the application of (territorial) law.

The applicants argued that once they were brought out of the British protectorate, they could no longer be legally held by British forces. The authority to deport them was, according to this argument, strictly territorial and could not extend to Gibraltar, the Atlantic Ocean, or to the German port they were approaching. As Pritt recounts, however, "the Vacation Judge, in the end, decided against us."[84] A deportation order, explained Jenkins, must entail the enforcement authorities that are necessary to carry it out. More fundamentally, the judge did not accept that the deportees were at the time of the *habeas* application held under British custody at all:

> the immigrants . . . were pressed to land there and they refused. They were told that, if they did not land, they would be taken to Hamburg. . . . these immigrants, having been given the warning and the choice, deliberately elected to go on in the ships . . . in my opinion, it would be possible to dispose of this case really on the short ground that, whatever the position was at any point of time before the arrival at Port de Bouc, there can now be no question of illegal restraint, since the immigrants remained *in the ships of their own free will.* (emphasis added)[85]

"For these reasons," concludes Jenkins, "a case for a writ of habeas corpus has not been made out."[86] The applicants were charged with trial expenses.

Within a heroic history of the *Exodus* as an assertion of sovereignty, Judge Jenkins plays the role of a villain. A remarkable aspect of his judgment is the fact he made no mention of what obviously moved Pritt and others who followed the case:[87] the recent atrocities against the Jews in Europe, and the role of the country they were being deported

---

[83] The order was given under the Palestine Defence (Emergency) Regulations of 1945 (the same law that Israel later invoked in expelling the Palestinians from the newly established state).

[84] Pritt, *The Autobiography of D. N. Pritt Part Two*, 267. A "Vaction Judge" is a fill-in judge that is supposed to dispose of urgent issues when a court goes on vacation.

[85] *R v. Sec of State for Foreign Affairs, ex Parte Greenberg* [1947] 2 All ER 550, para 2.

[86] *R v. Sec of State for Foreign Affairs, ex Parte Greenberg* [1947] 2 All ER 550, para 2.

[87] Herman, *An Unfortunate Coincidence*, 106.

to in those atrocities. The word "refugee" is not included in the text at all, although the passengers proactively communicated their identities to the British authorities.[88] One commentator even suggests that this lack of attention to the passengers' histories can be thought of as a kind of dehumanization.[89] However, the text of the opinion unwittingly discloses another kind of normative commitment and invites another interpretation.

Describing the applicants for the writ of *habeas corpus*, Justice Jenkins writes: "These six persons … set sail … with the intention either of getting into Palestine by stealth, or, if intercepted, of *embarrassing* the authorities who would then *have on their hands* a further 4,500 people to be dealt with somehow" (emphasis added). The judge describes this behavior with some contempt. But the challenge he exposes merits attention. It amounts to a rough outline of the binding nature of human rights – beyond transnational governance and beyond sovereignty. What are the underlying assumptions of planning to "embarrass" government officials by putting oneself "on their hands … to be dealt with somehow"? This is where Jenkins takes a small step away from Oppenheim, and the latter's assumption that the only possible source of rights is sovereignty. By raising this as a problem, the judge already assumes that the thousands simply cannot be *maltreated to any extent* – whatever positive law on this issue may be.

Every word in Jenkins's passage is critical. Among them is the image of *hands*. The figurative language captures something important about the scene Jenkins envisions. It implies human fragility: close the fingers into a fist and the refugees on your hands will perish. Challenging political authorities not to close their hands, unauthorized migrants are able to push the line between killing someone and letting her die.[90]

But the single most important word in Jenkins' opinion is "embarrassing." It only makes sense to talk about human rights once this potential embarrassment appears. Justice Jenkins was concerned that this embarrassment will somehow have coercive power over British authorities. Jenkins believed that when *President Warfield* left Europe, it exploited the unstated, tacit kind of law that bars the fingers from tightening up into a fist. Another way to describe this action would be simply to say that the Jewish migrants *relied* on such a law.

---

[88] While Pritt used the term "displaced Jews" in his oral argument, the judge ignored this nomenclature as well.

[89] Herman, *An Unfortunate Coincidence*, 107.   [90] See Chapter 4.

We therefore have more or less the same encounter, outlined by three lawyers with different backgrounds: a prominent professor and one of the main figures of nineteenth-century international law (Oppenheim); a chief legal adviser for a UN humanitarian agency (Weis); and a British Appellate Court judge (Jenkins). Oppenheim had a very clear-cut view about the respective rights and duties of the two sides of this encounter: they had none. Weis raised the issue as a question, hoping that international powers could be gradually moved to take responsibility. And Jenkins rejected the migrants' claims, but he hinted that there is a perceived duty at stake, not in some projected future, but in the present.

To be sure, the unauthorized migrants of the *Exodus* invoked this duty quite directly. In a handwritten letter addressed to the British agents during the deportation, they invoked their own humanity. The letter starts: "British soldiers and officers! You are waging battle against peaceful innocent people, which only crime consists in that they want a home just like hundreds of peoples!" (*sic*). The next lines are revealing:

> We have been dragged away with brutality from the shores of Palestine and for about two month already we are being led on the sea, locked in barbed wire just if we were dangerous criminals. Now you want get us off with force in Hamburg back to our enemies, back to the murder of people, which wanted to annihilate the world, and bestially destroyed our parents and children and exterminated more than a third of our people. You are sending us back to pains, suffering and downfall!! British soldiers and officers! Today you are compelled to do the same thing the Germans did before against whom you fought heroically!
>
> (*sic*)

Knowingly or not, the passengers of the *Exodus* repeated Harrison's most acerbic accusation, directed at his own government: "we appear to be treating the Jews as the Nazis treated them except that we do not exterminate them." A similar message was printed on a banner that was tied to the boat, making it as visible as possible. The message refers to characteristics of human life that belong to all humans as such, namely *family* and *hope*.

The human rights as encounter can be abstracted from this relationship, at an international border, between a powerless individual and a powerful official. The Jewish refugees posed a challenge to the British Navy: "you, and no one else, will decide if I will have a life worth living." This challenge is what Jenkins is talking about when he talks of *embarrassment*. When those who seek to pose such a challenge identify moral precepts to which a relatively powerful addressee claims to be bound, they can put the addressee in a position Max Weber labeled the *ethics of conviction.* Saying "you and no one else" captures the addressee in the position characterized by Weber (following Martin Luther): "here I stand, I can do no other."[91]

Following the first paragraph of Kaniuk's literary-historical account of the *Exodus* affair quoted above, the author continues:

> The State of Israel came into existence before it acquired a name, when its gates were locked to Jews, when the British fought against survivors of the Holocaust. It came into existence when its shores were blockaded – against those for whom the state was eventually designated – by forty-five model C warships, the most modern warships the British built toward the end of World War II, which hadn't managed to see service. The fleet was gigantic even by today's standards . . . It came into being when they closed its gates by means of tens of thousands of soldiers, thousands of police and intelligence agents from the CID, on land, in the ports, and throughout Europe, and by means of detention camps in Atlit and Cyprus.

While the first paragraph quoted above demonstrated powerfully the idea that human rights are only enforced within the context of sovereignty, here Kaniuk suggests a different sensibility. To be sure, he still stresses the importance of the state. But the curious thing about the passage is that the vindication of the Jewish cause is expressed by its negation. It is not enough to say that the narrative is constructed as one of the weak defeating the powerful. Such a conventional account would appear if Kaniuk would write that the doors of Palestine would eventually open for the passengers of the *Exodus* and is consistent with a story of a violent struggle for sovereignty.[92] Here, instead, the moment of founding is when those doors are still closed. The fact that the migrants were detained in Atlit (South of Haifa) and in Cyprus is somehow considered not as debasement but as victory.

This narrative of the rights of encounter is not about martyrdom. According to Kaniuk's narration, only after having been exposed to the Holocaust survivors' incredible will to survive did Harel decide the ship

---

[91] Weber famously called this an "ethics of conviction." See Max Weber, *The Vocation Lectures* (Indianapolis / Cambridge: Hacket Publishing, 2004), 92.

[92] It is encapsulated in other moments in the book, for example when he quotes the opinion of some of the Haganah leaders, according to which the migrant boats were "battering rams" with which British control in Palestine would be ousted. Kaniuk, *Commander of the Exodus*, 36.

would *not* fight the British forces unto death. He "wouldn't agree to become the architect of a new Masada, even in the name of a national myth for a resurrected generation." This position is contrasted with that of other *Haganah* operatives on board, who "stuck to the struggle" even after "having faced the eyes of the children that gazed at them day after day." But "the command he [Harel] accepted hadn't been to bring a ship full of corpses to Palestine."[93]

Though there were casualties, the story is more accurately framed under the general title of *embarrassment*. The embarrassment that Justice Jenkins identified in the encounter between the Exodus and the British Navy was exposed to third-party onlookers, thereby granting it a transformative political power. Precisely as Justice Jenkins feared, the actions of the British Navy were somehow encoded as illegitimate. And this development cannot be reduced to a violation of the rules of treaty law or of the law of an existing sovereign entity. Jenkins' reference to embarrassment speaks to the fact that there was indeed a source of law beyond sovereignty. Two components of this embarrassment are important here. First is a kind of self-embarrassment that comes from failing to be true to the self. We are led to believe that this embarrassment occurred or could have occurred immediately at the site of encounter. Second, however, is the embarrassment of not being true to the self as perceived by others. The invocations of humanity in the refugees' letter (only wanting a home) and of crimes against humanity (the comparison to "Germans") are presumably not intended only for the British "soldiers and officers." They already imply a potentially vaster audience. Turning to such an audience can still allow the encounter to generate a modicum of rights protection that relies on that audience's potential response. After World War II (and particularly in the wake of the Nuremberg Trials), the Western Bloc purported to form an alliance founded both on power and on principle. The encounter with the universal boatperson challenges that power inasmuch as it puts its fidelity to "principle" to a test.

Between Governance, Sovereignty, and Encounter

An obvious challenge to the "rights of encounter" is a reductionism that attempts to translate the enforcement stemming from encounter either to

---

[93] Kaniuk, *Commander of the Exodus*, 142–143.

transnational governance or to sovereignty. Law, this objection might add, is inextricably tied up with violence. The idea of law without violence falls into an empty utopianism at best and a deceptive denial of its own violence at worse.[94] This is what disturbed Lauterpacht with the UDHR. And it has been a looming concern for international lawyers ever since.[95] Arguing for the rights of encounter doesn't aim to reduce the importance of the rights of sovereignty or of those granted by transnational governance. Nor does it say that the violence of law is necessarily objectionable. But it is both conceptually and practically important to distinguish these rights of encounter from those discussed under transnational governance or sovereignty.

An argument reducing the rights of encounter to sovereignty would claim that the *Exodus* migrants were basically the instruments of a nationalist movement. In this view, the voyage was essentially a military operation made possible by partisan violence.[96] As one commentator had it, embarrassment was not more than one strategy among many that the Zionist movement employed.[97] The affair can only be understood as part and parcel of one policy that later led to orders given by Haganah leaders to expel the Palestinians. This created the Palestinian refugee problem, which is yet to be resolved. This position doubtlessly has some truth to it.[98]

---

[94] Paraphrasing Martti Koskenniemi's classic formulation. Martti Koskenniemi, *From Apology to Utopia: The Structure of International Legal Argument* (Cambridge: Cambridge University Press, 2006).

[95] The lack of enforcement was arguably a problem with certain normative claims in international law long before Lauterpacht. See, e.g., Stephen Neff, *Justice among Nations: A History of International Law* (Cambridge: Harvard University Press, 2014), 59. (explaining that "To many," natural law "existed only in the vaporous outpourings of scholars").

[96] At the end of World War II, Zionist leaders sought to make the postwar fate of the Jewish displaced persons (DPs) a major item on the international agenda, aiming to create a link, in the minds of global policymakers, between solving the problem of European DPs and the founding of a Jewish State in Palestine (Eretz-Israel). One means at their disposal was organized illegal immigration to Palestine by sea, namely, the *Ha'apalah*, or *Aliyah Bet*. See Aviva Halamish, "American Volunteers in Illegal Immigration to Palestine, 1946–1948," *Jewish History* 9, no. 1 (1995): 91.

[97] Aviva Halamish writes: "Illegal immigration had the potential to embarrass the British for callously preventing the entry of Jewish survivors of the Holocaust into their homeland, and thus making full use of the moral force of the Zionist cause" (Halamish, *The Exodus Affair*, xx).

[98] One historian has recently gone so far as showing that the 1951 Refugee Convention has "Israeli roots." See Gilad Ben-Nun, "The Israeli Roots of Article 3 and Article 6 of the 1951 Refugee Convention," *Journal of Refugee Studies* 26, no. 3 (2013): 1–25.

In answering the question whether or not unauthorized migrants were really part of a military campaign, some closer attention to what actually happened on the boat is required. The events demonstrate that the phenomenon was qualitatively different from war, even in the form of a partisan or revolutionary war. Only because the migrants on the boats *did not* come to fight against the British could their story have the "embarrassing" effect that Jenkins feared it might have. Particularly relevant here is the testimony of John Stanley Grauel, a former Methodist minister from Massachusetts, who was a volunteer aboard the boat.[99]

As Grauel explained, this non-belligerent stance was premeditated. One of the most contentious issues has been whether the Jews aboard the Exodus used firearms. Gruael testified that before embarkation from France, the crew searched all the refugees' belongings, making sure there would be no weapons on board. "Three pistols were found and thrown into the sea." When the British attacked with clubs, and "sprayed the Hurricane deck with three blasts from a machine gun," Grauel fought back with other refugees, throwing potatoes and canned goods at the British soldiers. The same descriptions appear in Kaniuk's account. "[T]he first three [British] invaders were locked inside the pilot deck, and youngsters previously trained for this purpose tossed crates and flung screws, tin cans, and rotten potatoes at them."[100] There is some form of retaliation here, but it importantly signals an *abstention* from a military overthrow of an existing legal order. Unauthorized migration becomes a paradigm of resistance – a word Harel uses repeatedly – but not a politics that extends war by other means.

Alternatively, the *Exodus* affair can be explained as a product of transnational governance. According to such an account, only because it was in the interest of transnational superpowers that displaced Jews find their way to the Middle East did their message finally prevail. This also has some truth in it. The *Exodus* had a considerable role in the transnational legal processes of the time.

Grauel, for example, testified before the United Nations Committee on Palestine (UNSCOP), which later cited his testimony as part of the

---

[99] For background about the volunteers, see Halamish, "American Volunteers in Illegal Immigration to Palestine, 1946–1948," 92. Halamish's analysis of the motivations of American Jewish volunteers is consonant with the analysis proposed here, inasmuch she shifts the main weight from nationalism to a kind of Universalist sense of guilt. This guilt is comparable to the Navy soldiers' alleged "embarrassment."

[100] Kaniuk, *Commander of the Exodus*, 136.

factual basis for its recommendation of the partition plan – leading to Israel's recognition by the United Nations in 1948. As Prime Minister Meir explained, Grauel was a "perfectly worthy gentile" and could therefore give the testimony: "no Jewish witness was to be believed." Though Meir credited Grauel for this achievement, her bitterness also expresses resentment toward networks of transnational governance. But the real response to reducing the *Exodus* affair to transnational governance is that it was only *because* the migrants generated the encounter that they were granted a position in a transnational sphere. Strictly from the perspective of transnational governance, there was no reason for the DPs to be transferred to Palestine. Nevertheless, they did achieve sovereignty there.[101] The rights of encounter are primary, and not secondary, to the rights generated by transnational governance networks.

In a letter to President Truman dated September 9, 1947, attorney Joseph Crown, secretary of the Lawyers Committee, wrote that "current reports of the brutality employed by the British Government in forcibly disembarking the Exodus refugees shocked the conscience of civilized humanity." Sending "tortured men, women and children back to the soil of Germany," he said, resembled the "callousness of the Nazi which was thought to have been destroyed." The final part of the letter establishes an obligation to human beings as such, based upon the recent history of human extermination. The response to this history and the enforcement of the rights of those who have been victimized by it should become part of American foreign policy: "Surely there can be no meaning to the sufferings of mankind during the recent war if such brutality and disregard for human rights and flouting of international authority is allowed to go unchallenged. Even at this eleventh hour it becomes the responsibility of the government of the United States to raise its voice on behalf of these defenseless peoples and to insist that they be permitted to enter Palestine."[102] Similar voices came from other actors outside of Palestine but also from the Jews living there.[103]

---

[101] See Shirley Jenkins, "Refugee Settlement in Australia," *Far Eastern Survey* 13, no. 13 (1944): 120.

[102] National Lawyers Guild Letter to President Harry S. Truman, September 9, 1947; Records of the National Lawyers Guild; Box 56b, Folder 8c; Tamiment Library and Robert F. Wagner Labor Archives.

[103] Zalman Rubashov, editor of the Hebrew newspaper Davar, termed Britain's behavior a "crime against humanity." Jewish Telegraphic Agency Daily News Bulletin, August 26, 1947.

The Human Rights Encounter

Imagine that you are not able to realize your idea of a life worth living.
You know that somewhere else – perhaps across the Mediterranean –
realizing such a life may be possible. But you are not allowed to traverse
the invisible border in the water.[104] So you decide to cross illegally and
seek a dignified life elsewhere. You know that on the high seas you can
move with no restrictions. But you also know that at some point, you
are bound to encounter an armed agent of the navy or the coastguard,
whose duty it will be to enforce the law. This official will be much more
powerful than you. What you may be able to do is put yourself on their
hands.

Now imagine that you are with the navy or coastguard, and you
encounter a flagless vessel on the high seas. You believe that if you
conduct your task and send the passengers of this vessel back to where
they came from, they will be exposed to a serious risk. They may not be
able to realize a life worth living. Or, they might be killed. Both sides of
this encounter are aware of the existential challenge it presents; it tests
their moral constitution. In the *Exodus* affair, presumably some members of the British Navy felt the command of the encounter with *bare
life*. This command is reflected, for example, in the poignant way
Lieutenant Commander Bailey, one of the commanders of the interception team, likens the ship to an animal: "*President Warfield* was
a phantom vision as it sailed at full speed with all its dead aboard in the
dark night, with two huge Zionist flags waving on the ship's masts,
illuminated by our large searchlights. Her siren wailing in the night
sounded like a wounded, lowing cow escaping to hide itself."[105] With
such a siren, a refugee can tell the border guard at sea: either allow me
in, and show fidelity to your principles, or show fidelity to your duty,
and violate your principles.

The powerful party in the encounter cannot exercise this judgment
without the power that the "powerless" party of the encounter exerts – the

[104] The fact that the line is in the water is only important here inasmuch as I'm thinking of
a territory from which sovereignty is absent. But this can also be land, and though the
world is divided between states, some areas maintain the same character as global no-
man's land. A beautiful illustration of this appears in *Inland (Gabbla)*, a 2008 film by the
Algerian director Tariq Teguia. One of the two protagonists is a female clandestine
migrant who has attempted to cross Algeria on her way to Europe. After she changes her
mind and decides to return to where she came from; in one of the final scenes she looks at
the open desert and announces that she sees the border. But there is nothing to be seen.

[105] Kaniuk, *Commander of the Exodus*, 141.

power of its very presence. "Presence" in this context should not be understood as of the body alone. Countless human beings on our planet do not have this relevant kind of presence, although they do have bodies. Presence must be claimed, for example, by stepping into the (coastguard's) searchlight. From that searchlight, the encounter also has to reach the third-party transnational audience, which may translate it into the necessary embarrassment. This is reflected, at the minimal level, by the *active* attempt to assert one's own right to a dignified life, regardless of citizenship, or lack thereof.

The father of legal positivism, John Austin, wrote: "A man is no more able to confer a right on himself, than he is able to impose on himself a law or a duty."[106] But human rights are not positive rights. In the theory of the *universal boatperson*, the powerless party violates the first part of Austin's assertion. The powerful party violates its second. Each party is dependent on the other in so doing.

---

[106] John Austin, *The Province of Jurisprudence Determined* (London: John Murray, 1832), 305.

2

What Is a Human Rights Claim?

The problem of the universal boatperson reemerged in 1975 as an enormous phenomenon of migrants taking to the sea (sometimes referred to as the Southeast Asian "exodus").[1] Could hundreds of thousands of "boat people" simply be ignored or "maltreated to any extent"?[2] Granted, many of them suffered horrific experiences. As writer Jonathan Schell described, "when the North Vietnamese took control of the South, in 1975, they created conditions such that tens of thousands of people preferred to escape into the South China Sea in boats, most of which never arrived in any destination."[3] According to UNHCR numbers, 200,000–400,000 Southeast Asian boat people died at sea. Others suffered starvation, rape, or police brutality. This, however, does not eliminate the triumph of a great number of others who survived, resettled in communities far away from home, and eventually gained access to newfound citizenships. They were sometimes able to transform a struggle for a life worth living into the freedom of participation in a political community of equals.[4] With their actions, these people demonstrated what it means to make a human rights claim.

---

[1] W. Courtland Robinson, *Terms of Refuge: The Indochinese Exodus and the International Response* (New York and London: Zed Books, 1998). For other examples, see, e.g., Elliot T. Tepper (ed.), *Southeast Asian Exodus: From Tradition to Resettlement* (Ottawa: The Canadian Asian Studies Association, 1980); Tai Van Nguyen, *The Storm of Our Lives: A Vietnamese Family's Boat Journey to Freedom* (Jefferson, NC, and London: McFarland & Company, Inc., 2009), 119; Bruce Grant, *The Boat People: An "Age" Investigation with Bruce Grant* (London: Penguin, 1980), 80.

[2] Lassa Oppenheim, *International Law* (New York and Bombay: Longman, Green, and Co., 1905), 366. See discussion in Chapter 1.

[3] Jonathan Schell, *The Real War: The Classic Reporting on the Vietnam War* (Boston: Da Capo Press, 2000), 18.

[4] I use the term "political freedom" in the positive sense, much indebted to the work of Hannah Arendt. For Arendt, freedom does not mean the ability to choose among a set of possible alternatives, or the faculty of free will – *liberum arbitrium*, which, according to Christian doctrine, was given to us by God. Arendt's freedom is twofold. On the one hand, it means the capacity to begin something new or do the unexpected, a capacity Arendt labels *natality*.

The Southeast Asian refugee crisis began well after the framing of the 1951 Refugee Convention. The United States had already committed to Convention-based refugee protection with its accession to the 1967 Protocol.[5] And the application of the Convention was expanded; with few exceptions, state signatories recognized that it applied regardless of the geographic limitation that had initially limited it to refugees from Europe. The ICCPR and the ICESR have also already been framed (1966), each of which promised to protect human rights – potentially the world over.[6] Yet the rights that international instruments conferred upon humans remained largely unenforceable. How, then, did the plight of the Vietnamese "boat people" come to be perceived as "a story of hope and positive human achievement"?[7] Legal frameworks that were put in place back then are today upheld as exemplary responses to maritime migrant and refugee flows.[8]

The United States evacuated significant numbers of people thought to be in danger in the 1970s. As an adversary in the Vietnam War, it had deep interests to protect its local allies and supporters.[9] These operations, however, fell short of the needs of enormous numbers of displaced people. Initially, neighboring countries hosted refugees. Refugee camps were erected on their territories with the assistance of international funding. As the situation deteriorated, however, the governments of the neighboring countries grew determined to stem the flow. Conditions in the camps worsened, and their navies and coastguards started pushing

On the other hand, it means the capacity of living within a community, among equals and participating in collective processes of self-government. See, e.g., Hannah Arendt, *The Human Condition* (Chicago: University of Chicago Press, 1998); Hannah Arendt, *On Revolution* (London: Penguin, 2006). Arendt didn't think such a positive form of participation is possible outside particular communities. This chapter aims to challenge the latter thesis.

[5] The United States was a key actor in the framing of the Refugee Convention but did not itself accede to the convention until 1967. It did not internalize it in domestic legislation until the 1980 Refugee Act. For a critique in the context of the Vietnamese refugee crisis, see Tang Thanh Trai Le, "The Legal Status of the Refugee in the United States," *American Journal of Comparative Law* 42 (1994): 578.

[6] On their importance in historical context, see Antony Anghie, "Whose Utopia?" *Qui Palre: Critical Humanities and Social Sciences* 22, no. 1 (2013): 63, 69–71.

[7] Former High Commissioner for Refugees Sadako Ogata's assessment in her foreword to Robinson, *Terms of Refuge*, vii.

[8] Guy Goodwin-Gillar, "Refugees and Migrants at Sea: Duties of Care and Protection in the Mediterranean and the Need for International Action" available http://www.jmcemigrants .eu/jmce/wp-content/uploads/2015/06/GSGG-Naples-Final-May2015.pdf (last accessed May 3, 2016).

[9] For an interesting recent portrayal of these events, see *Last Days in Vietnam*, a 2014 film by director Rory Kennedy.

refugee boats out of territorial waters and back to sea. The sea in turn grew lawless, and the "boat people" fell prey to rampant pirate attacks.

This crisis ignited an international legal process and a new legal response within a larger framework of transnational governance.[10] With much fanfare, the 1979 Geneva Conference introduced the *Orderly Departure Program* to address the crisis. The Program was a multilateral framework that sought to protect those who aimed to leave Vietnam, granting resettlement visas while preventing embarkations on perilous journeys. The new instrument of international law had considerable problems. But it demonstrated the positive potential of wide-scale transnational cooperation in the face of an ongoing emergency.[11] Courtland Robinson's *Terms of Refuge: The Indochinese Exodus and the International Response*,[12] hailed as "the definitive work" on this refugee crisis, documents the Geneva process and the events surrounding it. The book credits a variety of actors for the success: among them states, international organizations, and a variety of civil society actors.[13] But with few exceptions, existing literature about the process ignores the boat people or considers them as passive victims in the creation of a new international legal framework.[14]

This chapter argues that a precondition for human rights law is a human rights struggle. Human rights aren't naturally given. They are the result of active assertions of rights by persons who have no rights

---

[10] On the notion of "transnational legal process," see Harold Hongju Koh, "Transnational Legal Process," *Nebraska Law Review* 75 (1996). For a discussion of the notion of "transnational governance," see Chapter 1.

[11] See, e.g., James Hathaway, "Labelling the 'Boat People': The Failure of the Human Rights Mandate of the Comprehensive Plan of Action for Indochinese Refugees," *Human Rights Quarterly* 15, no. 4 (1993): 686 (contrasting the effective Orderly Departure Program to the ineffective Comprehensive Plan of Action); Judith Kumin, "Orderly Departure from Vietnam: Cold War Anomaly or Humanitarian Innovation?" *Refugee Survey Quarterly* 27, no. 1 (2008): 104–117 (arguing that "It proved to be both a quintessential Cold War program, developed and implemented chiefly because it was in the United States' interest, and an exceptionally forward-looking and innovative approach to resolving a refugee crisis and to addressing the asylum–migration nexus which so preoccupies States nearly 30 years later").

[12] Robinson, *Terms of Refuge*.

[13] Like the Évian conference discussed in the Chapter 1, it was a "transnational" process par excellence. See Phillip Jessup, *Transnational Law* (New Haven: Yale University Press, 1956), 2.

[14] This is symptomatic of human rights in the transnational governance vein. For a related discussion, see Balakrishnan Rajagopal, *International Law from Below: Development, Social Movements and Third World Resistance* (Cambridge: Cambridge University Press, 2003), 174. The *New York Times* alluded to a related tendency in a much more recent editorial. "Lost Voices of the World's Refugees," *New York Times*, June 13, 2015, available at www.nytimes.com/2015/06/14/opinion/lost-voices-of-the-worlds-refugees .html?smid=nytcore-iphone-share&smprod=nytcore-iphone (last accessed May 3, 2016).

within existing states. This struggle started from a condition of near lawlessness, created in Vietnam immediately after the American withdrawal from the country. What rights claims can be made in such radical conditions? I will show that the movement of persons can provoke a remedy by powerful states and can generate international legal process.

The chapter expounds upon some of the points already developed in the previous chapter. However, the chapter is also complementary to the previous chapter. A possible objection to the previous chapter is that the ultimate protection of rights was not of *human* rights at all. After all, the Zionist passengers of the *Exodus* ultimately established their own *state*. They protected themselves as citizens, not as human beings – and the question remains if there are any enforceable rights to speak of in international law, beyond those granted by states.[15] The Southeast Asian boat people, however, reveal the other side of the coin. Here, the remedy was not establishing a newfound citizenship and a new social contract. Rather, the remedy was creating a new transnational legal structure, the purpose of which was to open existing social contracts. Which one of these trajectories is pursued – establishing a new state or granting status within existing states – is less important than a more basic task: grounding a non-natural but extra-statist claim at the foundation of international law. Human rights originate from outside of the state and only then transform into claims identifiable in state-centric terms. Human rights claims stem from the existence Hannah Arendt labelled *bare life* – mistakenly stripping it from its political potential.

As will become much clearer in the next chapter, however, a human rights *claim* can only be coupled with a remedy when it meets a human rights *commitment*. Meanwhile, only general outlines of such commitments will be drawn. To ignite a transnational legal process, Southeast Asian "boat people" had to act in a way that implicated the conscience of their addresses. This conscience is closely tied with the identity and with the embodied presence of the addressee of the claim. It must be successful in demonstrating to the addressee of the claim that she is implicated by the claimant's plight.[16]

---

[15] Samuel Moyn made a similar point in his response to a previous version of Chapter 1. See Samuel Moyn, "The Embarrassment of Human Rights," *Texas International Law Journal: The Forum* 50, no. 1 (2015): 1, available at www.tilj.org/content/forum/14%20MOYN%20PUBLICATION.pdf (last accessed May 13, 2016).

[16] Elsewhere, I have formulated this as an existential dilemma: either treat people as humans and risk changing who you are (in terms of the composition of your population) or give up human rights and risk changing who you are (in terms of your constitutive commitments). See Itamar Mann, "Dialectic of Transnationalism: Unauthorized Migration and Human Rights, 1993–2013," *Harvard International Law Journal* 54, no. 2 (2013): 315.

For those who make human rights claims, a struggle for survival transforms into a struggle for freedom: either establishing a new social contract or opening and joining an existing one. For the addressee of the claim, conscience is often grounded in the idea of not colluding in the killing of others. It is thus much more immediately tied to the survival of the claimant, without any necessary regard to her freedom. Making a human rights claim thus turns out to be a struggle in which the claimant fights the addressee's urge to decouple the claimant's survival from her freedom. Practically, this often comes in the form of offering rescue without resettlement or access to citizenship. This case study demonstrates that human rights can become enforceable only through a negotiation between two forces: the boat peoples' efforts to make a place for themselves in the world, and states' efforts to govern or manage migrants transnationally and facilitate their survival. From the fall of South Vietnam, unauthorized migrants constantly pushed to assert their own freedom and survival, strenuously rejecting the push to decouple them.[17]

Limited but noteworthy international remedies emerged from the human rights encounters in the South China Sea. While many lost their lives, others found new homes: the largest number by far were resettled to the United States (823,000); significant numbers found themselves in Australia (137,000), Canada (137,000), France (96,000), Germany (40,000), the United Kingdom (19,000), and Japan (11,000). The political membership offered to these people should not be understood as the result of benevolence or of effective transnational cooperation. It was a result of the boat people's own struggles.[18]

Homo Homini Lupus

When the US military withdrew from Vietnam on April 30, 1975, the country was devastated.

Mass displacement began in Indochina before the war. But the United States carried out the most intense bombing campaign in military history

---

[17] For a demonstration of the emphasis on convergence of interests and "humanitarianism," see James L. Carlin, "Significant Refugee Crises since World War II and the Response of the International Community," *Michigan Yearbook of International Legal Studies* 3 (1982): 4.

[18] Thus, it is self-help as enforcement of human rights, relying on human rights as a law of encounter. On self-help more generally, see Oona Hathaway and Scott Shapiro, "Outcasting: Enforcement in Domestic and International Law," *Yale Law Journal* 121, no. 2 (2011): 252. Particularly salient here is their contention that "the properties which make law *law* are also those properties that make law morally valuable."

against North Vietnam.[19] As a *New York Times* correspondent explained, there was a "deliberate policy of creating refugees wherever possible."[20] Rural life was systematically destroyed, consuming soldiers, civilians, fauna, and flora alike.[21] The local economy and infrastructure in South Vietnam was made dependent on the US's military presence. Disease and illicit activities such as prostitution and drug abuse grew rampant, especially in Saigon.

Describing this period in his essay *The Real War*, Schell portrays the South as "a society entirely without inner cohesion, held together only by foreign arms, foreign money, foreign political will. When, deprived of that support, it faced its foe alone and the mirage evaporated, it was revealed for what it was – a loose collection of individuals."[22] "Panic" is everywhere in the descriptions of this disjointed society. As one South Vietnamese officer described the scene in the city of Danang: "Bands of children, hungry and thirsty, wandered aimlessly on the streets, demolishing everything which happened to fall into their hands. Danang was seized by convulsions of collective hysteria."[23] In another city, Nha Trang, a colonel, said that "[N]o one is in charge of the whole area. So everyone is thinking of running. That is all."[24] Schell's breathtaking essay captures a temporary Hobbesian state of nature, after the dissolution of American control.[25] Neighbors become beasts. Some jump at each other's throats. Others take flight.

---

[19] Edward Miguel and Gérald Roland, "The Long-Run Impact of Bombing Vietnam," *Journal of Development Economics* 96 (2011): 1.

[20] R.W. Apple, "Calley: The Real Guilt," *New Statesman* April 2, 1971, 449. Quoted in Noam Chomsky, "The Rule of Force in International Affairs," Review of Nuremberg and Vietnam: An American Tragedy, by Telford Taylor, *The Yale Law Journal* 80 (1971): 1456. Apple makes reference to an interesting invocation of the sea as a lawless space (a theme that reappears throughout this book). "An army general . . . explained the idea to me as follows: 'You've got to dry up the sea the guerillas swim in – that's the peasants – and the way to do that is blast the hell out of their villages so they'll come into our refugee camps. No villages, no guerillas; simple.'"

[21] On the use of herbicides in the Vietnam War, see Peter H. Schuck, *Agent Orange on Trial: Mass Toxic Disasters in the Courts* (Cambridge and London: Harvard University Press, 1986), 16–17.

[22] Schell, *The Real War*, 53.

[23] Schell, *The Real War*, 52.

[24] Schell, *The Real War*, 52.

[25] It is "Hobbesian" primarily in the sense that the "End for which Sovereignty was ordained" is frustrated. For an elaboration of what this means for Hobbes, see David Dyzenhaus, "Hobbes on the Authority of Law," in David Dyzenhaus and Thomas Poole (eds.), *Hobbes and the Law* (Cambridge: Cambridge University Press, 2012), 204.

Even before 1975, many found themselves scrambling to leave. The US evacuation plan started materializing in mid-April, when it was still discussed behind closed doors. The assumption in Washington was that "talking publicly about a big evacuation might make it more so."[26] Between April 3 and September 3, 1975, the United States evacuated around 110,000 displaced people from South Vietnam in "Operation New Life." About 3,300 children, who were thought to be orphans, were flown out of the country in "Operation Babylift" and transferred to adopting families. It quickly became clear that many had families at home.[27]

As its forces left Vietnam, the United States quickly found that it would not be as easy to leave its population. Among the iconic war images were those of refugees trailing on helicopter landing pads. "There were people, mostly families where the women and children did not get aboard the aircraft, who were lying in front of the fields of the airplane as it began taxiing," said one journalist describing the scene. "It's the most frightening experience I've ever had . . . *the fact of human beings turning into pure animals*. I've seen mob scenes before; this was outright *panic*" (emphasis added).[28] The crew of aircraft carrier Blue Ridge experienced this postwar encounter as they celebrated departure:

---

[26] Robinson, *Terms of Refuge*, 17. The underlying insight is clear: saving people in danger creates incentives to be in danger for those who want to be saved. This insight is consistent with a broadly economic theory of behavior, according to which people act rationally according to cost–benefit calculations and can be incentivized to act one way or another. It is also consistent with Arendt's understanding of bare life, a label aimed to describe humans that have been reduced to causation and cannot act purposively.

[27] A Ninth Circuit court explained the mistake as early as November 1975:

> it appears that some of the children have a living parent, and were merely left in orphanages for safekeeping (Vietnamese orphanages allegedly serve some of the functions of day care centers). The parent(s) may or may not know the child is alive, or where it is. Other children were allegedly released with the understanding that the parents would be reunited with the child here; still others were released by hysterical parents terrorized by the fear that the child would be murdered by the approaching forces.

See *Nguyen Da Yen* v. *Kissinger*, 528 F.2d 1194, 1197 (9th Cir. 1975); Barbara M. Brown, "Operation Babylift and the Exigencies of War – Who Should Have Custody of 'Orphans'?" *Northern Kentucky Law Review* 7 (1980): 81. On "Operation Babylift" see Dana Sachs, *The Life We Were Given: Operation Babylift, International Adoption, and the Children of War in Vietnam* (Boston: Beacon Press, 2010).

[28] Interview with United Press Correspondent Paul Vogel, available at www.upi.com /Archives/Audio/Events-of-1975/Fall-of-Saigon/ (last accessed November 14, 2013).

The Blue Ridge shuddered and moved forward, leaving the exhausted faces still pleading to be taken on board. A few hours earlier a few of us had watched as the bodies of two infants were lowered into the sea; *and in one last, disconsolate gesture which is embedded in my memory, a woman stood up and held out her baby as if to say, "At least take him"*; then she slipped and they both fell into the sea. (emphasis added)[29]

Seventh Fleet US Navy ships were initially positioned specifically to allow people on board. Other refugees reached neighboring countries and were held in refugee camps, waiting for an opportunity for resettlement – hopefully in the United States or in one of its allies. Within a week after the fall of Saigon, those who were evacuated began arriving in the United States. They were first held in Guam, and in four military bases in California, Florida, Pennsylvania, and Arkansas.[30] These arrivals were not uniformly well received, and in May President Gerald Ford voiced his disappointment: "I am primarily very upset, because the United States has a long tradition of opening its doors to immigrants from all countries. We are a country built by immigrants from all areas of the world, and we have always been a humanitarian nation."[31] The Vietnamese government framed these exits as treachery.[32]

The destructive effects of war and policies of the new revolutionary government were the initial driving force for unauthorized departures. But a somewhat different dynamic quickly developed. Vietnam was now at war with China. When the communists from the North overtook South Vietnam, about a million people of Chinese origin remained there. Their property was expropriated as part of the "socialist transformation." Many were sent to work and learn in rural areas in "reeducation

---

[29] John Pilger, "A Harsh Life, a Tired People," *Atlas World Press Review* January 1979, col. 1. Quoted in Claire Marechal, The Boat People Dilemma: A Duty to Rescue, A Right to Refuge? (L.LM. Thesis, Harvard Law School, 1979), 2. Compare to testimonies from the "Child Overboard Affair" in Australia (2001), described and analyzed in Chapter 4.

[30] Matthew Keenan, "Great Bend Opened Its Arms to Vietnam Refugees," *Journal of the Kansas Bar Asoociation* 78, December 1978: 14.

[31] Compare with Arendt's notion of "We Refugees" and its discussion throughout Chapter 3. See also John F. Kennedy, *A Nation of Immigrants* (London: Hamish Hamilton, 1964).

[32] Grant, *The Boat People*, 28.

> (Those who have committed numerous crimes against the revolution or against the population and have zealously served the US imperialists, and now, following the day or liberation, seek to leave the country in the wake of their masters, will be punished by law. Not included in this category are those who have been duped by enemy propaganda, taken fright, and have fled abroad.)

programs" – often in extremely poor conditions.[33] These activities were supposed to re-indoctrinate their corrupted selves into communism. While the country prohibited some from exiting, tens of thousands left, and "in 1978 and 1979 the boat people became an exodus that set off shock waves through the region and across the world."[34]

Gradually, it became the belief of policymakers in the West that Vietnam was not only keeping some people from leaving but also encouraging and facilitating departures.[35] The thought was that Vietnam was getting rid of people it did not desire, aiming to exacerbate and instrumentalize a regional crisis.[36] By the end of the 1970s, this policy drew harsh criticism, with distinct human rights fervor. One commentator found that "in forcing people to risk their lives at sea, Vietnam is practicing a form of genocide."[37]

---

[33] Hungdah Chiu, an international lawyer and a Chinese expatriate, explained this in a 1980 current developments piece in the *American Journal of International Law*. Hungdah Chiu, "China's Legal Position on Protecting Chinese Residents in Vietnam," *American Journal of International Law* 74, no. 3 (1980): 685–689.

[34] Grant, *The Boat People*, 82.

[35] Bruce Grant, an Australian writer who extensively interviewed Vietnamese refugees, explained the patchwork of legal and illicit activities:

> In the controversy about the officially approved exodus from southern Vietnam that developed after 1977, it is often forgotten that clandestine escapes continued at the same time as officially sanctioned departures. The latter started mainly to get rid of members of Vietnam's Chinese minority, although ethnic Vietnamese were able to buy their way into this channel. On the other hand, some Chinese continued to leave secretly, although Vietnamese made up the majority of the boat escapees.

See Grant, *The Boat People*, 28. Muamar Qadaffi had more recently made the explicit threat to do the same, and according to some accounts directed soldiers to send migrants to the Mediterranean in order to pressure European countries. See, e.g., Andrew Giligan, "Col Gadaffi 'Trying to Force Refugee Crisis' on Europe," *The Telegraph*, May 10, 2011, available at www.telegraph.co.uk/news/worldnews/africaandindianocean/libya/8505447/Libya-Col-Gaddafi-trying-to-force-refugee-crisis-on-Europe.html (last accessed May 4, 2016). ("The number of Libyan migrants entering Europe has exploded amid growing signs that Colonel Gaddafi's regime is trying to force a refugee crisis as a weapon against his NATO enemies.")

[36] See, e.g., David A. Martin, "Large-Scale Migrations of Asylum Seekers," *American Journal of International Law* 76 (1982): 598. The roots of this argument lie before the fall of South Vietnam; D. Edwin Schmelzer, "South Vietnamese Refugees: Pawns of Insurgency," *The Journal of International Law and Economics* 7 (1972): 89–101; Barry Wain, "The Indochina Refugee Crisis," *Foreign Affairs* 58 (1979–1980): 160–180; Hiroko Yamane, "Réfugiés Asiatiques D'Aujourdhui: vers un nouveau dessin des nations?" *Revue Française De Science Politique* 32, no. 3 (1982): 505–526.

[37] Barry Stein, "Geneva Conferences and Indochinese Refugee Crisis," *International Migration Review* 13, no. 4 (1979): 719.

The United States recognized, to some extent, its obligations toward those Vietnamese who worked for "any element of the US mission."[38] But the far greater number included members of the Chinese ethnic minority, and other displaced groups, literally innumerable as far as the administration was concerned. From its own perspective, it would neither be justified nor practicable for the United States to admit these multitudes to its own territory. And unlike the case with members of its "mission," the United States had no self-serving interest in doing so. Instead of focusing on the receiving end, argued Virginia law professor David Martin, international law should develop measures against refugee-sending countries.[39] The appropriate response to the boat people was to admonish Vietnam.[40] But Martin admitted that such a measure would not go far by way of finding a *solution* to the emergency unfolding: "Receiving states are caught on the horns of a difficult dilemma, torn between an impulse toward humanitarian response and a feeling that hospitality only invites the flow to continue until it may become unmanageable."[41]

The Vietnamese government, on the other hand, accused the United States of manipulating refugee flows and instrumentalizing them for American policy ends. The claim was articulated in a pamphlet published by Hanoi under the reprimanding title *Those Who Leave* (1979).[42] Addressed at a readership abroad, the thin booklet presented the government's defense against the allegations of human rights violations. From the Vietnamese perspective, the departure of boat people was an obstacle in building Vietnamese sovereignty.[43] The Vietnamese ambassador to France made a similar point: "millions of Vietnamese are too used to the

---

[38] Robinson, *Terms of Refuge*, 17.

[39] Martin, "Large-Scale Migrations of Asylum Seekers," 599.

[40] For an example of such admonitions, see "Vietnam," Ann. Hum. Rts. Rep. Submitted to Cong. By U.S. Dep't (1980): 714–720.

[41] Martin, "Large-Scale Migrations of Asylum Seekers," 609. In theoretical terms, this might also be restated as a dilemma between upholding human rights convictions and a cost–benefit calculation of what is in the United States' interest. This is the defining dilemma of the human rights encounter.

[42] *Those Who Leave: The "Problem of the Vietnamese Refugees"* (Hanoi: Published by Vietnam Courier, 1979).

[43] Far from a humanitarian drama, the idea is that the boat people represent, above all, an economic phenomenon of service-givers responding to a demand for their work: "At sea, they are picked up by ships which will take them to neighboring countries. For an 'intellectual', especially a technician with good qualifications, the journey will be free of charge, for the point is to perform a 'brain drain' to the detriment of Vietnam." *Those who Leave*, 22.

life of the past regime – consumption, lack of productivity, easy life owing to external help – they can bear no more the tremendous material difficulties, resulting from thirty years of war; so they flee."[44]

Rather than presenting a legal obligation toward humanity, argued Vietnam, human rights mar the liberated country's efforts to build an autonomous economy.[45] The United States, according to this story, used a combination of brute force and ideological influence to dismantle a dignified traditional life. If these strategies were not always meant to kill, they were intended to cause "forced urbanization" – and massive migration to Saigon. There, the values of rural life could be systematically and ideologically broken.[46] Dignified peasants would be crushed into docile consumers. Human rights are portrayed not only as the continuation of the war but also as expression of its ends – a capitalist economy.

The Vietnamese critique of human rights focused, among other things, on Vietnam's need to recover foreign aid.[47] The fact that the United States conditioned aid on Vietnam's human rights performance was, on the Vietnamese government's account, hypocritical: "the American leaders . . . seek to give a good conscience to the American people. Jimmy Carter has found the method: human rights . . . On 27 December 1976, the Los Angeles Times ran a big headline: 'No human rights, no aid!'" The problem with this American humanitarianism, argued Vietnam, is that

---

[44] The intervention of the Vietnamese Ambassador in France at "Antenne 2" (French Television), December 4, 1978. Le Monde, December 6, 1978, cols. 4 and 5. Quoted in Marechal, *The Boat People Dilemma*, 39.

[45] "The champions of 'human rights' in the West, from Jimmy Carter to the correspondents of Le Monde, are apt to forget those results which have given back to millions of Vietnamese their human dignity flouted by a century of French colonization and twenty years of American intervention. Human rights in a former colony are first of all the right to national independence; the right to choose a line of development which does not sacrifice its natural and human resources to the greed of multinational companies and that of a minority of landowners, capitalists, and agents of foreign powers; and the right to education, health care, and work. No equitable observer can deny that the present regime in Vietnam has made considerable efforts in this direction and has achieved results beyond the capability of any other regime in the present circumstances." Those Who Leave: The "Problem of the Vietnamese Refugees," *Those Who Leave*.

[46] As the pamphlet says, "The major political fact in this question is the vast anti-Vietnamese campaign launched throughout the world by the mass media of Peking and the West in a well-orchestrated manner." *Those Who Leave*, 33.

[47] The very first words of the booklet are a series of questions on "the people leaving Vietnam": "Who are they? Why are they leaving? How to settle the problem?" Treating these questions through a human rights paradigm, the government declares, is "a simplistic way by means of a few humanitarian tirades sprinkled with political slogans" *Those Who Leave*, 1.

it does not rely on a generally applicable rule:[48] "The same Western and Pekingese mass media that shed tears over the Vietnamese refugees are hushing up the fate of Palestinians forced into exile and have let the millions of victims of the 'Great Cultural Revolution' sink into oblivion. Human rights are not their true concern." To truly understand the refugee problem, one cannot stop at universally accepted principles. It is, rather, necessary to examine the "concrete social and historical circumstances" of decades of colonization and war. If new social and economic cohesion was to be built, this could only be done incrementally.

Against the background of these two narratives – the Vietnamese and the American – the boat people fell between the Cold War blocs into a space that seemed truly lawless. Focusing on the reeducation program, one legal scholar chose to describe this space as a social contract that had been voided for some of its members, "a type of domestic exile, in which many thousands of Vietnamese were excluded from the political community . . ." This, he concluded, has thrown them back into a kind of state of nature.[49]

The clash between the United States and Vietnam led the United States to resettle some of the Vietnamese. Though many were resettled in Western Bloc countries, the boats continued to leave in ever-increasing numbers. Thus, other governance efforts emerged. These were moved by the motivation to save lives. As early as 1975, UNHCR reached an agreement with Thailand, according to which the organization funded refugee camps on Thai territory.[50] In subsequent months UNHCR assisted unauthorized boats arriving in territories and islands belonging to Hong Kong, Malaysia, Singapore, and the Philippines. But the boat peoples' status in all of these places was precarious. In August 1975,

---

[48] *Those who Leave*, 34. Compare with Louise Holborn's call for a universal formalized refugee status in Chapter 1.

[49] His words might be useful here:

> Once the state has broken the political bond between itself and the individual, it has freed the individual from the moral necessity of acknowledging the legitimacy of its coercive power. Therefore, the state loses any legitimate basis for its exertion of coercive force over persons who have been excluded from the political community. Even continued residence in the territory of an oppressive state does not give rise to any implied consent to submit to the will of that state, if the continued residence is constrained by circumstances beyond an individual's control.

Stephen B. Young, "The Legality of Vietnamese Re-Education Camps," *Harvard International Law Journal* 20 (1979): 519–538, 536.

[50] Robinson, *Terms of Refuge*, 20.

President Ferdinand Marcos of the Philippines ordered the reprovision of a boat that arrived with eighty-four on board in order to send it to "sail to Hawaii." The order was rescinded after an appeal from the Catholic Bishops Conference of the Philippines.[51] A Thai directive provided that

> [i]n the event that people sneak into the country by boat, officials should detain the escapees and either force or tow the boat out of territorial waters immediately. If a boat has already reached shore, it should be helped with repairs, food, engine oil, medicines, and other necessary equipment. Then the boat should be towed out of Thai waters without delay (no more than 30 days after its arrival).[52]

In June 1979, the crisis reached an unprecedented boiling point. No positive law protected the "boat people." The Association of East Asian Nations (ASEAN)[53] declared they "have reached the limits of their endurance and have decided they would not accept any new arrivals." Those refugees that were already admitted to their territories would be sent out. Malaysia's Prime Minister, Mahathir Mohammad, had given an order to "shoot on sight" any Vietnamese found trying to enter Malaysian territory.[54] Other government officials later dismissed the comment as a misunderstanding.[55] As Robinson recounts, one suggested that Mahathir had ordered to "shoo on sight" the refugee boats.

Human Rights as the Protection of Survival

Beyond Cold War politicking, a legal debate about the plight of the boat people started to develop at the time between lawyers in the Western Bloc. While the United States had robust policy interests to engage in the evacuation and protection of the South Vietnamese, many other countries ended up participating. What motivated them was not only the American responsibility for the war, although the United States surely had its influence. There was a real normative stake in the discussion. The decisive factor that generated a new transnational legal process was that "civilized" countries just could not "shoo" people to death.

---

[51] Robinson, *Terms of Refuge*, 23.
[52] Robinson, *Terms of Refuge*, 43.
[53] Indonesia, Malaysia, the Philippines, Thailand, Singapore.
[54] A Malaysian daily newspaper, the *New Straits Times*, seemed to reflect the government's mood: "The crux of the issue is that the flow from Vietnam is no longer just a humanitarian problem. It has become as much a weapon of war as a softening-up raid by waves of bombers." Wain, "The Indochina Refugee Crisis," 168.
[55] Robinson, *Terms of Refuge*, 51.

Australian lawyers pioneered this legal debate. Australia didn't have the deep involvement the United States had in the Vietnamese plight but was very exposed to the issue because of its relative proximity.[56] As a signatory to the 1951 Refugee Convention, Australian lawyers considered their country constrained in ways that didn't apply to other regional actors. The first asylum seekers appeared at Australia's shores in 1977. But Australia's dilemma was not merely a matter of positive international law. The question, as Martin formulated it, was what to do with a "world that has not adequately adjusted to the individual-focused, European-centered approach of earlier years to deal with the massive influxes now experienced."[57] David Johnson's work illustrates the question. Johnson approached the subject from the point of view of an embodied and situated encounter.[58]

After having studied under Hersch Lauterpahct in Cambridge and serving as Dean of the University of London Faculty of Laws, Johnson accepted the chair in International Law at Sidney Law School. His article "Refugees, Departees and Illegal Migrants" appeared in the Sidney Law Review at the height of the boat people crisis.[59] It explores the sources of law available to Australia in its response to the unfolding catastrophe. It exposes the kind of embarrassment that the "boat people" were able to generate among Australian lawyers. And it articulates the premises that led to the adoption of the Orderly Departure Program, agreed upon at a 1979 conference in Geneva.

The British lawyer cited a report in the December 19, 1978, issue of the Sydney Morning Herald: "a fishing trawler crammed with 269 Vietnamese on board was escorted back to international waters by a Singapore Navy gunboat." The trawler "was believed to be heading for Australia by way of Indonesia." Johnson seconded the outrage expressed in an editorial on the subject. The reason why "a level-headed paper as the Sydney Morning Herald waxed almost hysterical about it," he wrote, was that the Australian government reached the conclusion that the Vietnamese government was "dumping its unwanted

---

[56] On Australia's initiative in this area, see: Martin, "Large-Scale Migrations of Asylum Seekers," 603. Explaining the inevitable defeat of the US military in Vietnam, Schell writes about the sheer distance between Vietnam and the United States, as a factor determining that the United States would have to inevitably leave.

[57] Martin, "Large-Scale Migrations of Asylum Seekers," 603.

[58] See also B. Martin Tsamenyi, "The 'Boat People': Are They Refugees?" Human Rights Quarterly 5 (1983): 348–373.

[59] David Johnson, "Refugees, Departees, and Illegal Immigrants," The Sydney Law Review 9, no. 1 (1980): 11.

citizens abroad 'in the full knowledge and awareness that tens of thousands more are rotting in refugee camps, helpless and hopeless, dependent on the reluctant charity of foreign nations on which they have no
claim *save that of humanity*'" (emphasis added). But what would that
claim of humanity be? The author was indeed baffled. Like Martin,
Johnson too first focused on sanctions directed at the human rights
violations at the root of refugee flows.[60] But that didn't prove particularly
helpful. The source of the problem Australia was now facing wasn't any
stable political structure.

Vietnam had no obligation under international law to prevent neighboring countries from exposure to Vietnamese refugees, admitted
Johnson, before grudgingly considering his own country's obligations.
His uneasy analysis here is indicative: refugees were still a kind of lacuna
in international law. It was not clear how, if at all, the Refugee
Convention filled the gap that Lassa Oppenheim identified back at the
turn of the century.[61] At first Johnson dismissed any obligations toward
the refugees under the Convention: "the obligations which the parties to
the Convention undertake are basically obligations to other States also
parties to the Convention. They are not obligations to the refugees as
such, enforceable by them under international law."[62] But Johnson is
quick to retract, at least partially: it "would be unwise to carry too far the
idea." He obliquely recognized that exceptional circumstances do include
obligations toward the refugees "as such."

As Johnson explains, a fundamental jurisprudential issue is at stake:
is international law "a system confined to regulating relations between
states," or does it have a "wider import"? The question is a philosophical
one: Do international legal obligations only stem from sovereignty, or is
a set of beliefs about what it means to be human also at their foundation?

---

[60] He urged world leaders "not just to register their outrage but to make crystal clear to the
Government of Vietnam that while it continues this policy it will receive no help, no aid,
no friendship." Johnson, "Refugees, Departees, and Illegal Immigrants," 14. Compare
with Martin, "Large-Scale Migrations of Asylum Seekers," 599 (arguing that "when large
numbers of refugees cross a border, the international limelight too often fastens on the
receiving countries; their actions are subjected to minutely critical scrutiny, while the
sending countries, the real sources of the problems, remain happily in the shadows.") This
discussion foreshadows a much more pervasive discussion of the "root causes" of migration – and of human rights violations – in the two recent decades. For an analysis and
a critique of this discourse, see Susan Marks, "Human Rights and Root Causes," *Modern
Law Review* 74, no. 1 (2011): 57–78.

[61] Oppenheim, International Law, 366. For discussion, see Chapter 1 above.

[62] This comports with the picture of human rights as generated by sovereignty, according to
which human individuals are not an independent source of law.

The question presents the old debate between positivism and natural rights. Wavering on this underlying perplexity, Johnson explains that "[I]t is not necessarily in the interests of humanity to press too far the duty of States to receive back their nationals." The authority he relied upon was Georg Schwarzenberger. Schwarzenberger, an international law expert mentioned in the previous chapter, was a British émigré who had been persecuted by the Nazis before moving to London. Johnson quotes him: "In cases of mass deprival of citizenship which, since the inter-war period, have given rise to the problem in its most aggravated form, the home State would likely to be only too willing to receive back such individuals, but, because of the fate awaiting them, civilized nations would hesitate to exercise their right of expulsion." Johnson probably knew about Schwarzenberger's personal history of statelessness.[63] Referring to Schwarzenberger's position, he adds that "by 'the fate awaiting' refugees returned to the country from which they fled he [Schwarzenberger] has in mind placing them in concentration camps or putting them to death." If the protection from extermination was what refugee protection meant, Johnson would endorse the idea.[64] But, he emphasized, that still wouldn't dictate any particular result in terms of *which* authority or jurisdiction should be responsible for any particular refugee. Johnson's appeal to humanity ascribes responsibility over refugees to *all* the world's nations. It therefore imposes them on no nation in particular.[65]

The universal boatperson is thus positioned as a threshold or test for law: what kind of rights, if any at all, stem from human existence –

---

[63] Schwarzenberger became stateless in 1939, and in June 1940 he was taken from his position in the New Commonwealth Institute for Justice and Peace, to be interned with 30,000 "enemy aliens" in Britain. After he was freed, Schwarzenberger expressed the opinion that his detention was justified. See Edgar Gold, review of Völkerrecht und Machtpolitik – Georg Schwarzenberger (1908–1991), by Stephanie Steinle, *Journal of the History of International Law* 5 (2003): 423.

[64] Though one Australian scholar made the positive law argument that a right to asylum must be granted to the Vietnamese refugees by non-signatories under human rights law, his position reads as far from conclusive. After surveying the relevant clauses from the United Nations Charter and the Universal Declaration of Human Rights, he writes, "there should be no problem in interpreting these provisions to cover the refugee." This conclusion, aspirational in tone, is followed by a call to adhere to "ethical" standards, a word that makes them sound like they are outside the pale of law.

[65] As Samuel Moyn has written, "Because they promise everything to everyone, they can end up meaning anything to anyone." Samuel Moyn, "Human Rights in History," *The Nation*, August 30/September 6, 2010, available at http://www.thenation.com/article/human-rights-history/ (last accessed May 4, 2016).

outside of state authority and beyond contractual obligation? When refugees appeared on the high seas beyond Australia's territory, they somehow could not simply be left to die en masse. With this prohibition, they entered the realm of law; not through reasoning about human nature, but through a particular understanding of recent history. A state may of course decide to grant a visa to a refugee. But would that state be answerable directly to the refugee?

The particular instance Johnson wrote about involved a fishing trawler that traveled to Australia through Singapore. Three passengers died on the way.[66] The Singapore police were not able to stop the trawler before it accessed the country's territorial waters. But Singapore was not a signatory to the Refugee Convention and did not admit refugees. The authorities provided the boat with fuel, food, and water and repaired its engine, before sending it on its journey. Johnson was concerned: countries like Singapore were forcing "civilized" countries like Australia to carry the weight of refugee admission. Malaysia too, he wrote angrily, introduced a systematic policy of forcing boat people back to sea, shifting the burden onto others, "especially Hong Kong, for whom the United Kingdom is also responsible."[67] In this narrative, Vietnam's neighbors made it necessary to push for transnational solutions. As another commentator wrote: "Both Malaysia and Thailand intended by their actions to shock the West into recognition of the problem and into more effective action to reduce the refugee camp populations of the region."[68]

But international law did not provide the instruments to deal with the refugee problem. "The present institutions, including especially the 1951 Refugee Convention, the 1967 Protocol and the Statute of the Office of the UNHCR, certainly represent a considerable improvement upon the ad-hoc arrangements that were set up to deal with refugee movements after the First World War and after the advent to power of the Nazis in 1933."[69] But these measures were not enough. New measures of

---

[66] Johnson, "Refugees, Departees, and Illegal Immigrants," 11.
[67] Johnson, "Refugees, Departees, and Illegal Immigrants," 56.
[68] Stein, "Geneva Conferences and Indochinese Refugee Crisis," 717.
[69] See also Edmond L. Papantonio, "The Right to Asylum and the Indochinese Refugee," *Fordham International Law Journal* 2 (1978–1979): 67:

> To speak of asylum in purely legal terms is to miss its essence, for it is a moral right that cannot be effectively enforced – the refugee is dependent upon the generosity of the state where he seeks refuge. One may argue that third countries' accepting refugees from countries of initial asylum tends

transnational governance were now required.[70] This time, Johnson promised, the objective of the international legislative instruments will truly be "the inherent dignity and the equality of all members of the human family."[71] The latter framing, of course, seemingly brings us back into the realm of natural rights. The point here is, however, that this understanding of nature was itself imbued with historical lessons and a situated experience. The next chapter will expand upon that aspect of the human rights *commitment*.

It is not by chance that Johnson returned to the transnational governance of the interwar period. As in that time, a transnational policy problem would be addressed through a network of governments, international organizations, and private actors: the UNHCR, the Intergovernmental Committee for European Migration (ICEM), the International Committee of the Red Cross (ICRC) – to name just a few.[72] But what would this new push toward transnational solutions look like? The first step was offshore detention.[73] The United States, Australia, France, and Canada were all to contribute resources to build a center on the Indonesian island of Galang, where they would be able to

> to stabilize these latter nations by reducing economic and social burdens on them as well as minimizing friction with their neighbors. Ultimately one cannot speak of legal obligations, but must rely upon the humanitarian sentiments of accepting nations to help restore to refugees the human rights they sought in fleeing their homelands.

The ad hoc arrangements are described concisely in Chapter 1.

[70] As late as 1982, Carlin emphasized the need for ad hoc responses to refugees and called for the creation of a "formalized" response (just like Holborn did in Chapter 1). It thus seems like this is more a feature of transnational governance than a bug. Carlin, "Significant Refugee Crises since World War II and the Response of the International Community," 22–23.

[71] This is the language of the preamble to the UDHR. He continues: "much remains to be done in this particular area of the law before the international community can be said to have realized in practice the goal set out in the first paragraph in the preamble of the Universal Declaration of Human Rights, namely 'recognition of the inherent dignity and of the equal equality of all members of the human family.'"

[72] Various other organizations also had important places at the table: the Intergovernmental Maritime Consultative Organization (IMCO), and the International Chamber of Shipping, for example.

[73] Johnson writes that "A possible and novel means of solving the problems of refugees from Vietnam was discussed at a meeting in Jakarta in May 1979. The meeting was attended by representatives of twenty-four countries, including Australia. The proposal was that a 'processing centre' should be established on the Indonesian island of Galang." Johnson, "Refugees, Departees, and Illegal Immigrants," 54–55. Compare to the British policy of detaining unauthorized migrants in offshore places like Cyprus, described in Chapter 1.

screen the refugees far away from home.[74] Vietnam preferred a program
under which people would leave its territory legally, guaranteed resettlement before leaving. In a conference in Jakarta, the Vietnamese representative suggested the departure of 10,000 refugees a month from
Vietnam, organized by the UNHCR.[75]

With the *Orderly Departure Program*, Vietnam's proposal was
adopted. The first agreement establishing the program was concluded
between UNHCR and Vietnam during discussions in Hanoi on May 30,
1979. It entrusted UNHCR with the responsibility to "make effort to
enlist support for this programme amongst potential receiving countries." No particular countries were mentioned. But the Geneva
Conferences that followed in June and July 1979 made the *Orderly
Departure Program* operational. British Prime Minister Margaret
Thatcher pushed for the meeting, the first of its kind in the United
Nations. Thatcher sought to alleviate Hong Kong's burden.[76] Vice
President Mondale headed the American delegation. Mondale opened
the conference in a celebratory note, citing Évian:[77]

> Forty-one years ago this very week, another international conference on
> lake Geneva concluded its deliberations. Thirty-two "nations of asylum"
> convened at Évian to save the doomed Jews of Nazi Germany and
> Austria ... We have each heard similar arguments about the plight of
> the refugees in Indochina.[78]

---

[74] The response to Southeast Asian refugees thus became the important precedent in later
efforts to extra-territorialize refugee processing.

[75] He denied that his country was "guilty of collusion," and claimed the situation was in
fact seriously harming his country. Johnson, "Refugees, Departees, and Illegal
Immigrants," 55.

[76] The colony was struggling to accommodate the influx of some 56,000 people in the first
six months of 1979. Robinson, *Terms of Refuge*, 51.

[77] If Schell is to be believed on this, Americans were virtually obsessed with WWII
analogies. Schell, *The Real War*, 24. This has remained a tendency ever since, at least
for some commentators; see, e.g., Leon Wieseltier, "By Doing Nothing in Syria, Obama
Ensured There Is Nothing We Can Do," *The New Republic*, November 8, 2013, available
at www.newrepublic.com/article/115534/washington-diarist-takes-obamas-syrian-
stance (last accessed May 4, 2016). On Évian, see also Chapter 1.

[78] When Ted Kennedy came back to the Senate to report on the new international legal
framework that was achieved, he too returned to the same historical moment:

> Forty-one years ago this week, diplomats from many countries met at
> Evian, along lake Geneva, to consider the desperate plight of thousands of
> Jews in Hitlers's Germany. For several days the diplomats met, and they
> talked; but they did not act. Tens of thousands of helpless human beings
> perished – opening the door to the deaths of millions more in the holo-
> caust that followed. Last weekend the world met once again in Geneva to

The rhetoric generated legitimacy and sway for what was basically a large fundraising event.[79] The idea was to redistribute Vietnamese population around the globe. And Vietnam, which the United States derided as persecutor of its own population, could for this purpose rise to become an equal member at the negotiating table.[80] Instead of leaving by boat, people seeking to leave Vietnam could now enlist in UNHCR offices in the country and obtain resettlement visas. They were encouraged to spread across numerous destinations around the globe. A sign in one local office advertised Malawi, a country where boat people would enjoy warm weather, similar to home.[81] In return for international assistance in emigration programs, Vietnam promised to try to prevent people from leaving the country on perilous journeys by sea. Albeit the Western reprimand of communist despotism, the revolutionary country was initiated into an increasing global network of world governance. But the multifarious groups of refugees and migrants were not represented. As Arendt observed with regard to earlier transnational governance efforts, the international conference was more about saving migrants from themselves than about granting them a stake in their own future.

Toward the end of June 1979, communist authorities in South Vietnam began to impose severe preventive measures on would-be migrants. These included public warnings that anyone caught at sea trying to escape would be shot. Coastal patrols were intensified and large rewards were promised to those who informed officials about secret departures.[82] Thus, inconsistencies cropped up in human rights protections. UN Secretary-General Kurt Waldheim lucidly recognized these problems. Like Johnson, who pointed to international cooperation in order to realize the principles laid out in the UDHR, Waldheim too referred to UDHR. Perhaps more aware of the details of such

consider the humanitarian crisis of hundreds of thousands of Indochinese refugees and to respond to the urgent plight of the "boat people" floundering throughout Southeast Asia, but, unlike Evian, the world did not just talk, it acted.

"Refugee Crisis in Southeast Asia: Results of the Geneva Conference," *U.S. Senate*, July 26, 1979.

[79] Robinson, *Terms of Refuge*, 53.
[80] Compare with Cambodia, which was not invited, because of the genocide that took place there.
[81] Compare to the initiative to send Jewish DPs to Australia, discussed in Chapter 1. A. Grenfell Price, "Refugee Settlement in the Tropics," *Foreign Affairs* 8 (1940): 660.
[82] Grant, *The Boat People*, 58.

cooperation, he was not as sanguine about the relationship between the UDHR and the Geneva framework:

> [W]e face a certain dilemma. The United Nations of course stands for the proposition that individuals wishing to leave their country have the right to do so. At the same time, as a practical matter, we obviously do not wish to see an exodus of persons anywhere in the world who depart from their countries in a manner which would put their lives in jeopardy.[83]

The Secretary-General referred to Article 13(2) UDHR: "Everyone has the right to leave any country, including his own, and to return to his country." UNHCR pushed a transnational legal process that culminated in the Geneva Conference, where this provision was compromised. The solidifying understanding of human rights put emphasis on order.[84] In Waldheim's transnational governance, the underlying premise represents a preference for life (saving refugees from drowning) over freedom (hearing their claims and granting or denying remedy accordingly).[85]

Financial incentives had a crucial role in sending Vietnamese citizens and others to new lives around the globe. When countries felt that preventing "boat people" from taking to the sea was important enough a task for them, they raised budgets to facilitate the global redistribution of humans. Since the war, Vietnam had refused to normalize its relationship with the United States, claiming that it was entitled to reparations.[86] In Geneva, Vietnam repeated this demand, but agreed not only to cooperate with the *Orderly Departure Program* but also to have American officers on the ground, facilitating it. A limited level of cooperation without full-blown normalization of diplomatic relations was granted in return for something short of reparations, but still significant: Vietnam could now outsource a part of its expenses on migration. Vietnam was not the only country that could enjoy such funding.

---

[83] Quoted in Robinson, *Terms of Refuge*, 58.

[84] Note that it was not so much that the exclusive benchmark for legality was sovereignty. That could be a fair description of the ASEAN countries' positions. As the ASEAN countries explained in Geneva, they pushed refugees back to sea when they felt that their sovereignties were in peril.

[85] Earl Harrison's postwar reprimand that the allies would adopt any treatment of DPs short of their extermination had now become more or less official human rights policy.

[86] As one member of an American delegation to Vietnam told the Senate, "We indicated that we hoped the end of that road would be normalization of relations. However, as we moved down that road we first ran into the demands for huge amounts of aid which were termed 'demands for reparations.' We turned those down flatly." Geneva Conference Hearing, p. 13.

The ASEAN countries, or "countries of first asylum," as they were called, obtained contributions for refugee-holding facilities – and a greatly increased number of resettlement visas. Camps and other facilities, including prisons, were employed to augment the protection of life.

A reduction of unauthorized migration was reported almost immediately after the Geneva Conference. But in the years to come, when crises in neighboring Cambodia and Laos exacerbated, unauthorized refugee flows from Vietnam continued, in which Vietnamese citizens were only a fraction. Transnational governance was modified accordingly. In some areas asylum-seeking migrants were *refouled* – pushed back to where they came from – and exposed to life threats. By and large, however, the transnational network that developed in order to manage these flows found ways to protect survival.

A remarkable example was the "humane deterrence" policy announced by Thailand in January 1981 and supported by the UNHCR and the United States.[87] This policy was designed to assist the Thai government in its attempt to manage refugee flows coming from Laos, which in 1979 and 1980 entered the country at an annual rate of almost 90,000. "Humane deterrence" meant that the migrants would be sent to an austerity camp and taken out of the resettlement stream for an indefinite period. The measure was supported by UNHCR and the United States as "humane," because the fundamental premise of refugee protection – refugees would not be returned to persecution – was observed.[88] This nomenclature – *humane deterrence* – encapsulates much of what is at stake in this understanding of human rights. On the one hand, it sanctifies "humanity" as a value. On the other hand, in its emphasis on "deterrence," it reflects an understanding according to which "humanity" is best governed by "carrot-and-stick" – and in large numbers rather than individually. The conditions in camps became a major site of the negotiation of the scope and requirements of human rights.[89] In some places, there could be

---

[87] Astri Suhrke, "Indochinese Refugees: The Law and Politics of First Asylum," *Annals of the American Academy of Political and Social Science* 467, The Global Refugee Problem: US and World Response (1983): 102–115, 106.

[88] And at least in the opinion of one author, "humane deterrence" is implicitly also an efficient way to distinguish between refugees and other unauthorized migrants. In this account, this policy reduced significantly the number of lowland Lao passing the border – a group of people who unlike the highlanders were not in real danger in Laos. Suhrke, "Indochinese Refugees," 107.

[89] This is why one author calls boat people "prisoners of international politics." John Knudsen, "Prisoners of International Politics," *Asian Journal of Social Science* 18, no. 1 (1990): 153.

funding for acceptable conditions in camps, but governments intervened in order to keep them as rudimentary as possible. Such policies, it was assumed, would discourage future refugees.[90]

The *Orderly Departure Program* ended in 1989, with another new transnational legislative initiative, the *Comprehensive Plan of Action*. This program, also adopted in Geneva, was specifically designed to deter the movement of boat people from the region.[91] A US-led transnational governance network continued to grant preferential treatment to migrants from Vietnam until 1994, when the "era of the boat people" was "declared over."[92] This policy change corresponded with the restructuring of the Vietnamese market and the country's accession to the World Trade Organization (WTO). The United States raised the trade embargo over Vietnam. Sadako Ogata, the United Nation High Commissioner for Refugees, explained: "the international community will not and cannot pay indefinitely to provide free food, free housing and free medical care for these people." Those who were resettled attained both survival and some measure of freedom as members – *citizens* – of new polities. Camp inmates, who managed to secure measures of survival on UNHCR's bill but were not resettled would now have to fend for themselves. Sometimes, the line drawn between the groups had to do with the refugee definition in international law – dividing between political and economic refugees. In the majority of the cases, however, the result was more arbitrary. It depended not least upon the boat people's determination and will in asserting their own aspirations for both freedom and survival.

From Survival to Freedom

Is survival all that human rights have to offer? As already mentioned quickly in the introduction to this book, Arendt's work on refugees and the stateless is often taken to suggest exactly that. Arendt wrote about the

---

[90] The strategy worked not only on the way in but on the way out as well: "those countries that are most inhospitable to their refugees succeed in getting more of their refugees accepted for resettlement." Stein, "Geneva Conferences and Indochinese Refugee Crisis," 719.

[91] Interestingly, it is this program and not the Orderly Departure Program that is often cited as the model for addressing the contemporary "refugee crisis." See e.g. T. Alexander Aleinikoff, "Rethinking the International Refugee Regime," *Yale Journal of International Law* 41 (2016): 6.

[92] Henry Kamm, "Vietnam's Exodus Is Declared over," *New York Times*, February 17, 1994.

interwar period.[93] This was a period of tremendous cooperation between governments, international organizations, and civil society actors. At Évian, and then in the treatment of the DPs after the war, her point was proven. The post-Vietnam War era was remarkably similar. Here too, a momentous refugee crisis led to intense cross-border cooperation. Here too, an innovative and multilateral legal framework was introduced. Here too, the principle organizing these innovations was bare life, or the life of humans lacking any form of political participation. There was a significant measure of American commitment to an anti-communist agenda motivating the decisions. But to the great dismay of many anti-communist South Vietnamese, the military defeat signaled the end of the willingness to pursue this commitment. The Geneva processes did not rely directly on the actions of its beneficiaries and provided them with no avenues for making claims with regard to the bureaucracy that would manage their lives. Leaving the account of human rights at that, however, would ignore the perspective of the boat people. For the boat people, the claim of survival was more than just a will to stay alive. It was rooted in their own agency and in a demand for freedom. While the latter was not always attained, human rights cannot be thought of without an account of the former; which is precisely what Arendt attempts to do, when she regards refugees as bare life and dismisses the agency that they had. In the previous chapter, I have shown that such agency sometimes allowed them to establish newfound sovereign entities; this chapter is about the converse result, namely, that refugees claim their own agency with respect to transnational governance.

Much like in Arendt's theorization, in the authoritative histories of the post-Vietnam War period, such as Robinson's *Terms of Refuge*, the boat people's accounts barely appear. Implicitly, we are told that their experience of human rights is irrelevant. States initiated their responses in relation to one another. The management of boat people resembles the management of a natural disaster, more than it does the government of people. At best, the efforts of boat people to carve their own access into the workings of transnational governance are portrayed as inauthentic and fraudulent. Examples include the use of "flags of convenience"

---

[93] For others, this period became the constitutive moment for international refugee law and human rights more generally – that, for example, is Paul Weis's contention, expounded in Chapter 1. The more orthodox view is of course that the constitutive moment was in the postwar moment. See Anne Marie Slaugther and William Burke-White, "An International Constitutional Moment," *Harvard International Law Journal* 43 (2002): 1.

belonging to Central American countries such as Honduras and Nicaragua; and the acquisition of forged documents and basic skills in Cantonese designed to convey that one is ethnically Chinese, which ostensibly made it easier to leave. Such actions may indeed amount to manipulations of positive law, and their corollaries will be discussed in some detail in the subsequent chapters. Meanwhile, it is important to highlight that they also reflect a considerable *understanding* of the law.[94]

The accounts that boat people produced offer another perspective on this engagement with international law and human rights. There is a rich nonacademic literature that reflects an imagination of human rights far removed from that limited to survival. While survival remains crucial, it is always acquired through autonomous action and is never simply *given*. Survival is tied to this autonomy in the most significant and urgent way, in encounters on water, not least because of the danger of drowning: under age-old customary rules governing the relationships between seafarers, the question of survival cannot be eliminated or ignored.[95]

Consider, for example, the personal stories published in Tokyo under the title *Boat People: Today's "Untouchables"* (1978).[96] Tran Hoang described the hunger that a long journey on rickety boats inflicted on him and on his fellow passengers after they left Vietnam. Seemingly in line with Arendt's insistence on the objectification of the displaced, Hoang's account is initially introduced as driven by the laws of physics, rather than by purposive political action. The figurative language compares the boat to "helpless leaves adrift in calm or stormy seas ..." Hoang "tells of his surviving drift to freedom on Malaysia's shores." He describes what it meant to float helplessly: "Lack of food and water for day after day and night after night, leaves humans devoid of all restraint, but that of trying to survive," he writes. "A tiny bit of food becomes the difference between life and death, and starving people have no inhibition. Thank God that we drifted ashore before we devoured one another."[97]

This emphasis on physical forces is in some tension with another account. Le Kim Ngan worked in the University of Saigon before he

---

[94] Wain, "The Indochina Refugee Crisis," 172.
[95] In that sense, the space the boat people fell into was not entirely lawless, as suggested in the outset of the chapter. Even its apparent "lawlessness" was constructed and conditioned by law.
[96] Isamu Ando, *Boat People: Today's Untouchables* (Tokyo: Sophia University, 1978).
[97] Ando, *Boat People*, 58.

decided to leave Vietnam. He expresses astonishment with the solidarity that he found, beyond ethnic or national affiliation, in the moment of encounter:[98]

> Convinced that freedom was something that one should be willing to live and fight and die for, I planned a way of escape from Vietnam . . . On the afternoon of September 6th, we were saved by the MIGHTY, a Japanese ship. I cried . . . we all cried. Why do they treat us so kindly, though they are a different race? And, on the other hand, why do our people, who are of the same race, why do they treat us so cruelly?

The sixteen-year-old Tran Hue Hue had a particularly remarkable story, which later garnered considerable attention internationally.[99] Here, too we find an account of being reduced to the elements. Hue recounted how a few seagulls did not sustain a group of forty-nine, after they ship-wrecked on a tiny atoll in the South China Sea in 1979. For a while they were able to hunt the birds with their bare hands. But this nutrition did not suffice, and members of the group gradually starved to death. As the number of survivors fell, she said, the remaining few developed a newfound solidarity: "We loved one another very much. We shared our food. We slept in the same corner and treated one another as blood relatives. And we were no longer a crowd, so the seagulls came back. In the day, when the seagulls flew away, we slept. When they came back in the evening to sleep, we tried to catch them."[100] Hue was the only one of the shipwrecked refugees who survived to tell this story.

This emphasis on survival is juxtaposed with a deliberate engagement with international law, especially when authorities that can grant a form of remedy are present. Such an appeal to international law was voiced, among other refugees, by Hoang: "Night and day, over and over, we drifted slowly on the seas, with ships from free nations frequently passing by," he recalls. Equating with murder a lack of response to the refugees' call, he invokes a rule of international maritime law. His words here are a bare-boned legal argument: "Deck hands waved limp greetings, as they were forced along with the murderous decision of their captain. The International laws of the sea, obliging ships to go to the aid of those in distress, were ignored, not by one, but by all."[101]

---

[98] Ando, *Boat People*, 54–55.
[99] Her story was rendered into a biography. See Peter Townsend, *The Girl in the White Ship* (New York: Holt Reinhart, 1981).
[100] Grant, *The Boat People*.
[101] Ando, *Boat People*, 58.

Tran Phoc Hau, Captain of a boat called the *Song-Be 12*, recounts a more activist engagement with international law and specifically the rules of jurisdiction in territorial waters. Hau wrote his memories just a few months after his trawler reached the Darwin, Australia (November 29, 1977).[102] The passengers of the *Song-Be 12* were not authorized to depart from Vietnam. With pride and amusement, Hau tells the story of how these people won their freedom. The boat was scheduled to leave Saigon for a domestic destination. The passengers conspired to divert from the planned route and "race" into Australian territorial waters. The problem was that three Vietnamese soldiers were assigned to guard the journey. Hau and his crew decided to exploit the soldiers' vulnerability – their love of whisky.[103] Just a few hours after leaving, at 10 am, they were invited to dine and were tempted to a glass of "their cherished drink."[104] The story has the flavor of revolutionary action.[105]

---

[102] Hau begins his story by describing the South Vietnamese capital after the American withdrawal. "The smell of death, anxiety and fear pervades the city of Saigon after two and a half years of the new government's rigid rule. It is a dead city if judged by human rights, freedom and decency."

In a way it specifically employs human rights to criticize the communist Vietnamese regime; this testimony nicely ties into the (very different) discussion developed contemporaneously in places like the US Congress. The description seems to echo a popular image of totalitarianism behind the iron curtain: "People walk hurriedly and singly wherever you look. Life could change radically in a moment with the next person you meet. Even a close relative cannot be trusted. His existence may depend on providing the government's agent with information of a close one . . . the new regime has arranged all that."

[103] This is inserted as a symbol of Western freedom – and the communists' hypocrisy.

[104]
> Two glasses of whisky with sleeping drug as a mixer were enough to have the Government agents sleeping like babies. While the crew at lunch, the Song Be 12 was turned toward Vung Tau, and we now acted boldly and were determined to carry out our well laid plan. Our leader group had tied the three sleeping men and set aside the two loaded CKC rifles and a K-52 colt. Then we called the crew, one by one, for a thorough briefing of our escape that we had executed perfectly until now.

Boat People, pp. 24–25.

[105] And is in some respects not unlike stories Yossi Harel of the *Exodus* told Kaniuk (discussed in Chapter 1). Harel recounted how the *Exodus* was able to leave the port in Marseilles: "By order of the authorities, two French customs officers remained aboard the ship, but the Protestant minister John Grauel treated them to whiskey. By midnight they were in a happy mood, at which point Grauel handed them a few more bottles and sent them on their merry, warmhearted way." Yoram Kaniuk, *Commander of the Exodus* (New York: Grove Press, 2001), 122.

Rather than establishing new sovereignty, the passengers sought to assert their own dignity under international law. They identified the 1951 Refugee Convention as a norm that can be appealed to, engaged with, and put into action.[106] The span of territorial waters is taken into account. "The 120 ton, 36 meters vessel raced to Australia with 179 aboard. History will recall the ingenuity and courage of the Captain and his friends. You'll delight in this story and pictures, by the Captain of the happy hi-jackers!"[107]

The refugees, says Hau, tied the soldiers to a post only after they dozed off on a mixture of whiskey and a sleeping pill. The ship first reached a refugee camp in Malaysia, where other refugees seem to have perceived its journey as a distinctly political event: "2,000 Vietnamese living in this temporary camp danced and shouted with joy when they saw our ship and sensed what we had done." Here Hau inserts a signal: "Kill the communists, some impulsively suggested. But cool heads took charge. To do so would have marred the ideals for which we had fled."[108] The invocation of a commitment to the protection of captive soldiers has an important role. It sends the message that the Vietnamese refugees – while enforcing their own human rights – are not only beneficiaries of human rights but are also bound by them. They are not a security risk and cannot be categorized as an enemy.

Another paradigmatic story of encounter appears in a testimony by one Hung Truong, in a compilation titled *Voices of Vietnamese Boat People: Nineteen Narratives of Escape and Survival*.[109] The testimony characteristically proceeds from a life of persecution in Vietnam to a happy ending represented in the form of a fulfilling family life in a new home in Arkansas. The protagonist's action as the Captain of a small boat is at the center of this narrative. He explains the way in which he deployed survival in order to reach the promised land of freedom. His testimony is titled "Drowning the Boat," and it recounts two separate occasions in which their boat encountered merchant ships that did not want to take them on board. In order to leave these boats no other option,

---

[106] From this perspective, asylum-protecting territories are not only there for refugees to be "thrown" into. They become a forum for adjudicating claims to justice, coming from anywhere or anyone on earth; they assume a kind of "universal jurisdiction," which is not applied by their own domestic prosecution but by people who require the remedy.

[107] Ando, *Boat People*, 19–20.

[108] Ando, *Boat People*, 26.

[109] Mary Terell Cargill and Jade Quang Huynh (eds.), *Voices of Vietnamese Boat People: Nineteen Narratives of Escape and Survival* (Jefferson, NC: McFarland & Company, Inc., 2000).

Truong and a friend decide to tear a hole in their own boat and let water in.[110] The first merchant ship they meet takes their boat on board and fixes it, leaving them no choice but to continue their journey. The movement from survival to freedom is epitomized by the confrontation between the boat people and the merchant ship: if the latter decides not to help the boat people, it has no other choice but letting them drown. If the latter does pick them up, this does not yet mean access to freedom within a new collective. But it may be the first and most rudimentary step toward such freedom. Truong explains:

> When we arrived in our little boat at the second oil rig, we said, "please help us." Those on top of the oil rig said, "No, no." They didn't want to accept us either. So I tied my boat to a big boat near the oil rig. And I waited until midnight. I told everybody to go up onto the oil rig. They were crying. But they climbed up any way they could. They went up to the first floor and then to the second.
>
> When I saw that they were safe, I took my big hammer and I hammered out the floor. As I hammered, I cried. I told that boat: "That's my friend. That's my heart." Because that boat had helped me escape from Vietnam. It had helped me get away from pirates and get away from the thunderstorm. After that, I jumped on the rig, and I watched the boat go down into the water. I cried, and then I said: "That's okay. Thank you." And then I jumped onto the first floor of the oil rig and climbed to the second.[111]

In *Voices of Vietnamese Boat People*, Truong is photographed in his house in the American South. But this safety was of course not everyone's plight. After journeys at sea, more and more of the refugees and migrants found themselves languishing in camps and detention centers in the region. Here, opportunities to engage in more conventional politics were richer: there was more time for using words. Here too, human rights were deployed as a way of asserting claims that drew a direct line between defending the inmates' survival and their freedom. Even where freedom in its fullest sense was absent, some form of agency was always present.

The population of Hong Kong refugee camps published political periodicals, expressing opposition to the government in Vietnam, "under the theme of human rights." The title of a recent essay documenting these periodicals, "Visions of Resistance and Survival from Hong Kong

---

[110] Compare with Chapter 4.
[111] Cargill and Huynh, *Voices of Vietnamese Boat People*, 80–81. Compare with "self-harm," as described in Chapter 4.

Detention Camps", emphasizes the inextricable tie between freedom and survival.[112] The author documents the relationships the publishers of these Vietnamese-language journals had with major news venues in the West such as *Time* magazine and *The Economist*, as well as with UNHCR, all of which helped fund their activity.[113] The covers of the periodical *Tự Do* ("freedom") are indicative of the political imagination at work. In one of them appears an image of the Statue of Liberty, alongside the adjoining plea: "Do Not Abandon Me, Liberty!"[114] Another shows two hands breaking their handcuffs on the background of a large boat sailing on a sunny horizon.[115]

On the Malaysian island of Bidong, the population of the camp engaged in education. This also took the shape of proto-political activity in which they prepared themselves to act in a transnational context. One Reverend Bao opened a library in the cabin of a refugee boat, complete with a balcony overlooking the sea: "the chants of an English class conducted by one of his volunteer teachers could be heard: 'Take me to Kennedy square', 'Where is Haymarket?,' 'Where is the taxi?'"[116] When one journalist interviewed him, the reverend was planning vocational training for the 1,800 unaccompanied children in the camp.[117] He was preparing them to be active members of societies in which they would perhaps not initially be members. This would not hamper them from *seeking* membership.

The Vietnamese refugees in the Thai camp Songkhla made a particularly interesting attempt to engage both domestic and international law. Affected by the many incidents in which pirates targeted refugee boats, they decided to appeal to the authorities for protection. When this didn't work, three authors from the camp put together an

---

[112] Daniel C. Tsang, "Visions of Resistance and Survival from Hong Kong Detention Camps," in Yuk Wah Chan (ed.), *The Chinese/Vietnamese Diaspora: Revising the Boat People* (London and New York: Routledge, 2011), 103. The very last lines of his essay call for an exploration of "resistance and survival in the Hong Kong Vietnamese detention camps" (113).

[113] Tsang, "Visions of Resistance and Survival from Hong Kong Detention Camps," 104. Tsang is a librarian in UC Irvine and a self-avowed radical in the contexts of gay rights and Asian-American identity politics, formerly an anti-Vietnam War activist. See David Reyes, "UCI Lecturer, Mentor Out 'to Change Society'," *The Los Angeles Times*, March 14, 1994, available at http://articles.latimes.com/1994-03-14/local/me-33903_1_asian-american (last accessed May 22, 2013).

[114] Compare with repeated appeals to Emma Lazarus's words in Chapter 3.

[115] Tsang, "Visions of Resistance and Survival from Hong Kong Detention Camps," 104.

[116] Grant, *The Boat People*, 79.

[117] Grant, *The Boat People*, 79.

English publication titled *Pirates on the Gulf of Siam*.[118] The book is organized around testimonies, similar to a contemporary human rights report.[119] Presenting itself as coming directly from the victims, however, it has an added urgency.

But this form of engagement was of course not an altogether happy story. As the years passed, camps provided their inhabitants with little more than life itself. Such characterizations appear in the late 1980s, when migrants remained interned sometimes for years or were identified as not entitled to protection – and turned back. In accounts of screening procedures introduced to select people for resettlement, migrants are described as docile, mute, and passive. But as the 1980s turned into the 1990s, the shrinking scope of protection also provoked unrest. One study focusing on refugees in Hong Kong showed how reporting on refugee protests systemically underplayed its political nature, explaining spurts of violence simply as power struggles within groups in the camp. In February 1990, an incident in which authorities used tear gas and 300 were injured was presented in local media as a clash between two rival groups. In another case that year, 4,000 refugees responded to rumors about a new return policy by marching around their dormitories. Hunger strikes became a preferred way to protest against repatriation. Artwork from the Hong Kong camps included poignant depictions of these strikes,[120] which bring together freedom and survival perhaps in the most direct way imaginable: starving oneself in order to gain freedom highlights the choice of the authority confronting the strike, namely, to protect survival and prevent freedom.[121] It thus became another way of generating the human rights encounter.[122]

What Is a Human Rights Claim?

During the years of the Indochinese boat people crisis, there was no agreement between actors that used human rights arguments about the

---

[118] Nhat Tien, *Pirates on the Gulf of Siam: Report from the Vietnamese Boat People Living in the Refugee Camp in Songkhla-Thailand* (San Diego: Van Moch Graphics and Print, 1981).

[119] Compare also to Earl Harrison's report discussed in Chapter 1.

[120] Tsang, "Visions of Resistance and Survival from Hong Kong Detention Camps," 105.

[121] Through a hunger strike, an individual can therefore assert a form of sovereignty even in the face of a sovereign state.

[122] See discussion in Chapter 4 as well.

content of these rights.[123] For boat people, human rights claims rested on an inextricable bond between freedom and survival, the urgency of which stemmed from a perceived risk to one's life. The United States had a similar position, at least initially. Its reception of some Vietnamese, accompanied by commentators' reprimand of the Vietnamese government, was framed not only as a project of lifesaving. It was rooted in an imagination of American political freedoms. But this commitment was limited, and if it were not for the boat peoples' actions, it would not have led to the kind of reaction on the transnational level. Indeed, within transnational governance networks, human rights were about a much more thin commitment to being "civilized."[124] The meaning of being civilized turned out to be saving lives, while *suppressing* claims about freedom.[125] Considering the gap between the two accounts of human rights, it becomes necessary to ask: What is at stake in the difference between them?

A memoir written by one Vietnamese-American author begins with a heartfelt dedication: "To my father, who delivered us to the land of the free."[126] But the legal history of the 1979 Geneva conference does not mention this author's father or any other actual boatperson for that matter. It may seem strange to suggest that this father should become a protagonist of international legal process. International law, one might say, is not about the aspirations of individuals or their personal choices, dramatic as they may be. Even within the traditional human rights

---

[123] If one believes, like some critical legal theorists, that rights never have any definite content, this would of course be utterly unsurprising. See Martti Koskenniemi, *The Politics of International Law* (Oxford: Hart Publishing, 2011), 135–136.

[124] I assume a dichotomy here, which may not be entirely accurate. Were there not members of transnational governance networks that genuinely worked for both the survival and the freedom of boat people? Perhaps. A good example might be the flotilla Medecins du Monde sent to protect asylum seekers from pirate attacks, led by Bernard Kouchner. Michel Foucault famously delivered a speech titled "Confronting Governments: Human Rights," in which he celebrated the initiative, casting it in what seems to me as the terms of both "freedom" and "survival." See Michel Foucault, "Confronting Governments: Human Rights," in James Faubion (ed.), *Essential Works of Michel Foucault 1954–1984 Vol. 3: Power* (London: Pegnuin, 1994). See also an excellent essay on the affair, Jessica Whyte, "Human Rights: Confronting Governments?" in Matthew Stone, Ilan Rua Wall, and Costas Douzinas (eds.), *New Critical Legal Thinking: Law and the Political* (New York: Routledge, 2012), 11–31.

[125] On the "dark side" of the "civilizing mission," and how it shaped international law more generally, see Antony Anghie, *Imperialism, Sovereignty and the Making of International Law* (Cambridge: Cambridge University Press, 2007).

[126] Van Nguyen, *The Storm of Our Lives*. Compare with Harold Koh's frequent invocation of his own father discussed in Chapter 4.

literature, which recognizes the status of individuals regardless of their citizenship, this status is conceived of as one that merits "protection." This word is indicative, as "protection" is passive – and denies the more active notion of "participation." Such limitations of the scope of international human rights law, though extremely prevalent, merely reflect a *particular* orientation toward international law.[127] They are not at all necessary, and the underlying theoretical assumptions they reflect were not always in place.[128] From the perspective of the boat people, their choices were about their survival and their demand to access freedom. Though only roughly articulated in the vocabularies of law, such questions are not easily severable from legality.[129] Surely the issues in question in the dedication, namely territory ("land") and liberty ("free"), are categories not at all foreign to law.[130]

Linking survival to freedom was doubtlessly important in the personal narratives boat people told themselves. But were their actions powerful enough to exert *influence* on transnational legal process? Given the asymmetry between them and the governments convened in Geneva, it may seem to make little sense to say that boat people pushed governments to costly action. But it is hard to imagine that something like the

---

[127] Hathaway and Shapiro call this orientation the "Modern State Conception of law," proceeding to criticize it. See Hathaway and Shapiro, "Outcasting," 268. As Antony Anghie has argued, the universalization of the relationship between sovereigns, as the only relationship worthy of counting as "international law," had the effect of "suppressing and subordinating other histories of international law and the peoples to whom it has applied." See Anghie, *Imperialism, Sovereignty and the Making of International Law*, 5 and chapter 2 more generally.

[128] As Stephen Neff explains, for the Stoics "the entire human community must be seen as one single outsize city-state of *polis* – as, in the Greek terminology, a 'world-city' or *kosmopolis* ..." The life of all creatures is conceived of one organism, in which every creature's actions play a role. See Stephen Neff, *Justice among Nations: A History of International Law* (Cambridge: Harvard University Press, 2014), 43.

[129] Perhaps the most important positivist theorist of law, H.L.A. Hart, seems to struggle to some extent with the question if protecting survival is a necessary objective of law. See H.L.A. Hart, *The Concept of Law* (Oxford: Oxford University Press, 2012), especially chapter 9, as well as Leslie Green's useful introduction.

[130] This is of course a paraphrase of the American national anthem, The Star-Spangled Banner. On territory, see Paul Kahn, *The Cultural Study of Law* (Chicago and London: University of Chicago Press, 1999), 55. (Kahn writes: "The Rule of law is always rule over a defined territory. Morality may be without borders, but law's rule begins only with the imagination of jurisdiction. We have moral, but not legal, obligations to those beyond our borders." From the present perspective, Kahn's observation requires one amendment: human rights' imagination of jurisdiction is tethered to our bodies, not only to territory. That is why the encounter can in fact create legal obligation beyond the border, as discussed in Chapter 1.)

Orderly Departure Program would develop but for the interference boat people generated. The relevant policies were only adopted reluctantly: there was no choice but to do *something*. By putting in place an alternative path to freedom, which did not demand taking to the sea, world governments made boat people de facto negotiators on issues of transnational governance. Even without relying on discourse, boat people sent a message about their needs and interests. And their message was taken into account.

Another objection to the claim that the actions boat people took enforced their rights rests upon a certain requirement of reason in politics.[131] Even if they did somehow employ international law to save themselves, it is highly unlikely that they had *deliberate* involvement in the *Orderly Departure Program* and other remedial measures. I have claimed that their actions allowed them to be participants in the relevant transnational legal process even without sending delegates to the negotiation table. But they may have not even *known* it existed. A necessary condition for engagement with politics, in this view, is a reasonable actor, whose decision-making process joins means to ends.[132] This condition informs much contemporary political theory, premised on the social contract.[133] And it may indeed be a necessary condition for making political claims founded upon citizenship within a sovereign state.[134] But this condition does not delineate an appropriate limitation for political claims founded upon membership in humanity – the

[131] This requirement is explained by Max Weber in his conceptualization of an "ethics of responsibility." See Max Weber, *The Vocation Lectures* (Indianapolis: Hackett Publishing, 2004).

[132] Such an actor cannot be motivated by fear, which is "a primal, and so to speak, subpolitical emotion." Raymond Aron, *Main Currents in Sociological Thought I: Montesquieu, Comte, Marx, Tocqueville, the Sociologists of the Revolution of 1848*, trans. Richard Howard and Hellen Weaver (Gardens City: Doubleday, 1968).

[133] Most importantly the work of John Rawls, *A Theory of Justice* (Cambridge: Harvard University Press, 1999). My criticism of liberalism here relies to considerable extent on Paul Kahn, *Putting Liberalism in Its Place* (Princeton: Princeton University Press, 2005), 120 (Kahn discusses Rawls's conception of "public reason":

> Those who cannot engage in public reason are not entitled to participate in the construction of public norms. Yet, because the public norms are to be the product of reason, we can aspire to universal agreement on their content. Anyone who cannot raise him or herself to the level of public reason suffers, from the perspective of liberalism, a kind of political pathology.

[134] Ultimately, however, I believe the sovereign state too premised on the version of the social contract developed in this chapter, in Chapter 3, and in the Conclusion to this book.

membership the universal boatperson asserts. Hers is a form of participation on the transnational or extranational level. Rather than assuming
a preexisting political community or state, it relies on human rights law
and is grounded upon the human rights encounter.

Thomas Hobbes's political thought is useful in clarifying what is at
stake in politics and law beyond citizenship. Hobbes may be the greatest
theorist of the relationship between politics, law, and self-preservation,
and indeed of the relationship between freedom and survival.[135]
Hobbes's approach on the relationship between freedom and survival
will be contrasted to Arendt's.

The role of survival in Hobbes's theory of social contract has been
much commented upon.[136] Its general outlines are one of the most
familiar narratives in Western political philosophy: in the state of nature,
humans live in the condition of bare life. Unprotected by any sovereign
power, they fear for their own lives, which are "nasty, brutish, and short."
And "the accumulated anguish of individuals who fear for their lives
brings a new power into the picture: the leviathan."[137] This delegation of
violence in return for protection typically ends up awarding members of
the social contract with more than mere survival or bare life. Civil society
grants them a certain kind of political freedom.[138] The moment of
passage from the state of nature to civil society allows us to conceptualize
bare life as a political category that encapsulates a fundamental form of
political action.[139] Hobbes conceives human life as always already political. Even before accession to the social contract, life is set within the

---

[135] For a discussion of two different ways to understand the centrality of self-preservation in
Hobbes's oeuvre, see Thomas Nagel, "Hobbes's Concept of Obligation,"
The Philosophical Review 68, no. 1 (1959): 68–83.

[136] See, e.g., Corey Robin, "Fear: A Genealogy of Morals," *Social Research* 67, no. 4 (2000):
1085, 1087.

[137] Carl Schmitt, *The Leviathan in the State Theory of Thomas Hobbes: Meaning and Failure
of a Political Symbol* (Chicago: University of Chicago Press, 2008), 33.

[138] Citizens under Hobbes's Commonwealth are free in the sense of being governed by
"Good Lawes":

> By a Good Law, I mean not a Just Law: for no Law can be Unjust. The Law
> is made by the Soveraign Power, and all that is done by such Power, is
> warranted, and owned by every one of the people; and that which every
> man will have so, no man can say is unjust. It is the Lawes of the Common-
> wealth, as in the Lawes of Gaming: whatsoever the Gamesters all agree on,
> is Injustice to non of them. A good Law is that, which is *Needfull*, for the
> *Good of the People*, and with all *Perspicuous.*

    Thomas Hobbes, *Leviathan* (Cambridge: Cambridge University Press, 1991), 239.

[139] Compare with the account of this passage suggested in Chapter 3.

realm of power and people respond to each other's threats and interests. In the state of nature humans are subject to each other's power and exert power (limited as it may be). It is for this reason that Hobbes recognizes a form of Natural Rights, according to which "there be some rights which no man can be understood by any words or other signs to have abandoned or transferred."

Life in the Hobbesian state of nature is characterized by a constant experience of fear. This fear explains how bare life becomes, for Hobbes, the origin of political action, rather than its negation. Corey Robin explains: "the fearful are focused on their own conception of the good ... Fear is thus the foundation of purposive agency. It focuses us on our long-term aims and pulls us back from risky behavior that might make it impossible for us to fulfill those aims."[140] Political experience does not necessarily begin from a comfort in which needs are met and one can discuss the structures of collective life. One is pushed to politics in order to protect oneself and to improve one's position in conditions of dearth. Thus, by tying fear to agency, Hobbes also ties survival and freedom. This doesn't reduce fearful action to causation. To the contrary, the actor still has a space to decide if and how to protect her survival. Robin suggests that this results in an aversion from risk. But in certain radical conditions of fear, *assuming* risk is entirely consistent with the theory. Risk appears as a possible way to increase the probability of survival for one's self and one's most immediate relatives and loved ones. While acting to protect their survival, the refugees speaking in the testimonies attempted to constitute their own freedom. Some succeeded. The decision to do so has foundational import for the theory of human rights.

Return to the descriptions of panic we found in Schell, referenced above. In *The Real War*, Schell memorably described the South Vietnamese Society as a "collection of individuals," a description that echoes Hobbes.[141] This is not the individuality of a reasonable actor weighing means against ends and deliberating over collectively beneficial policies in a safe remove from material needs. In the power lacuna that remained at the end of April 1975, the Vietnamese society is described as hopelessly fragmented, confused, and nightmarishly disoriented. Members of this society are edging close to the life of animals, in the Hobbesian sense of "*homo homini lupus.*" Remember the children lying

---

[140] Robin, "Fear: A Genealogy of Morals," 1092.
[141] Schell, *The Real War*, 53.

in front of a taxiing aircraft. The frequent reference to children empha-sizes the magnitude of the tragedy, and points to the powerlessness of bare life.[142]

Like the Hobbesian state of nature, the Vietnamese postwar environ-ment is characterized by a pervasive, generalized fear. Like the motion of the uncontrolled boat floating on water, in these emergency conditions, deterministic necessity and free action become nearly indistinguishable. However, they are never in fact one and the same. Was it the force of the elements pushing the boat people to step into boats and become "helpless leaves adrift in calm or stormy seas"? We don't know. The only fair way to answer is to adopt the testimonies of boat people.[143] From their perspectives, they have invariably contributed to obtaining their own remedies. Even in the most limiting of constraints, they always did something that *could have not been done* (or the other way around). These little actions reflect how in their movement out of the Hobbesian state of nature, fear brought about a new kind of politics.

The movement to a proto-political position is reflected in a poignant way in Hue's testimony. Hue described the *love* that developed between the survivors on the atoll island in the South China Sea.[144] They shared their food. They slept in the same corner and treated one another "as blood relatives." The experience is fashioned in her testimony through a blend of will and submission. Both experiences point to the same direction of mutual help among the members of the group. Existence is wholly absorbed in the ebbs and flows of the ocean and the cyclical movement from sunrise to sunset. It is not based on a social contract but on a shared fate and a shared struggle. Though Hobbes's theory of the state of nature is often depicted only in its darkest tonalities, it is in fact amenable to such an experience of shared fate.

There is a kind of equilibrium in Hue's story between the seagull coming back to the island and the starving humans trapped on it.

---

[142] Like animals, children cannot be held accountable for their actions and are closer in that way to nature. Like animals, they cannot join as full members to a social contract. But even if children do not have voting rights in a community of citizens, this does not mean they do not have rights. In fact, it doesn't even mean that minors do not participate meaningfully in their own societies or have stakes in their own futures. This suggests that the source of the rights of noncitizens, like the rights of children, cannot be found in the capacity to participate in a particular polity and must be established elsewhere.

[143] Even if these were given after the fact and are probably colored by hindsight, this particular coloring is not irrelevant. What we are after here is how their actions *appeared to them*, not how they appeared from the perspective of some of disinterested bystander.

[144] On Love, see Kahn, *Putting Liberalism in Its Place* (2005), 143–290.

Humans try to nourish off the seagulls' bodies. They therefore scare them away. Only when the number of human survivors falls, the seagulls come back. The cycle is complete when the seagulls incarnate the members of the group that have perished. The universal boatperson moves between the human and the inanimate and between the tides of the sea. She approaches the life of an animal.

It is such animal life, not an autonomous and unconditioned reason, that allows Hoang to resist killings when he says: "A tiny bit of food becomes the difference between life and death, and starving people have no inhibition." There is a solidarity that continues to exist even when the will seems to be taken by natural causation.[145] The life of animals does not have to be associated with a war of all against all. Though nowhere near an idyllic picture Jean Jacques Rousseau may have painted of his state of nature, it is different from the description of "[B]ands of children, hungry and thirsty . . ."[146]

---

[145] Contrast with *Regina* v. *Dudley and Stephens* [1881–1885] All E.R. Rep 61 (Queen's Bench, December 9, 1884). Lord Coleridge writes:

> To preserve one's life is generally speaking, a duty, but it may be the plainest and the highest duty to sacrifice it. War is full of instances in which it is a man's duty not to live, but to die. The duty, in case of shipwreck, of a captain to his crew, of the crew to the passengers, of soldiers to women and children, as in the noble case of The Birkenhead – these duties impose on men the moral necessity, not of the preservation, but of the sacrifice, of their lives for others, from which no country – least of all it is to be hoped in England – will men ever shirk, as indeed they have not shrunk. It is not correct, therefore, to say that there is any absolute and unqualified necessity to preserve one's life. "Necesse est ut eam, non ut vivam," is a saying of a Roman officer quoted by Lord Bacon himself with high eulogy in the very chapter on Necessity, to which so much reference has been made. it would be a very easy and cheap display of commonplace learning to quote from Greek and Latin authors – from Horace, from Juvenal, from Cicero, from Euripides – passage after passage in which the duty of dying for others has been laid down in glowing and emphatic language as resulting from the principles of heathen ethics. It is enough in a Christian country to remind ourselves of the Great Example which we profess to follow.

[146] Schell, *The Real War*, 52. In a glorious passage, Gilles Deleuze and Felix Guattari return to the work of French-Jewish author Valdimir Slepian, to explain how the drive to fulfill needs may make one creatively embrace animality (rather than being pushed to animality by being reduced to needs alone):

> I'm hungry, always hungry, a man should not be hungry. So, I'll have to become a dog – but how? This will not involve imitating a dog . . . For I cannot become a dog without the dog itself becoming something else. Slepian gets the idea of using shoes to solve this problem, the artifice of the

To be sure, in Hobbes's political theory, it is not just any fear for survival that will lead humans to unite under sovereignty. The fear that leads to the establishment of a commonwealth is people's fear of each other. Once sovereignty is established, citizens will fear sovereignty. But for the commonwealth to remain stable, their new fear must have a lesser intensity. It is precisely for this reason that it can be thought of as a form of freedom. The commonwealth must appear to be preferable to the state of nature.

The definition of a refugee under the 1951 Refugee Convention and its Protocol refers to fear, but this is not the Hobbesian fear. International law requires refugees to have a "well-founded fear" for one of five reasons: race, ethnicity, religion, political opinion, or membership in a particular social group. The definition envisions refugees through their citizenship and their membership in sovereignty. The *sovereign* is the paradigmatic persecutor, not one's fellow human beings (as in the Hobbesian state of nature).[147]

Like the 1951 Refugee Convention, the *Orderly Departure Program* too excluded "economic refugees." Access to refugee status was only possible if the asylum seeker suffered fear of her sovereign. At certain phases of the *Orderly Departure Program*, the boat people were screened for resettlement under the criteria of the Refugee Convention and Protocol. Though many suffered from sources of fear recognized in the Refugee Convention, most presumably did not. The devastation of war and the resulting hunger are two sources of fear that are not recognized in the Convention. The war in Vietnam produced a multitude of people who were not persecuted individually (as the Convention requires), but who de facto were no longer members of any social contract. They were in the position of Hobbesian bare life in the state of nature, not in the position of Convention refugees. The energy that fueled the international legal

---

shoes. If I wear shoes on my hands, then their elements will enter into a new relation . . . But how will I be able to tie the shoe on my second hand, once the first is already occupied? With my mouth, which in turn receives the investment in the assemblage, becoming a dog muzzle, insofar as a dog muzzle is now used to ties shoes.

Gilles Deleuze and Felix Guattari, *A Thousand Plateaus: Capitalism and Schizophrenia* (Minneapolis and London: University of Minnesota Press, 1987).

[147] Though in some jurisdiction persecution by private entities has been recognized under the Convention, this too is not the mutual fear of the Hobbesian state of nature. For this jurisprudence too assumes that every person has a particular citizenship. Persecution by a private entity can only be recognized when it is conceived as a failure of the sovereign to grant protection.

transformation that leads to the *Orderly Departure Program* was not the fear recognized by the Refugee Convention, but something else.

Hobbes goes into detail in describing how in the state of nature power is divided more or less equally among individuals: without social hierarchies, we are all weak and stupid more or less to the same degree. A contemporary application of Hobbes, however, may start from a different premise. Law already exists; the institutions of "civil society" have been erected. However, for the universal boatperson, law is a destructive force. The assumption of a fundamental equality of power between all individuals therefore also does not hold: those parts of the world that are organized in well-functioning commonwealths are powerful. Those parts of the world in which sovereignty has failed, disintegrated, or never emerged in a social contract, are by comparison powerless.[148] In order to obtain some measure of participation, the latter must do one of two things. They can either find ways to inflict the fear of a Hobbesian state of nature even on those living in proper Commonwealths;[149] or they can address powerful political entities in ways that are still available to them as bare life. But what are the political means available to bare life, short of violence?

When migrants approach a border behind which "civil society" has been established, they hope that at least their *survival* will be protected by law that is *not their own*. If they are admitted into the realm of law, this can end up granting them more than just survival. Sometimes they gain political freedom in the form of citizenship. Access is granted under a condition of emergency – the risk of drowning in the sea. In such conditions, powerful parties legally committed themselves to respond to the presence and call of distress that bare life can voice. But, as legal theorists have long recognized, emergency has the tendency of establishing a new norm: once emergency grants them access, citizenship is normalized and regularized access.[150] When a state of nature appears out of an international crisis like postwar Vietnam, some people's fear can lead them from survival to freedom. This

---

[148] On the notion of a well-ordered sovereign and its place in international law, see David Singh Grewal, "The Domestic Analogy Revised: Hobbes on International Order," Yale Law Journal 125(3) (2016): 618–680.

[149] This may be a partial explanation of the extra-sovereign violence that transnational terrorist organizations wield.

[150] The problem was most famously introduced by Carl Schmitt in Carl Schmitt, *The Concept of the Political*, Enlarged edition (Chicago: University of Chicago Press, 2007) and reintroduced by Giorgio Agamben, *State of Exception*, 1st edition (Chicago: University of Chicago Press, 2005). In the context of Southeast Asian refugees, one author went so far as writing that refugees "are emergencies." See Tepper (ed.), *Southeast Asian Exodus*, 5.

remedy will of course be available only as long as powerful parties continue to observe the legal duties they have toward bare life.

It is within this paradigm of the political action of bare life that the personal choices and aspirations of boat people must inform an account of human rights. Remember Truong, who made it impossible to get rid of himself and his fellow passengers, by tearing a hole in their own boat. This led him first to a refugee camp and finally to resettlement in Arkansas. It contributed to the formation of the transnational cooperation from which other Southeast Asians also benefitted. In this story we have seen how the boat people discovered that transnational political participation could stem from bare life. In some circumstances, membership in humanity is more protective than membership in one's particular community. This insight is encapsulated in Ngan's question: "Why do they treat us so kindly, though they are a different race? And, on the other hand, why do our people, who are of the same race, why do they treat us so cruelly?"

Just like in the Hobbesian social contract, in its modified version proposed here, violence is delegated to sovereignty. That is why Hau decided to employ nonviolence.[151] His choice doesn't necessarily reflect the judgment that violence is *wrong*.[152] To the contrary, violence is an inherent part both of enforcing the rights of sovereignty and of transnational governance networks. But because sovereignty claims a monopoly over the legitimate use of violence, employing violence would immediately encode the actor as *challenging* sovereign authority. Human rights claims must appeal to values that sovereign authorities recognize as genuinely *their own*. To remain merely human – and thus entitled to the rights reserved to bare life – one must not be perceived as a criminal, an enemy, a revolutionary, or a terrorist.[153]

Against Hobbes's emphasis on survival, one might take Hannah Arendt's view of political life as removed from material needs.[154]

---

[151] This is also the position the *Exodus*'s migrants decided to take when they used potatoes as weapons.

[152] Compare with Chibli Mallat, Philosophy of Nonviolence: Revolution, Constitutionalism, and Justice beyond the Middle East, 1st edition (Oxford and New York: Oxford University Press, 2015).

[153] Interestingly, the Brussels Salvage Convention (1905), the first international legal instrument to codify the rule of rescue at sea, specifies that it does not matter if a person in need of assistance at sea is an enemy: "Every master is bound, so far as he can do so without serious danger to his vessel, her crew and passengers, to render assistance to every-body, even though an enemy, found at sea in danger of being lost." Brussels Salvage Convention, Art. 11.

[154] According to which "every citizen belongs to two orders of existence." Arendt, *The Human Condition*, 24.

In her magnum opus, *The Human Condition*, Arendt argued that political action within a bounded community requires the basic needs of the actors to already have been met. This thesis is echoed in *On Revolution*, where mass poverty is thought of as an obstacle to the very possibility of political life.[155] Only when free of concerns for their own survival, citizens are able to deliberate in the public sphere and give themselves their own law. "The touchstone of a free act is always our awareness that we could also have left undone what we actually did," writes Arendt. The actions described in the testimonies above meet this initial test. But Arendt continues by saying this is "not at all true" where "bodily needs, the necessities of life process" are in question.[156] Hue demands of us a concept of human action that remains critically tied to bodily needs.

The Common Origin of Freedom and Survival

Is it really necessary to decide between a Hobbesian reading of politics in which the Southeast Asian boat people are the protagonists and an Arendtian one in which they could only be the recipients of aid?

Think of this photo (Figure 1), which appears in *The Vietnamese Boatpeople: Today's Untouchables*. The picture shows a boy, bare-bodied but for underwear and a necklace. The boy stands sternly in front of the camera. The frame measures his height from head to toes. The fact that the boy has only one arm immediately stands out. The caption attached reads: *"Bui Quang Dung, four year old freedom fighter! Liberation day, April 30, 1975 'freed' one arm ..."*

The date in the caption is the date of the United States' withdrawal and the establishment of the new socialist regime. This is the regime that the book as a whole portrays as an oppressive, persecuting regime. But the date renders the title "freedom fighter" somewhat confusing. Was the child a "freedom fighter" for the independence of Vietnam? Or is he a symbol, rather, of a flight for freedom, in which people fought to leave the country? The date stands at one and the same time both for Vietnam's liberation and for the beginning of the "Indochinese Exodus."[157] The two heroisms – insurgents fighting for independence and refugees fleeing

---

[155] Arendt, *On Revolution*.
[156] Hannah Arendt, *The Life of the Mind* (New York: Harcourt, 1978), Part II: Willing, 5.
[157] This is the title of Robinson, *Terms of Refuge*.

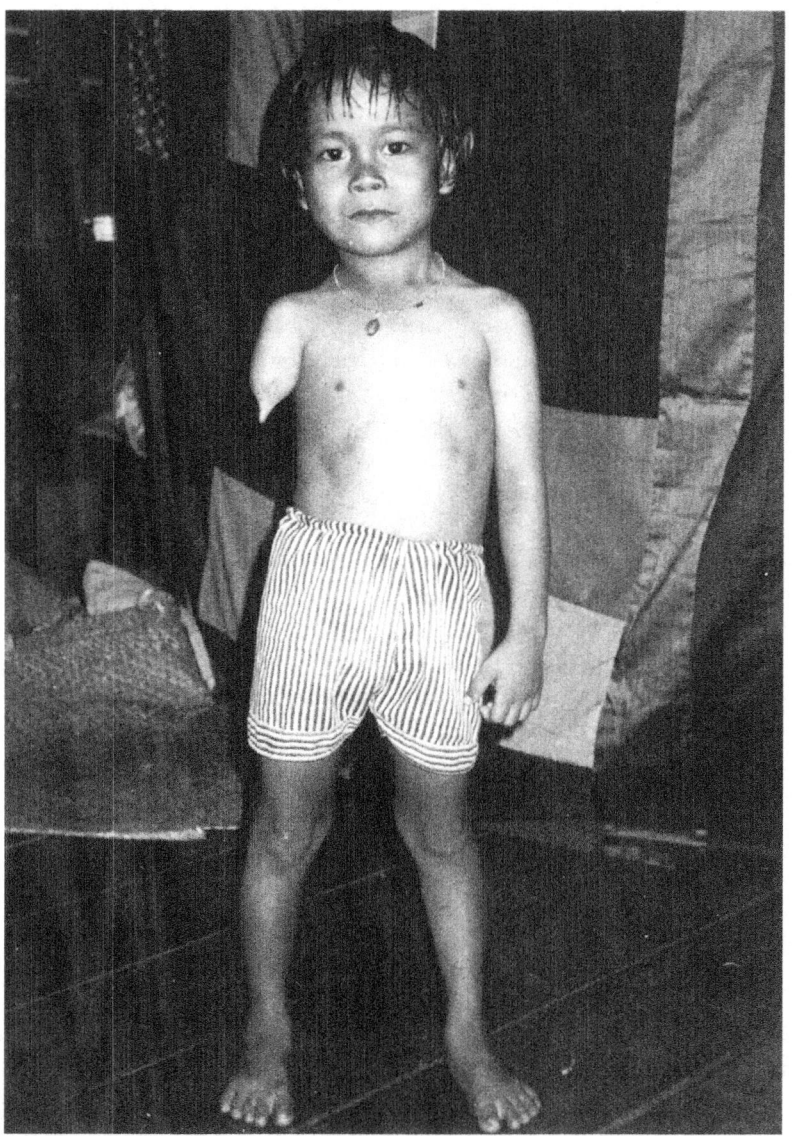

■ Bui Quang Dung, four year old freedom fighter ! Liberation day, April 30, 1975 "freed" one arm...

■ Em Bùi Quang Dũng 4 tuổi, ba năm trước đây em đã bị cụt mất một tay trong ngày "hòa bình" 30-4-75, với cánh tay đau buốt vì xương non cứ tiếp tục mọc dài thêm.

■ Enfant Bui Quang Dung, 4 ans. Il y a trois ans il avait perdu son bras le jour de "Paix" 30 Avril 1975 ; ce bras continuait à lui faire mal, l'os ne guérissant toujours pas...

■ ブイ・クァン・ユン 4 歳。 3 年前の解放の日、昭和50年 4 月30日片手を失ない、今は骨が伸びるため毎日痛みを耐えている。

Figure 1   Four-year-old freedom fighter
(photographer unknown)

from persecution – are rendered into two sides of one coin.[158] In the terms developed in the previous chapter – one side means asserting the rights through sovereignty, and the other means asserting the rights through transnational governance.[159] The previous chapter tells a history in which the rights of sovereignty were pursued. This chapter tells a history in which some people preferred the rights of transnational governance. The boy's body delineates that "zone of indistinction," to use Giorgio Agamben's term, between *physis* and *nomos*, in which neither option has already been taken up. This zone can be filled with an act of unaccountable killing (as Agamben emphasizes). It can also be filled with responsibility toward the other (to use Lévinas's language). It is only for the powerful party in the human rights encounter to decide. But as long as the powerful party claims to adhere to human rights, the latter option is the only one that is available to her. What will come *after* such responsibility is a difficult question. This chapter has shown that sometimes the political action of bare life on the transnational sphere can lead to real institutional change. This is only one way in which it can lead from the survival of bare life to the freedom of citizenship.

But perhaps even more interesting is the part of the caption telling us that this boy freed only "one arm." Here, the text is irreverently humorous. It proposes to the viewer: imagine the boy as a freedom fighter who has made a sacrifice for his community. The missing arm is the price of freedom. What the boy gained by losing it is the integrity of other parts of his body. The missing arm stands as a metaphor for multiple other

---

[158] The same intuition is expressed by the following testimony by a single parent with three children who arrived in the United Kingdom in 1989:

> Before the fall of Saigon, I was on the opposite side to the Communists. After that I suffered quite a lot of hardships. I only did odd jobs for my livelihood because I had no right under the new regime. What I needed was freedom for myself and children. However, I did not think much about leaving my home country, it meant leaving my own family. At that time, there were two ways to have freedom – fighting or leaving. Somehow at the very late stage of the "boat people," finally I managed to flee from my home country to seek freedom.

Quoted in Karen Duke and Tony Marshall, *Vietnamese Refugees since 1982* (London: Home Office Research and Planning Report, 1995), 17–18.

[159] This is consistent with Hobbes's assertion that "every sovereign hath the same Right, in the safety of his People, that any particular man can have, in procuring his own safety." Hobbes, Leviathan, 244.

bodies: those who have died for the liberation of Vietnam and those who have drowned in the sea while trying to escape. This play with a double meaning of sacrifice – in fight or in flight – is the sharpest articulation of the common origin of freedom and survival. This common origin is the foundation and source of human rights, whether they come to be institutionalized in sovereignty or in transnational governance.[160]

The Politics of Human Rights Claims

In the aftermath of the United States' withdrawal from Vietnam on April 30, 1975, hundreds of thousands of migrants took to the sea, hoping to be saved and resettled in countries in the Western Bloc. In 1979, the United States and the UNHCR initiated multilateral discussions on this issue, which resulted in the *Orderly Departure Program*. This program sought to stem the flow of boats leaving Vietnam, granting Southeast Asian persons who wished to leave their countries opportunities to apply for visas. While this program has been recognized as a success of transnational governance, the boat people are ordinarily not considered as actors in the transnational legal process that generated it. This chapter challenges that assumption, arguing that these maritime journeys should be understood as a paradigmatic example of human rights claims.

From the perspective of the transnational actors sitting around the table in Geneva and negotiating the *Orderly Departure Program*, it may have seemed like boat people were passive victims of an international crisis, rather than actors within it. I have argued, however, that it is unnecessary and unjustifiable to adopt that perspective as our own. It represents no more than a preference for a particular kind of politics, one that assumes a preexisting and more or less functioning basis of sovereignty. But limiting the view of politics to that worldview requires adopting a political ontology that fails to reflect the experiences of many of the affected groups. At the bottom line, the *Orderly Departure Program* likely would not have been launched were it not for the actions of boat

---

[160] This logical extreme is precisely where sensibilities demanding protection of survival (and not freedom) are likely to reappear. The boy becomes a symbol of the normative outlook aiming to protect refugees from themselves. The humorous caption demands the viewer to approve of the child's sacrifice – of his exposure to the risks at sea. But from the perspective of the protection of bare life, or the vindication of survival, the viewer may feel inclined to guard the child from becoming a freedom fighter. On children's agency and human rights, see David Oswell, *The Agency of Children: From Family to Global Human Rights* (Cambridge: Cambridge University Press, 2012).

people. Even if they didn't know about the Geneva talks, boat people contributed to pushing powerful actors not to ignore their problem.

I argued that human rights claims do not originate in states or transnational organizations. Human rights claims are the claims of those who seek the protection of human rights. Making human rights claims remains political action even if it is not engaged from a position of reason but responds to need, necessity, and fear.[161] When one makes a claim of survival, that claim relies on one's agency and can sometimes lead to freedom. Hobbes made this argument in the clearest way, in texts that very much defined the Western philosophical tradition. Contemporary liberal theory has instead followed a different assumption: politics is constituted by reason. The underlying assumption is that one's needs have already been met. Looking at the boat people, I urge a return to the Hobbesian perspective, but in a slightly different form. Today, conditions of a "state of nature" are by no means caused by natural events. If, as Robert Cover wrote, the sea represents an imagined law of nature, one might prefer floating in the sea to the conditions in areas such as postwar Vietnam.[162] Hobbes believed we exit such conditions by establishing civil society through a social contract. Today, that is often not possible. Migration becomes a self-help human rights remedy, parallel to giving one's right to violence to the sovereign.

---

[161] The purpose here was not to make an argument about the nature of free will: "Genealogy is not metaphysics; its concern is not to answer the problem of free will, but to understand its conceptual shape, trace the passage of these concepts from metaphysics to politics, and investigate the remnants of this tradition within our current beliefs about law's rule." Kahn, *The Cultural Study of Law* (1999), 75.

[162] Robert Cover, *Justice Accused* (New Haven: Yale University Press, 1975).

3

What Is a Human Rights Commitment?

In May 1941, Hannah Arendt arrived in New York. She was thirty-two years old, broke, and knew little English. But it wasn't long before she started to publish her essays and reviews in the new language. Among these early works was "We Refugees" (1943), a short and personal piece she penned for the Jewish-American *The Menorah Journal*.[1] Her experiences of persecution are reflected in this essay. Yet Arendt was now in the safety of a new society. Though still stateless – Arendt became a naturalized citizen of the United States in 1950 – she began to enjoy her membership in the American social contract. In some of her later work, Arendt celebrated the constitutional tradition of the society she now became part of.[2] Comparing the American to the French revolution, she painted a magnificent portrait of the American Founding Fathers, who appeared as the architects of the paramount democracy in modern times.[3]

In 1941, it may have looked to Arendt like a commitment to realize the rights of noncitizens could be incorporated as part of the American social contract. This proposition was fundamentally and dramatically put to a test at the US Supreme Court fifty years later, as the Cold War came to an end.[4] Noncitizens at American borders were no longer Europeans or allies from a faraway war. Like the growing number of unauthorized migrants landing at the borders of Europe around the same time, they came from the developing world and were propelled by a mixture of persecution and economic dearth. US policymakers believed the country had no interest in admitting them.

---

[1] Hannah Arendt, "We Refugees," in Marc Robinson (ed.), *Altogether Elsewhere: Writers on Exile* (London and Boston: Harvest, 1996), 110. Originally published in *The Menorah Journal* 31 (1943).

[2] Hannah Arendt, *On Revolution* (London: Penguin, 2006). Specifically, see Arendt's discussion in the chapter entitled *Novus Ordo Saeclorum* (starting p. 179).

[3] See, e.g., Arendt's almost intimate reference to "the Founding Fathers' enthusiastic and sometimes slightly comical erudition in political theory." Arendt, *On Revolution*, 121.

[4] *Sale* v. *Haitian Centers Council*, 823 F. Supp. 1028 (E.D.N.Y. 1993) (hereinafter: *Sale*).

Facing Haitian refugees, the US Supreme Court did not find that noncitizens could enforce their rights by appeal to the American social contract. The Court did not even uphold the minimal idea of human rights as protection of survival, explained in the previous chapter. Instead, the Court allowed the executive branch to close the country's doors. Under a bilateral agreement with Haiti, migrants were interdicted on the high seas and sent back to the risk of persecution. *Sale* v. *Haitian Centers Council* (1993)[5] was the famous (or rather infamous) case that upheld this arrangement. Arendt's observation in *Origins of Totalitarianism*, discussed in the introduction to the book, was confirmed: In conditions of perceived crisis, states will sidestep "The Rights of Man."[6]

This result raises the question of this chapter: What does it mean to be committed to human rights law? The idea that the American social contract entails certain duties toward all persons could at best be an aspiration; in actual fact it proved untenable. In our own time, U.S. executive-branch lawyers have repeatedly defended the position that obligations under the International Covenant on Civil and Political Rights (ICCPR) do not apply to noncitizens outside US territory.[7] This, it has been argued, creates a "legal black hole" in which no law applies.[8] Yet, is it true that no legal obligations exist toward all humans?

The *source* of a human rights commitment is not a government's commitment – constitutional, treaty-based, or otherwise. Human rights commitments have a separate source. Individuals, inasmuch as they are

---

[5] *Sale.* On the global influence the case had, see Itamar Mann, "Dialectic of Transnationalism: Unauthorized Migration and Human Rights, 1993–2013," *Harvard International Law Journal* 54, no. 2 (2013): 315–391.

[6] See also Otto Kirscheimer, "Asylum," *American Political Science Review* 53, no. 4 (1959): 994. Arendt's fascinating emphasis on particularly transnational aspects of this process appears in her discussion of "an independent foreign policy of the police." *The Origins of Totalitarianism* (New York: Harvest, 1977), 288 (compare with the discussion of American foreign policy below).

[7] See, e.g., Charlie Savage, "U.S. Seems Unlikely to Accept That Rights Treaty Applies to Its Actions Abroad," *The New York Times*, March 6, 2014, available at www.nytimes.com /2014/03/07/world/us-seems-unlikely-to-accept-that-rights-treaty-applies-to-its-actions-abroad.html, and related Memorandum from October 19, 2010 by the United States Department of State, available at www.nytimes.com/interactive/2014/03/07/world/state-department-iccpr.html?_r=0.

[8] Johan Steyn, "Guantanamo Bay: The Legal Black Hole," *The International and Comparative Law Quarterly* 53, no. 1 (2004): 1–15. See also: Owen Fiss, *A War Like No Other: The Constitution in a Time of Terror*, ed. Trevor Sutton (New York: New Press, 2015), 53–55; and compare with Fleur Johns, *Non-Legality in International Law: Unruly Law* (Cambridge: Cambridge University Press, 2015), 69–108.

committed to human rights, are committed to two concomitant forms of law. One entails duties toward fellow citizens under the social contract. The other entails duties toward all human beings. This chapter explains the dualism through a reading of Arendt's "We Refugees." Contrary to the assumption that "We the People" can be the source of rights for noncitizens, the two sources of law remain radically discordant. This discord will be further explored in the next chapter, through the actions and testimonies of border enforcement agents off Australian shores. For now, suffice it to say that "We Refugees" is about the debt citizens of functioning polities have toward those who have not obtained the protection of any social contract. Rather than being reducible to any particular social contract, human rights commitments are about the rights of the stateless – de facto or de jure.[9]

The act of forming a community bound by a social contract excludes some people from membership. It is, therefore, an act of constitutive violence.[10] By giving themselves their own law, members of a social contract take that capacity from others. This act of initial exclusion can be associated with a variety of different violent practices. Acts of political founding have often followed from colonial expropriation or displacement of indigenous populations, enslavement, or the extermination of groups with competing claims of membership. At the basis of all of these is a fundamental distinction between members and non-members, citizens and aliens. Border enforcement carries the same constitutive violence to the present.[11] Human rights commitments follow from this constitutive violence and signal a recognition of its arbitrariness, which carries with it duties to those left with no effective citizenship.

Two forms of legal obligation flow from this constitutive violence. Positive law is the law citizens give to each other by mutual promises. Human rights law complements this foundational exclusion by the realization that some duties exist toward humans as such. In the context of refugee and migrant reception, this insight is encapsulated by the recognition that in some circumstances, the social contract must be

---

[9] Compare with Jacques Rancière, "Who Is the Subject of the Rights of Man?" *The South Atlantic Quarterly* 103, no. 2 (2004): 297–310 (Rancière writes that "the Rights of Man turned out to be the right of the rightless, of the populations hunted out of their homes and land and threatened by ethnic Slaughter").

[10] See Walter Benjamin's famous essay, "Critique of Violence," in Walter Benjamin, *Selected Writings: 1913–1926* (Cambridge and London: Belknap, Harvard University Press, 1996), 236.

[11] See discussion in Nick Vaughan-Williams, *Europe's Border Crisis: Biopolitical Security and Beyond* (Oxford: Oxford University Press, 2015), 8.

opened toward new members. "We Refugees" is best read as a concise formulation of this discord between two sources of law.[12]

"The History of All Other Nations"

In *Origins of Totalitarianism*, Arendt argues that refugees and stateless people pose a danger to political communities.[13] Stripped of citizenship rights, she refers to them as *bare life*. Refugees in the interwar period not only reflected the ways in which "The Rights of Man" were unenforceable; they foreshadowed their abolition.[14] Whether they were the beneficiaries of humanitarian assistance or the targets of arbitrary police control, refugees could not find the protections of any state.[15] They were at best reduced to mere survival and at worse subject to the "Final Solution." They lived like "mere savages" and could not exercise political freedom. As already discussed in previous chapters, Arendt famously makes this argument in one of the book's chapters in particular – an essay titled "The Decline of the Nation State and the End of the Rights of Man."[16]

The most immediately observable difference between "We Refugees" and *Origins* is not in the content of the argument, but in the authors' voice. In "We Refugees," Arendt doesn't consider refugees from the scholarly remove that characterizes *Origins*. She is writing about Jewish refugees in the first-person plural to an audience that includes others with a similar background. Significantly, she is writing from New York, after many of the peers she is talking to also fled to the United States. The German-Jewish philosopher fled from Nazi persecution in Germany, then from Vichy's France, and finally arrived in Manhattan. From a position of relative safety, she reflects upon her displacement and

---

[12] Compare with Leora Bilsky, "Citizenship as Mask: Between the Imposter and the Refugee," *Constellations* 15, no. 1 (2008): 72–97.

[13] Arendt, *The Origins of Totalitarianism* (1977), 302. (The language here is striking: "The danger is that a global, universally interrelated civilization may produce barbarians from its own midst by forcing millions of people into conditions which, despite all appearances, are conditions of savages.")

[14] Arendt, *The Origins of Totalitarianism* (1977), 280, 293 ("The first great damage done to nation-states as a result of the arrival of hundreds of thousands of stateless people was that the right of asylum, the only right that had ever figured as a symbol of the Rights of Man in the sphere of international relationships, was being abolished").

[15] Arendt, *The Origins of Totalitarianism* (1977), 295.

[16] Hannah Arendt, *The Origins of Totalitarianism*, New edition (New York: Harcourt, Brace, Jovanovich, 1973), 267.

persecution. She writes a blueprint for a theory of human rights premised on refugee identities.

The essay features the memorable Mr. Cohn from Berlin, who had always been a German "super-patriot," "150% German." When in 1933 he was forced to leave, Cohn found himself in Prague. Very soon he became "as true and loyal a Czech patriot as he had been a German one." In 1937, the Czech government began to expel its Jews, and he adjusted to Austrian patriotism. Next came being French. After all Cohn had gone through, becoming French was perhaps the most impossible feat of all: "I think I had better not dilate on the further adventures of Mr. Cohn. As long as Mr. Cohn can't make up his mind to be what he actually is, a Jew, nobody can foretell all the mad changes that he will still have to go through."[17]

Reading "We Refugees," it may seem like being a refugee is as far as a human can get from political participation. This conclusion is consistent with the characterizations of *bare life* in *Origins*.[18] Consider Arendt's bitter comments on the growing suicide rates among Jewish refugees. These are not acts of martyrdom or sacrifice. Suicide is not about choosing death over life for a higher cause or even about claiming personal sovereignty over one's own existence.[19] Jewish refugees in the United States left the world from the privacy of their own apartments. Arendt invites her readers to imagine they are sitting at small Manhattan windows, taking their lives only after apologizing to the world for having ever existed.[20]

But in its final passage, "We Refugees" takes an unexpected turn with the scintillating flavor of politics. It concludes by an oblique reference to the constitution of a political community based upon refugee identities.[21] Here, in contrast to arguments in her later work, a private experience of

---

[17] Arendt, "We Refugees," 117.

[18] This is also the conclusion Giorgio Agamben reaches in his reading of "We Refugees" (translated by Michael Rocke), and available at www.faculty.umb.edu/gary_zabel/ Courses/Phil%20108-07/We%20Refugees%20-%20Giorgio%20Agamben%20-%201994 .htm (last accessed May 11, 2016).

[19] See discussion of suicide in Albert Camus, *The Myth of Sisyphus: And Other Essays* (New York: Knopf Doubleday Publishing Group, 2012). See also Giorgio Agamben, *Homo Sacer: Sovereign Power and Bare Life*, trans. Daniel Heller-Roazen, 1st edition (Stanford: Stanford University Press, 1998), 136.

[20] Arendt, "We Refugees," 114 (They "apologize for the violent solution they have found for their personal problems").

[21] See Itamar Mann, "We Refugees or: What Is a Jewish Political Space?" *Theory and Criticism* 37 (2010) [Hebrew], available at http://theory-and-criticism.vanleer.org.il/En/ NetisUtils/srvrutil_getPDF.aspx/13X3lz/%2F%2F37-2.pdf (last accessed May 11, 2016).

exile suggests a particular point of access *into* politics.[22] Arendt gives only vague advice on how to obtain such access. The refugee or stateless person must cease covering up the fact that she can never be fully assimilated into the nation-state. She must create a space in the public sphere for her identity as a refugee. This program, it is crucial to realize, already requires some level of personal security. It is hard to imagine how one might pursue it from the confines of a prison cell or from shelter in an attic. This agenda can make sense only to those who have been given some respite from persecution. In other words, Arendt calls for preserving the refugee and stateless identities even after being granted membership in a polity.

The cryptic passage in which Arendt explains how refugee identities can provide a point of access into politics merits close reading. "Those few refugees who insist upon telling the truth, even to the point of 'indecency,' get in exchange for their unpopularity one priceless advantage: History is no longer a closed book to them and politics is no longer the privilege of gentiles." The prescriptive part of the text is a demand addressed directly from a refugee to other refugees who have all obtained the safety necessary to act politically within a community of members: Keep your identity, she tells her fellow would-be citizens: "Refugees driven from country to country represent the vanguard of their peoples – if they keep their identity. For the first time Jewish history is not separate but tied up with that of all other nations. The comity of European peoples went to pieces when, and because, it allowed its weakest member to be excluded and persecuted."[23] Arendt's pledge to tie the history of one people "with that of all other nations" is a pithy formulation of what it means to have a human rights commitment. The imperative is directed at individual members of functioning social contracts. It requires them to remember their existence before they acceded to the social contract, in terms of belonging to a people that didn't have the protections of positive law. It requires of them openness to the claims of strangers who are not members of the social contract, when in dire risk or need.

"A Nation of Refugees"

Arendt's "We Refugees" can be read in historical context. American political culture in the early 1940s made a vocabulary of anti-

---

[22] Hannah Arendt, *The Human Condition* (Chicago: University of Chicago Press, 1998), 22–78.
[23] Arendt, "We Refugees," 119.

assimilationism readily available for her. As frequently recounted, in the nineteenth and early twentieth centuries, European immigrants who dreamt of freedom contributed to the United States' rise to global prominence. The familiar narrative is one about immigrants who in the face of racism and xenophobia pursued their dreams and helped build American prosperity. Immigrants could often retain the cultural values they came with – sometimes for generations.[24]

For example, in a 1936 celebration of the fiftieth anniversary of the Statue of Liberty, Franklin Delano Roosevelt called for a preservation of immigrants' foreignness: "We take satisfaction in the thought that those who have left their native land to join us may still *retain here their affection for some things left behind* – old customs, old language, old friends" (emphasis added).[25] Franklin Delano Roosevelt's posture was fashioned as a direct opposition to the racial ideologies that had taken hold in Nazi Germany.[26] European nationalism at the time posited the value of homogenous societies that would ultimately be traceable to a common source. The president aimed to distinguish the United States not only from European totalitarianism but also from old-world nationalism more generally.[27]

Thus, it is quite possible that Arendt believed the United States could accommodate Mr. Cohn. In this pluralist society, Jewish refugees would be able to "tell the truth" about their pasts, becoming a "vanguard" of their (newfound) American people. An interview Arendt gave years later in 1973 supports this claim. The first question the interviewer asked her was about her initial impressions upon arriving to the United States at the age of thirty-two. "The United States is not a nation-state," announced Arendt. "It is impossible for a European to understand this simple fact."[28]

---

[24] See Susan Martin, *A Nation of Immigrants* (Cambridge: Cambridge University Press, 2011); See also Robert Fleegler, *Ellis Island Nation: Immigration Policy and American Identity in the Twentieth Century* (Philadelphia: University of Pennsylvania Press, 2013); For a beautiful little book engaging this political myth through poetry, literature, and photos, see Georges Perec and Robert Bober, *Ellis Island* (New York: New Press, 1995).

[25] Fleegler, *Ellis Island Nation*.

[26] Fleegler, *Ellis Island Nation*, 36–37.

[27] Compare with Judith Resnik, "Law as Affiliation: 'Foreign' Law, Democratic Federalism, and the Sovereigntism of the Nation-State," *International Journal of Constitutional Law* 6, no. 1 (2008): 33–66, 50 (discussing the way examples from "foreign" law helped American judges distinguish the United States from European totalitarian regimes).

[28] Arendt was asked what was her main impression of the United States when she arrived in 1941. Her answer seems indicative. Arendt explains:

In a state without a nation it would be possible to integrate without assimilating. The United States would allow Arendt to become an equal citizen without giving up her refugee identity, in a way that was simply unimaginable for Mr. Cohn during his European trials. According to this hypothesis, *The Rights of Man* failed in the interwar period to grant protections to humans who lacked effective citizenship because they were promised by *nation-states*. If the United States was not a nation-state, perhaps no such failure would be necessary: The rights of all humans could, after all, be grounded in the social contract. To say "We the People" would in effect be saying "We Refugees."

By the 1970s, however, the global political context in which Arendt spoke was very different. Longstanding perceptions of a divide between an old Europe and a new America had evaporated. The United States solidified its position as by far the most powerful member of the Western Bloc. A nation of "We Refugees" was about to encounter *bare life* in a way that would cast "We the People" as a question. Who are Americans, and what do "We" stand for?

When Secretary of State Cyrus Vance addressed Congress to explain the 1979 Geneva Conference and the *Orderly Departure Program*, discussed in the previous chapter, he alluded to statements such as FDR's. This narrative was now anchored in the politics of the Cold War, in which a central tenet of United States foreign policy was to admit refugees from behind the iron curtain.[29] Also at work was nostalgia for the United States as a haven for persecuted Europeans. Vance reconfirmed "We are indeed a nation of refugees" adding: "What we have found with the Vietnamese [that] we have taken in from Indochina is, they have turned out to be hard working, diligent, and good and strong

Mon impression dominante ... Well. See, this is not a nation-state. America is not a nation-state and Europeans have a hell of a time understanding this simple fact, which after all, they could know theoretically; it is, this country is united neither by heritage, nor by memory, nor by soil, nor by language, nor by origin from the same ... There are no natives here. The natives were Indians. Everyone else is a citizen and these citizens are united only by one thing, and that's a lot: that is, you become a citizen of the United States by simple consent to the Constitution. The constitution – that is a scrap of paper, according to French as well as German common opinion, and you can change it. No, here it is a sacred document, it is the constant remembrance of one sacred act, and that act is the foundation.

See Hannah Arendt, *Hannah Arendt: The Last Interview and Other Conversations* (New York: Melville House, 2013).

[29] Ira J. Kurzban, "A Critical Analysis of Refugee Law," *University of Miami Law Review* 36 (1982): 865.

productive people."[30] Economic benefit somehow united between universal aspiration and particular affiliation.[31] The *Orderly Departure Program*, according to this narrative, was the upshot of a quintessentially American set of values, marrying between capitalism and human rights.[32] Could American history, as Arendt seemed to

---

[30] United States, Refugee Crisis in Southeast Asia results of the Geneva Conference: hearing before the Committee on the Judiciary, United States Senate, Ninety-Sixth Congress, first session (Washington: US Gov. Print. Off., 1979): 22 (Hereinafter: Geneva Conference Hearing).

[31] President Gerald Ford, Vice President Walter Mondale, and President Jimmy Carter were only some of the others who made comparable remarks. In his 1980 presidential debate against Ronald Reagan, Carter invoked this idea with respect to domestic racial integration. In his October 28, 1980, debate against Ronald Reagan, President Carter said:

> Ours is a nation of refugees, a nation of immigrants. Almost all of our citizens came here from other lands and now have hopes, which are being realized, for a better life, preserving their ethnic commitments, their family structures, their religious beliefs, preserving their relationships with their relatives in foreign countries, but still holding themselves together in a very coherent society, which gives our nation its strength. In the past, those minority groups have often been excluded from participation in the affairs of government. Since I've been President, I've appointed, for instance, more than twice as many black Federal judges as all previous presidents in the history of this country. I've done the same thing in the appointment of women, and also Spanish-speaking Americans. To involve them in the administration of government and the feeling that they belong to the societal structure that makes decisions in the judiciary and in the executive branch is a very important commitment which I am trying to realize and will continue to do so in the future.

Available at www.debates.org/index.php?page=october-28-1980-debate-transcript (last accessed May 11, 2016).
For Vance, however, the rule informed the United States' relationship particularly with non-citizens (an orientation more appropriate for the word "refugees"). This emphasis helped the United States claim normative force beyond its own citizenry and within the transnational networks of the time.

[32] Vance said:

> We are a Nation of refugees. Most of us can trace our presence here to the turmoil or oppression of another time and another place. Our Nation has been immeasurably enriched by this continuing process. We will not turn our backs to our traditions. We must meet the commitments we have made to other nations and to those who are suffering. In doing so, we will also be renewing our commitments to our ideals – and to ourselves.

Geneva Conference hearing, 8. Thirty years later, Hillary Clinton could still proclaim: "We are not just a nation of immigrants, we are also a nation of refugees." Speech delivered at the 2010 World Refugee Day, 2010, available at www.rescue.org/blog/a-nation-refugees. By putting "immigrants" first, she seemingly confirmed what now appears as an established divergence between the two ideas. For a certain period in the

suggest, truly be tied up to "the history of all other nations"? The question whether popular sovereignty, based on a social contract, could embody the iteration "We Refugees" goes to the basic question what is the source of law.

The Haitian Challenge

Three years before Vance spoke to the Congress about Vietnam, Albert Blaustein struck a similar note in a talk at the American Society of International Law (ASIL). Blaustein recounted the following encounter: "On December 12, 1972, the amazed sunbathers on Pompano Beach, north of Miami, witnessed . . . invasion. They were Haitian blacks, sixty-five of them, dressed in rags, who had just traveled eight hundred miles across open water in a battered fishing smack; nineteen days on the open sea without charts and without even a compass. They claimed political asylum."[33] He described *bare life*. As Arendt described it later in *Origins of Totalitarianism*, this was the life of "savages."[34] Blaustein had been invited to speak on a panel that was to imagine what might refugee protection look like, come the year 2001. Though somewhat bizarre, his talk was remarkably representative of salient popular sentiments. "My fellow immigrants and descendants of immigrants," he greeted his listeners before proceeding to argue that the potential of uncontrolled entry of immigrants could spell the United States' demise.

Blaustein was a law professor at Rutgers and an experienced human rights lawyer. He had traveled the world as "constitution writer-for-hire."[35] After his first overseas assignment drafting a constitution for South Vietnam in 1966, Blaustein helped write the constitutions of Bangladesh, Liberia, Zimbabwe, and Fiji. With the end of the Cold War, he would serve numerous Eastern European countries.[36] To this

Cold War, however, the two ideas were one and the same. Clinton noted that two of her predecessors as Secretary of the State, Madeleine Albright and Henry Kissinger, were themselves refugees.

[33] Clyde Ferguson Jr., Albert Blaustein, John Thomas, James Wilson Jr., Dale de Haan, and Richard Plender, "Refugees: A New Dimension in International Human Rights," *Proceedings of the Annual Meeting (American Society of International Law)* 70 (1976): 63 (hereinafter: "Ferguson et al., 'Refugees,'").

[34] Arendt, *The Origins of Totalitarianism* (1977), 302.

[35] His son therefore gave him the title of "a Jewish James Madison." See http://articles.philly.com/1994-08-22/news/25841867_1_constitution-poland-job-title (last accessed May 11, 2016).

[36] Richard Perez-Pena, "Albert P. Blaustein, a Drafter of Constitutions, Dies at 72," *New York Times*, August 23, 1994, available at http://articles.philly.com/1994-08-22/news/25841867_1_constitution-poland-job-title.

panel, Blaustein came mainly in his capacity as a modern-day Malthusian and cofounder of the Washington-based organization *Zero Population Growth*. Blaustein staunchly believed that global overpopulation and resource scarcity were the main problems the world would face for years to come. Taking the exercise assigned to the panel quite literally, he assumed the posture of a prophet: "[M]y role is that of Jeremiah. And know ye that I am skilled in modern prophecy."[37] Like Jeremiah anticipating the fall of Jerusalem, Blaustein warned of imminent destruction. The ancient Jews did not listen to Jeremiah's call to return to God's way. Americans still stood a chance to prevent their own country's demise. The damning side of Blaustein's "prophecy" focused on the demographics of immigration. He provided data about population growth and resource scarcity around the world, alongside growing immigration pressures – legal and illegal – from "underdeveloped" countries. He stressed the high birthrate in Latin American communities and the spike in illegal immigration to the United States. This, he said, would pose challenges to the American economy and to the just distribution of wealth among citizens.

Blaustein explained that the developing immigration crisis was *global*. Its most decisive symbol was mass unauthorized migration by way of the sea. Citing Jean Raspail's 1973 best-seller, *The Camp of Saints*, Blaustein used extravagant imagery to explain what was at stake: "This is the story of the Last Chance Armada, the story of a million starving Indians who take over on a hundred dilapidated ships in Calcutta harbor and eventually invade the Côte d'Azure . . . Read the story billed as 'a chilling novel about the end of the white world'." The speaker shared Raspail's concerns that poor immigrants of color would inundate the United States and the West.[38] "By 1990," he said, "it is expected that Spanish Americans will outnumber the so-called white population of Los Angeles."[39] The United States had a global role in responding to the crisis: "as Americans and as caretakers of Western civilization we must act for our self-preservation . . ." Blaustein thus emphasized the tension between the "nation of refugees," which first emerged in the

---

[37] Ferguson et al., "Refugees," 58.

[38] Jean Raspail is an ultra-conservative French Catholic, whose novels include visions of Catholic monarchical restoration. In 2004, he wrote an article for Le Figaro titled *The Fatherland Betrayed by the Public*. He was sued by the International League against Racism and Anti-Semitism for "inciting racism and hatred," but a court did not allow the action to go forward.

[39] Ferguson et al., "Refugees," 58.

context of largely European immigration, and a growing concern about entries from the "developing" world.[40]

Against this alarmist background, Blaustein's argument made an unexpected turn. "Like the Jeremiah of old, I prophesy doom – but only if we turn away from our responsibilities and burn incense to Baal."[41] Here, he reverted back to the "nation of refugees." His reasoning was similar to Vance's. Precisely in order to defend itself from the imminent waves of immigration, the country must observe its commitment to the protection of refugees. It is not the risk to the economy but the risk to self-defining values that would ultimately be the real danger to the nation. "When we cease to be the land of refuge and asylum, we will cease to be America." Washington will be secure if only the United States avoids such "un-American would-be solutions as domestic passports/ identity cards."

The Haitian "invasion," Blaustein discussed, was a harbinger of what was yet to come. For him, the new boat people represented the latest episode in a drama that had been unfolding since Jewish refugees drowned in the Mediterranean after World War II. The drama continued:[42]

> I talk of ships. Once, back in 1942, there was a ship called the *Struma*. Its 769 passengers and crew, all Jews, went from port to port vainly seeking admission – vainly seeking refuge. Over and over again they were ordered away – to go back – even though going back meant death in Germany. In February 1942, the ship was sunk. One member of the crew escaped death. That was all, and so we vowed that this could not and would not happen again. For years I have been predicting the sequel . . . I had a vision and still envision ships in the night, over-loaded with people from India, Bangladesh, and Indonesia stopping off the Australian shore.[43]

---

[40] Compare with arguments conservative politician Pat Buchanan made years later in Patrick Buchanan, *State of Emergency: The Third World Invasion and Conquest of America* (New York: St. Martin's, 2007); and to the leading academic voice that made these arguments, Samuel Huntington, *Who Are We?* (New York: Simon & Schuster, 2005). More recently, presidential nominee Donald Trump has voiced the same sentiment with his proposals to do away with birthright citizenship in the United States.

[41] Ferguson et al., "Refugees," 63.

[42] Compare with Jessica Tauman. Discussing the MV *Tampa* affair, in which hundreds of Afghan rescuees were not allowed to land in Australian territory, Tauman dramatically invoked the *St. Louis*, a boat of refugees of Nazi persecution, who were not allowed to land in the United States during World War II. Jessica Tauman, "Rescued at Sea, but Nowhere To Go: The Cloudy Legal Waters of the *Tampa* Crisis," *Pacific Rim Law and Policy Journal* 11, no. 2 (2002): 461–496, 496. On the MV *Tampa*, see Chapter 5.

[43] Ferguson et al., "Refugees," 62–63.

As Blaustein anticipated, the number of Haitian arrivals constantly grew. Political destabilization on the island substantially increased the number of boats from Haiti starting in the 1980s. President Ronald Reagan first steered the US government's response to the crisis through executive-driven transnational legal solutions. The policy began with Executive Order 12,324 on the "Interdiction of Illegal Aliens":[44] The United States Coast Guard was authorized to interdict ships on the high seas suspected of carrying illegal immigrants. In conjunction with that Order, the United States concluded a bilateral agreement with Haiti, permitting it to patrol the country's coastal waters and to intercept Haitian vessels suspected of carrying illegal migrants.[45] Such vessels could now be returned to Haiti. The encounter between American citizens and Haitian boat people landing on their beaches would be prevented. The United States followed the example of Southeast Asian countries that had tried to prevent the influx of Vietnamese "boat people" only a few years earlier.[46]

The bilateral agreement provided for return only upon the asylum seeker's consent.[47] This meant that after interdiction, Haitian migrants were transferred to a Coast Guard cutter, carrying representatives of the

---

[44] Exec. Order No. 12,324, 3 C.F.R. 181 (1981–1983). On the importance of this policy, see Guy Goodwin-Gill, "The Right to Seek Asylum: Interception at Sea and the Principle of Non-Refoulement," *International Journal of Refugee Law* 23, no. 2 (2011): 443–457.

[45] Compare with Chapter 4.

[46] Guy Goodwin-Gill, "Refugees and Responsibility in the Twenty-First Century: More Lessons Learned from the South Pacific," *Pacific Rim Law and Policy Journal* 12, no. 1 (2003): 23–47, 29. As recounted in Chapter 2, "the West" admonished the ASEAN countries vehemently for their unruly practices. As one author euphemistically wrote at the time, it was clear the new policy was "contrary to the kind of policy the United States asks friendly governments in Southeast Asia to adopt toward Indochinese arrivals." Thus,

> It has been argued by American critics that first asylum in the ASEAN countries could be jeopardized by two recent initiatives in U.S. refugee policy. First, the Reagan administration's policy of interdicting Haitian boat people, and case-by-case asylum determination of Salvadoran and Haitian applicants, it is claimed, are contrary to the kind of policy the United States asks friendly governments in Southeast Asia to adopt toward Indochinese arrivals.

> Astri Suhrke, "Indochinese Refugees: The Law and Politics of first asylum," *Annals of American Academy of Political and Social Science* 467 The Global Refugee Problem: US and the World Response (1983): 102–115, 110.

[47] The requirement of "consent" can be understood as a tacit recognition that by controlling the movement of refugee populations, the United States is engaged in a form of *governing* foreigners. According to this view, a radically asymmetric encounter already implies the government of non-citizens. See, the US Declaration of Independence: "That to secure

State Department, the Immigration and Naturalization Services (INS), and often a Haitian Creole interpreter. "Screening" mechanisms were set up to identify bona fide asylum seekers while still on the high seas. Some of those who could not be returned to Haiti were held in an offshore detention facility in Guantánamo Bay.[48] This policy not only allowed the US government to manage the number of refugees it wanted to admit but also raised serious concerns about *refoulement*. Advocates for the refugees questioned whether it was possible for an asylum seeker to establish "well-founded fear" under such circumstances and challenged the policy in US courts. In the ten years this screening procedure was in place, only twenty-eight out of 25,000 intercepted boat people were deemed "refugees" rather than economic migrants.[49] If that was not enough, George H.W. Bush cracked down even more severely on Haitian migrants. In 1992, with Executive Order 12,807, Bush authorized the Coast Guard to return all fleeing Haitians with no process at all.[50] Through the course of the legal challenge to these measures – initially the one employed by Reagan and later the more stringent one employed by Bush – the narrative of "We Refugees" was put to a test at the US Supreme Court.

Litigating the Haitian Challenge

Korean diplomat Kwnag Lim Koh initially moved to the United States in order to continue his education. He taught in the Seoul National University in the late 1940s but decided to pursue higher degrees and enrolled in programs at Harvard and Rutgers. After the Korean April Revolution in 1960, with the apparent rise of democracy, Koh was drawn into politics and became a diplomat at the Korean embassy in Washington. When a military government overthrew the new democracy, Koh became an exile and the family sought refuge in New Haven, Connecticut.[51] As his son Harold Hongju Koh later described, their father consoled his children: "Don't worry. This is a nation of refugees, a nation built by immigrants. What it says on the Statue of Liberty are not

---

these rights, Governments are instituted among Men, deriving their just powers from the consent of the governed."

[48] Compare to Cyprus in Chapter 1, Galang and Bindong in Chapter 2, Nauru and Papua New Guinea in Chapter 4, and Lampedusa in Chapter 5.

[49] For some commentators, the whole policy was premised on determining collectively that Haitians were economic migrants.

[50] Exec. Order No. 12,807, 3 C.F.R. 303 (1992).

[51] Howard Kyongju Koh and Carolyn Kyongshin Koh Choo, *Koh Kwang Lim: Essays in Honor of His Hwegap, 1980* (New Haven: East Rock Press, 1982).

just words, but a sacred promise, and that promise will protect us."[52]
When Koh the son told his father's story in his frequent lectures and
addresses, he too presented the idea of a "nation of refugees" as
a paradigmatic example of a commitment to human rights.

The Korean diplomat's son went on to a stellar legal career. After
clerking for Justice Harry Blackmun in the US Supreme Court,[53] Koh
joined the faculty at Yale Law School, later becoming the school's Dean.[54]
After serving as legal advisor to the State Department in President Barak
Obama's first term, he returned to his position at Yale. The story of the
asylum his father found in the United States became professionally
significant particularly in one context early in his career: Koh represented
the Haitian Refugee Council, a nongovernmental organization that
sought to assert the Haitian refugees' rights in the United States, and
particularly their right to asylum under the 1980 Refugee Act and the
1967 Protocol. As counsel, Koh argued in front of the US Supreme Court
challenging Executive Orders 12,324 and 12,807.

Apart from a discussion of the status of treaties under the Supremacy
Clause of the US Constitution, the case raised no significant constitutional issues. Yet, for this legal team, which included Former Secretary of
State Cyrus Vance, the case involved the meaning of "We the People." If,
as Blaustein positioned them, the Haitian refugees presented the paradigmatic challenge of globalization to the constitutional narrative, Koh
was there to defend it. The defense was delivered not only in the name of
his clients and not only in the name of law. Like the Vietnamese-
American author of the memoir mentioned in the previous chapter,
Koh declared he carried out the task in the name of his father.[55]
The terminology he used in Court was quite strong:

> At the close of my argument before the Supreme Court, I decided to say,
> "Your honor[s], ... ours is a nation of refugees. Most of our ancestors
> came here by boat. If they could do this to the Haitians, they could do this
> to any of us." By so saying, I wanted the Justices to remember that *the
> Haitians are us*. I wanted to remind them that by living this case, *our
> nation has relived its past*. I wanted to remember, as my father did, what it
> means to love the law and to be faithful to it: never to forget that ours is

---

[52] See Harold Hongju Koh, The Haitian Refugee Litigation: A Case Study in Transnational
Public Law Litigation, 18 Md. J. Int'l L. & Trade 1, 2 (1994).

[53] See *A Tribute to Justice Harry A. Blackmun*, 108 Harv. L. Rev. 19 1994–1995.

[54] He is currently back at Yale Law School as Sterling Professor of International Law.

[55] Tai Van Nguyen, *The Storm of Our Lives: A Vietnamese Family's Boat Journey to Freedom*
(Jefferson, NC and London: McFarland & Company, Inc., 2009).

a nation of refugees, a nation committed to the rule of law and not to individuals, a nation that still believes in principle, and not just politics. (emphasis added)[56]

On June 21, 1993, the Supreme Court rejected Koh's arguments in an eight to one decision. Justice John Paul Stevens, writing for the majority, found that the duty of *non-refoulement* did not extend to the high seas. Choosing a textual interpretation of the Convention centered on the fact that the French verb *"refouler"* means "to expel" or "to deport," he held that its obligations were strictly territorial. One cannot be deported before being admitted to a country.[57] Justice Blackmun dissented. According to Blackmun, the policy Executive Order 12,807 introduced – the interdiction of unauthorized Haitian migrants at sea and their return to Haiti – violated the Convention's central provision, the rule of *non-refoulement*.[58] Both opinions apply positive law, but only Blackmun took up the idea that the nation's "refugee identity" could have legal consequence.

Drafting *Sale*, Justice Stevens staved off any discussion beyond positive law. Responding to the Haitian Centers Council's argument, he clarified that the case will not be decided based on a *moral* judgment: "In spite of the moral weight of that argument, both the text and negotiating history of Article 33 affirmatively indicate that it was not intended to have extraterritorial effect."[59] This formulation did not initially satisfy Justice Antonin Scalia. In a note to Stevens, he wrote: "For my taste, that comes too close to acknowledging that it is morally wrong to return these refugees to Haiti."[60] Stevens declined the request

---

[56] Koh Hongju Koh, "The Haitian Refugee Litigation: A Case Study in Transnational Public Law Litigation," *Maryland Journal of International Law and Trade* 1 (1994): 20.

[57] Stevens wrote:

> The drafters of the Convention . . . may not have contemplated that any nation would gather fleeing refugees and return them to the one country they had desperately sought to escape; such actions may even violate the spirit of Article 33; but a treaty cannot impose uncontemplated extra-territorial obligations on those who ratify it through no more than its general humanitarian intent. Because the text of Article 33 cannot reasonably be read to say anything at all about a nation's actions toward aliens outside its own territory, it does not prohibit such actions. Sale, at para. 64.

[58] Convention Relating to the Status of Refugees, art. 33, April 22, 1954, 189 U.N.T.S. 137.

[59] *Sale*, at para. 54.

[60] "I would prefer that sentence to read 'Whatever the moral weight of that argument' . . ." wrote Saclia. The notes are located in Justice Blackmun's papers in the Library of Congress.

to revise the text, and Scalia joined Stevens' opinion nonetheless. The two justices were in agreement on the only point that really mattered: If there was a moral issue here, it did not control the result. The underlying principle is the "separation thesis," according to which law and morals are fundamentally distinct. Blackmun's final and dramatic note, on the other hand, deviates somewhat from this positivism. His reading of treaty and statute is informed by a moral idea of what the American polity is: "The refugees ... demand only that the United States, *land of refugees and guardian of freedom*, cease forcibly driving them back to detention, abuse, and death. That is a modest plea, vindicated by the treaty and the statute. We should not close our ears to it" (emphasis added).[61]

Though written nowhere in the Constitution, Blackmun embraced the narrative of a "nation of refugees" (suggested to him by his former clerk). He explained: "The convention that the Refugee Act embodies was enacted largely in response to the experience of Jewish refugees in Europe during the period of World War II. The tragic consequences of the world's indifference at the time are well known. The resulting ban on *refoulement*, as broad as the humanitarian purpose that inspired it, is easily applicable here, the Court's protestations of impotence and regret notwithstanding."[62]

Responding to the Supreme Court's decision in *Sale* v. *Haitian Centers Council*, some onlookers agreed with Blaustein's warnings. They concluded, more or less seriously, that the decision signaled America's demise. The majority opinion supposedly violated principles that American identity rested upon. Take for example this letter, saved among Blackmun's papers in the Library of Congress, from one Alana B. Levy. The letter is dated August 5, 1992:

> I am ashamed and embarrassed to be a citizen of a country which turns its back on the Haitian Refugees! Did we not turn our back on Jewish refugees in World War II with deadly results? Did our ancestors not come from humble backgrounds seeking political and religious freedoms, and the promise of America? How can we blindly send these people back to their doom, and still proudly call ourselves *Americans?*[63] (emphasis original)

---

[61] *Sale*, at para. 125.
[62] *Sale*, at para. 123.
[63] The emotional response to the violation of human rights as one consisting of shame or embarrassment is already familiar from Chapter 1.

The shame Levy expressed here recalls the embarrassment discussed in Chapter 1 and invoked in the Introduction to this book. A cartoon from the Chicago Tribune, also cut and filed among the Justice's papers, offered a lighter version of the same lamentation. Like Koh's father, the cartoon cited the words of Emma Lazarus. But here, the lines on the foot of the Statue of Liberty were "voided." Off walked a little judge, nose peeking from under a pile of wig and robe, "Haitian decision" in hand.

Human Rights and Self-Interest

What would be required for "We the People" to be credibly posited as "We Refugees," and still remain "of the people, by the people, for the people"?[64] The question is about the possibility of grounding human rights in a domestic constitutional legal order, that of the United States.

Alongside the pledge of mutual alliance in one social contract, citizens would choose a certain modicum of obligations toward all humans through their respective mutual promises. In this view, the United States' social contract turns out to be about a commitment both to citizens and to humans in general. This suggests a theory of human rights, which I will call "the constitutionalist model": Human rights are defined first and foremost as that part of a polity's social contract that postulates fundamental legal responsibilities toward all non-members. At least since the Declaration of the Rights of Man and of the Citizen (1789), this is the most dominant way of understanding human rights. In the postwar world, the idea emerged that human rights would constrain sovereignty, even popular sovereignty based on the social contract. But inasmuch as positive human rights law relied on state consent, expressed through treaty or through customary international law, a social contractarian view is still the dominant one. In the words of Vance, Blaustein, and Koh, we found various versions of this idea (though it did not exhaust the terminology any one of them advanced). This, I assumed, is also a reasonable reading of Arendt's short essay from 1943 – and of Blackmun's dissent.

Sale reviewed practices that governed an encounter between government agents and noncitizens beyond territorial sovereignty. One party to this encounter was the coastguard of the world's most powerful

---

[64] These are Abraham Lincoln's famous words from his Gettysburg Address.

country, and the other was made of multiple impoverished refugees and migrants. The Court found that United States law had nothing to say about these people's claims. As long as agents of the United States act outside US territory, they are permitted – theoretically and practically – to kill people with impunity. We are in Oppenheim's world – as described in Chapter 1 – in which noncitizens outside of sovereign territory can be "maltreated to any extent."[65] Koh brought the political imagination of a "nation of refugees" to court in the most direct manner imaginable. For him, to say that "We the People" are "We Refugees" was to make a legal argument. The majority granted this argument no weight whatsoever.[66] Yet the view that human rights stem from the social contract still seems to dominate a certain political imagination, especially in the United States. This is true whether we think domestically, where human rights are often thought of as constitutional rights; or if we think internationally, where human rights law is thought of as a set of treaty-based obligations.

In the 1990s discussion of Haitian refugees, the constitutional model was intertwined in various ways with another idea about human rights, also still very much at work today. This can be called the "foreign policy model."[67] Within this paradigm, human rights are a concern primarily relevant to the executive branch. This genre of human rights talk appeared in Koh's academic commentary and advocacy work, as well as in the work of other human rights activists at the time. Like the constitutionalist model, this genre too stems from a belief that commitments toward citizens and commitments toward noncitizens both emerge from the American social contract. It is encapsulated in Blaustein's pronouncement above that Americans are the "caretakers of Western civilization." Though Blaustein's terms may sound somewhat crude to contemporary ears, similar arguments still have considerable traction among American policymakers, both liberal and conservative.[68]

---

[65] See Chapter 1.

[66] See Robert Cover's classic discussion of American positivism in the context of Slavery: Robert Cover, *Justice Accused* (New Haven: Yale University Press, 1975), 25–28.

[67] The "foreign policy model" has a long intellectual history in the United States. Perhaps its sharpest iteration is Hans J. Morgenthau, *Human Rights and Foreign Policy* (Washington, DC: Council on Religion and International Affairs, 1979). See more generally the materials compiled in Oonna Hathaway and Harold Koh, *Foundations of International Law and Politics* (New York: Foundation Press, 2005).

[68] This was reflected recently, for example, by the appointment of Samantha Power to the position of United States Ambassador to the United Nations. See Samantha Power, "A Problem from Hell": America and the Age of Genocide (New York: Basic Books, 2013).

Virginia Law Professor David Martin relied on the foreign policy model in a 1992 talk, soon before *Sale* was decided.[69] Like Koh, Martin often crossed the line between policymaking, scholarship, and advocacy. Under President Carter, he served in the State Department's Human Rights Bureau.[70] The title of his talk posed a question: *Kurds and Haitians: From Refugee Legalisms to Humanitarian Intervention?*[71] His comments were set against two historical examples. The first example was the response to 1.5 million Kurds who fled Iraq after Saddam Hussein cracked down on a rebellion in the North of the country in 1992. About one-third of these refugees reached Turkey. At a certain point, Ankara "refused to allow more than 20,000–40,000 vulnerable people down from the mountain."[72] Ignoring the refugees would potentially stain the reputation of world superpowers. Television coverage was by now much more comprehensive than it was in 1979. And the plight of the Kurds would be broadcast to a global audience, who, Martin thought, will be clamoring for response.

[69] David Martin, "Kurds and Haitians: From Refugee Legalisms to Humanitarian Intervention?" *Proceedings of the Annual Meeting (American Society of International Law)* 86, no. 1 (1992): 623–630. Martin's work on the Vietnamese boat people is concisely considered in the previous chapter.

[70] "In those days our allies seemed only too happy to treat our efforts as foolishly idealistic . . ." Martin, "Kurds and Haitians," 624.

[71] Turning to a 1987 position paper by the Swiss government, Martin walked through the potential reasons for pursuing a human rights policy in the context of unauthorized migration. Among other things, the Swiss paper contained a call to "do more in dealing with source-country conditions, as a way of ameliorating migration pressures." It asked for "more consistent human rights initiatives and enhanced support for economic development in the Third World." It assumed such measures would prevent migration from occurring in the first place, which was the real task for human rights. See Martin, "Kurds and Haitians," 624–625.

[72] Martin drew an interesting parallel between this situation, and the late 1970s context examined in the previous chapter:

> If you think that sounds like Malaysia or Thailand in 1979, I would agree. And if the world community had considered the Kurdish crisis with a 1979 mindset, it probably would have seen only two basic options: first, ignore the situation – turn the other way as the countries immediately and inescapably involved force desperate people back across the border; or, second, start a massive program for distant resettlement, of the kind that still persists for Indochinese refugees.

This, said Martin, was a "rather depressing range of options." Martin, "Kurds and Haitians," 625.

But what options beyond ignoring this crisis did the United States have?[73] British Prime Minister John Major came up with what appeared to Martin as the right solution: creating conditions in the home country "where the asylum seekers could at least live in relative safety." This called for a military operation: "[I]t amounted to humanitarian intervention, to use the term that law journal debates ordinarily employ." This, Martin explained, "was in fact a bold human rights initiative, taken, one could say, for selfish reasons: to avoid having to resettle the Kurds in the West or otherwise to bribe or cajole Turkey to take them in ... Iraq's protestations about sovereignty were curtly overridden."[74] Simply letting the Kurds die was not an option for the "civilized world." This model, argued Martin, should be employed in the context of unauthorized migration from Haiti. His words turned out to be prescient: On June 16, 1993, the Security Council adopted Resolution 841, implementing the Iraq-inspired model in the context of Haiti.[75]

Randall Robinson too thought within the foreign policy model. One of the most dynamic advocates for the Haitian migrants, in April–May 1994 he went on a hunger strike, protesting the policies the Supreme Court

---

[73] "Distant resettlement" is dismissed off hand, leaving it for the reader to surmise that it would be too costly, too risky, or too unpopular politically to take a massive population in. The *Orderly Departure Program* could not be reconceived for the benefit of the Kurds.

On Thursday November 21, 2013, Deputy High Commissioner in UNHCR, and formerly Dean of Georgetown Law Center, Alexander Aleinikoff, spoke at the Center. Aleinikoff echoed the underlying point. As he explained, in the postwar period the solution for refugees was becoming members in their host countries; in the Cold War it was resettlement; at present it is life in camps. Aleinikoff pointed to the fact that at present the challenge is to help refugees create their own economies in camps without integration in the local communities (which do not have the political will for that). Mustering additional political will for resettlement, as in the Cold War, was off the table.

[74] "Selfish Reasons for Human Rights Policy" is also Martin's subtitle, and he makes clear this is his main point.

[75] He thought the 1951 Refugee Convention, which the *Sale* litigation centered upon, was outdated. As he explained, a central premise of the Convention – that refugee populations could only be granted remedies once they crossed the border – rested on the long-superseded sanctity of sovereignty. Rather than an economic burden or a challenge to self-defining commitments, the Resolution's language took an additional step and rendered the refugees into a *security* issue. With the subsequent Resolution 940 of July 13, the Security Council proceeded to authorize military action against Haiti under chapter 7 of the United Nations Charter, in order to reinstall Aristide. A settlement was reached with US representatives after the Haitian military leadership found out that a US invasion force was on its way and that paratroopers would land in a few hours. Aristide consequently returned to Haiti, on October 15, 1994. See Kurt Mills, "Refugees as Impetus for Intervention: The Case of Haiti," *Refuge* 15, no. 3 (1996): 16.

upheld in *Sale*.[76] For Robinson, the rejection Haitian migrants confronted was a story of racism against Blacks.[77] As he explained, the United States had a global role. The distinctive question "human rights" raised was how should that role be realized. During the Cold War, the primary instrument of influence in Africa was development aid. But such aid was focused only on a few countries and was given to leaders, not peoples. "These countries have largely become the economic, political, and human-rights basket cases of the African continent largely because the leaders of these countries that received our aid worked for us."[78] Robinson thus made the transition: from aid to warfare. Moving to events that unfolded in Rwanda, he pointed out that when push came to shove, the United States could not muster the determination to put its own troops on the line.[79] Such steps were necessary if human rights were to be realized in Africa and in the Caribbean.[80]

In the context of litigation, Koh was far from Martin's dismissive views about the Refugee Convention, as he was from Robinson's understanding of a "global color line" (to paraphrase W.E.B. Du Bois). However, his prescriptive work at the time amounted to a theory of America's role in

---

[76] See www.nytimes.com/1994/05/09/world/hunger-strike-on-haiti-partial-victory-at-least .html.

[77] It was during his strike that Clinton finally reached the decision to resume asylum screening on a boat anchored in the Caribbean, and Clinton's aide called Robinson personally to deliver him this news. Many credited Robinson personally for putting an end to the policy of *refoulement*, among them Bush's (disapproving) Vice President, Dan Quayle: "This is a foreign policy by hunger strike, and that is not a way to conduct foreign policy," he said.

[78] Randall Robinson, "The Obligation to Rescue," *Social Research* 61, no. 1 (1995): 7–12, 9.

[79] While Robinson's self-proclaimed commitment was to the rights of people of color the world over, he also admitted that the United States could not deploy anywhere there was a crisis. He therefore saw his own role as activist primarily in the dissemination of information, which he thought would somehow compel Americans to push for response: "One cannot overestimate the impact that electronic journalism has on the American body politic." Robinson, "The Obligation to Rescue," 9.

[80] Both Martin and Robinson saw human rights through the prism of United States foreign policy. They both emphasized attempts to rescue victims of human rights abuses abroad, if need be, by military intervention. There are important differences between their two perspectives, both in style and in content. The important commonality, however, is the way that in both their political imaginations the United States had the role of a *global enforcement agency for human rights*. This role is thought of as a touchstone of American identity in a post-Soviet world. Robinson couldn't be clearer on this: "[W]hat kind of nation will we be? Over the last thirty years, American foreign policy has been driven largely by a single imperative – the imperative of Soviet containment. That no longer applies. Now, at this crossroads, for what do we stand?" Robinson, "The Obligation to Rescue," 9.

the world, sharing important assumptions with both commentators. He theorized the ways in which aid, economic sanctions, and war related to each other as complementary tools of American foreign policy. He particularly believed in marrying self-interest and universal values. Koh too demanded harsh sanctions against Haiti – if need be military ones. The United States, he said, had gotten its priorities reversed. It should have adopted the most aggressive measures against the Haitian government – while accommodating those fleeing from it. Instead, it cracked down on migrants but turned a blind eye toward the government's abuses. Far from being an extra burden on the United States, correcting these priorities would have been advantageous for the country.

President Clinton, explained Koh, identified the Haitian challenge when he was running for office: "United States foreign policy simply cannot be divorced from the moral principles we believe in."[81] But when he took office, Clinton continued the policies of the previous administration. "The Haitian refugee situation," wrote Koh, "presented the Clinton administration with both a challenge and an opportunity: the challenge of succeeding where its predecessor had failed and the opportunity to do so in a way that would signal a return to – not a rejection of – our most fundamental American values."[82] When the United States was not acting upon "fundamental American values," Koh believed advocacy should be redirected toward transnational institutions: primarily (but not exclusively) foreign and international courts. The latter could push the United States toward the enforcement of its own values: human rights.[83]

Perhaps the most compelling argument within the "foreign policy model" came from the executive branch, which defended high seas interdictions as saving the lives of noncitizens. As one observer described it, "The Clinton administration's attorney implored everyone present to concede that forced repatriation is tantamount to a life-saving policy, preventing death at sea."[84] In making this argument, the executive considered differing aspects of the Haitian interdiction policy.[85] Some

[81] Harold Hongju Koh, "The 'Haiti Paradigm' in United States Human Rights Policy," *Yale Law Journal* 103 (1993–1994): 2391–2435, 2434.

[82] Koh, "The 'Haiti Paradigm' in United States Human Rights Policy," 2435.

[83] Koh, "The 'Haiti Paradigm' in United States Human Rights Policy," 2406. (Suggesting that "adverse Supreme Court decisions are no longer final stops, but only way stations, in the process of 'complex enforcement' triggered by transnational public law litigation.")

[84] Carl Anderson, "Justice Blackmun's Query Said It All: Reflections on Haiti, Refugees, and the U.S. Supreme Court," *Hybrid: A Journal of Law and Social Change* 1 (1993): 73–77, 73.

[85] The Court paraphrased the argument: "[The government] had to choose between allowing Haitians into the United States for the screening process or repatriating them without

militated toward allowing the unauthorized migrants to lodge asylum requests in the United States. Others pushed decision makers to deny that option. A "human rights policy," in this vision, accepts that the lives of noncitizens have *some* normative significance. But the lives of noncitizens figure within a consequentialist judgment: They compete against the interests of citizens and – perhaps more interestingly – against those of *other* noncitizens.[86] It could therefore turn out that returning asylum seekers to the risk of persecution would be better *for them*; it would deter *other* asylum seekers from the dangerous voyages at sea.[87] The administration's position had an important affinity with other versions of the foreign policy model. Human rights were American interests that could be implemented through a continuum running from diplomatic engagement, to development assistance, to war.

Within the foreign policy model, however, opposing policy outcomes can be thought of equally as cases of human rights enforcement and human rights violation.[88] Taking the administration's argument seriously would mean that the repatriation policy could represent human rights commitments as much as a policy granting each migrant an asylum hearing. Or in the case of Martin, Robinson, and Koh, a war in which Haitians would be involuntarily subject to a risk of death could be protective *for them*.[89]

---

giving them any opportunity to establish their qualifications as refugees. In the judgment of the President's advisers, the first choice not only would have defeated the original purpose of the program (controlling illegal immigration) but also would have impeded diplomatic efforts to restore democratic government in Haiti, and would have posed a life-threatening danger to thousands of persons embarking on long voyages in dangerous craft *[emphasis added]*. The second choice would have advanced those policies but deprived the fleeing Haitians of any screening process ... The wisdom of the policy choices made by Presidents Reagan, Bush, and Clinton is not a matter for our consideration." *Sale*, at para. 9.

[86] This argument had profound and global effect on the ways in which policies of high seas interdiction developed around the world. Its last major (and fascinating) iteration is the Australian governmental report: Report of the Expert Panel on Asylum Seekers (2013) available at http://artsonline.monash.edu.au/thebordercrossingobservatory/files/2015/03/expert_panel_on_asylum_seekers_full_report.pdf (last accessed May 12, 2016).

[87] Compare with the governance efforts described in Chapter 2.

[88] This is Martti Koskenniemi's view more generally about human rights discourse. See, e.g., Martti Koskenniemi, "Human Rights Mainstreaming as a Strategy of Institutional Power," *Humanity: An International Journal of Human Rights, Humanitarianism, and Development* 1, no. 1 (2010): 47–58.

[89] This idea of a military intervention supposedly motivated by human rights is extremely familiar today, both from liberal theory and perhaps more painfully from practice. Its justifications appear, e.g., in the work of philosopher John Rawls. Contemporary

Like the constitutionalist model, a theory of human rights as foreign policy depletes the iteration "We Refugees" of any identifiable content. The foreign policy model is more accurately described as pragmatic judgment, not as a human rights commitment. The Supreme Court rejected the constitutionalist mode of equating "We Refugees" to "We the People" when the Executive no longer asserted it as a US interest. In both cases, human rights are not conceived of as binding duties, and at best are recommendations for good policy. They cannot be defined as "law." "Human rights" in both these models are the rights of American sovereignty and those of the American people. They may express American political will to assist non-members, but they also have the potential of expressing that will in the form of violence against non-members. Confronting the Haitian asylum seekers, the hypothesis according to which "We Refugees" could be identified with "We the People" was refuted.

"We Refugees"

I would like, however, to suggest another reading of "We Refugees," which does entail a commitment to the rights of noncitizens.

Immediately after ceasing to be a refugee, Arendt remembered all too well the experience of displacement. It was from this position on the border between *bare life* and citizenship that she invoked "We Refugees" in the first person plural. From here it was possible not only to recognize but also to experience the way that noncitizens in dire need pose a normative claim upon members of exclusive political communities. From this position, one becomes much less likely to believe that *bare life* truly is mute. Human rights commitments depend on the realization that political life inevitably exists not only within but also outside of member-ship in a social contract.

Social contract theory begins from a finite group of individuals who constitute a sovereign entity. Constitutional law, at least in the United States, begins from the imagination of a concrete historical rendition of the social contract, a constituent assembly drafting the Law of the Land. The human rights perspective suggested in "We Refugees" stems from the realization that this act wields violence toward those who do not become members. These can be members of indigenous

instances included the 2011 coalition invasion in Libya, which also had the prevention of migration in its background.

communities whose polities predated the establishment of a sovereign government recognized by international law. They can also be migrants and other people in movement who are excluded by the definition of a closed, delimited, territory. Such violence imposes a burden on those who enjoy membership in the exclusive clubs of citizenship. This foundational violence continues to the present whenever a border is enforced. The upshot is that every citizen must ask whether, and to what degree, this original violence can be justified with regard to particular non-members. European positive human rights law tells us exactly this. The provisions that are "non-derogable" remain even in the face of emergencies "threatening the life of the nation." There are some forms of violence which one should not engage in, even at the price of risking the cohesiveness of the social contract.

The iteration "We Refugees" amounts to a way of positioning the self. It puts the self in the liminal place of "Jews," from which it is possible to see the arbitrariness of inclusion within a club of citizenship. From this perspective, there is no state of nature prior to the social contract. There are, rather, unequally distributed social contracts, from which one finds one's self excluded.[90] "The Jew" for Arendt is synonymous with a person who remains unprotected by sovereignty and has no links to any identifiable social contract.[91] She is the victim of the foundational violence of state building. But at the same time, "the Jew" is the *citizen* that Arendt addresses, when she demands of her peers not to conceal their identities. Saying "We Refugees" is occupying both these positions at once, without uniting them in a common source of law (as both the constitutionalist and the foreign policy models attempt to do). Alongside the bonds of a particular

[90] In *A Nation of Immigrants*, John F. Kennedy does address the initial encounter between the colonial settlers and Native Americans. "Will Rogers, part Cherokee Indian, said his ancestors were at the dock to meet the Mayflower." This, however, poses no problem for the imagination of a "nation of refugees": "some anthropologists believe that the Indians themselves were immigrants from another continent who displaced the original Americans – the aborigines." Though by no means offered as settled expert authority, this is enough to do away with the claim of indigenousness. While deployed to deny the violence that the founding of the United States inflicted upon Native Americans, these lines may also present a challenge to contemporary Americans. Their positions too can never be naturalized. John F. Kennedy, A Nation of Immigrants (New York: Harper Collins, 2008).

[91] Though Arendt talks about "Jews," no particular group of refugees is privileged as the "original" model. Arendt's justification for her focus on the Jews is first and foremost personal. Yet it is not exclusive.

community, "the Jew" will always have a duty toward those who have been left outside.[92]

Saying that duties toward noncitizens are *legal* may seem to run directly against Arendt's text.[93] Arendt insists that "the Jew" has fallen into a lawless space: "But before you cast the first stone on us, remember that being a Jew does not give any legal status in the world. If we should start telling the truth that we are nothing but Jews, it would mean that we expose ourselves to the fate of human beings who, unprotected by any specific law or political convention, are nothing but human beings."[94] This emphasis on lawlessness falls in line with the imagination of positive law as the only source of law.

But Arendt's words here are crucial. The statement is made in the second person and is addressed from the author to her reader. The idea of truly having "no legal status" comes with a particular kind of positioning of the reader: "before *you* cast the first stone on us" (emphasis added). The reader is inserted into a position in which it is not just *anyone* that is encountering "the Jew." The reader is encountering a Jew, and it is *she* that is invited to harm her. For those who reject the option of throwing the stone, that rejection of violence is not simply an act of grace. It is adherence to human rights law.

---

[92] Compare with Stewart Motha's beautiful description of an encounter with a Tamil-speaking cab driver in Paris. Motha revisits Arendt's "We Refugees" and concludes:

> Some years ago I encountered a stranger in Paris – that celebrated cosmopolitan city of exiles. A friend and I were making our way to the Palais de Justice for a function to mark the launch of the International Criminal Court. When we tried to hail a taxi, a modest unmarked car pulled up in front of us. We informed the driver of our destination and he offered to take us there for a price yet to be agreed. He spoke French and Tamil. I speak English, Sinhala, and not enough French to get by. It soon became clear that this man was a Tamil who had left Sri Lanka in circumstances very similar to my own. Despite feeling that I shared much in common with him, we did not share a language. But the joy our encounter brought me was immeasurable. I was on a road with a stranger but the ever-present sense of estrangement dissipated. This was the pleasure of exile – no illusion or dogma, just the simple sense that the only "home" I wanted and needed that night was in that car with this man.

Stewart Motha, "The Redundant Refugee," *Critical Legal Thinking*, November 6, 2015 available at http://criticallegalthinking.com/2015/11/06/the-redundant-refugee/ (last accessed May 12, 2016).

[93] As well as against Giorgio Agamben's reading of the text: Giorgio Agamben, "We Refugees," available at www.faculty.umb.edu/gary_zabel/Courses/Phil%20108-07/We%20Refugees%20-%20Giorgio%20Agamben%20-%201994.htm (last accessed May 11, 2016).

[94] Arendt, "We Refugees," 118.

"Refugees driven from country to country represent the vanguard of their peoples ..." The use of the plural form, "peoples," suggests a plurality of relevant experiences. Yet there is a methodological justification to begin an account of universal obligations from one's own particular history. The exclusion that the Jews have suffered in Europe is the exclusion Arendt is best acquainted with, and her non-positive human rights commitments stem from this particular experience. The human rights commitment, in other words, is a situated and embodied one, not one that seeks to be grounded in a viewpoint that is outside of one's own particular identity.[95]

Blackmun's dissent can perhaps be read beyond the constitutionalist model, along the same lines. According to this reading, when Blackmun returns to the framing of the Refugee Convention, he doesn't mention the relevant history simply in order to provide the framers' intent. He is referring to the violence the convention responded to. He echoes Koh's reference to his parents' experience by replacing the Korean diplomat with the Jewish refugees of World War II. This experience is tied by way of analogy to that of Haitians seeking to reach Florida. While each of these narratives is different, each overflows territoriality and any closed definition of membership. Exposure to these narratives does not simply result in pity or sorrow for the victims. The narratives implicate their addressees' own identity. In the human rights encounter, the claim may meet a commitment. The committed authority, says Blackmun, must provide some form of the "right to be heard."[96] The claim and the commitment, however, do not always match. If they don't, a human rights remedy can be denied.[97]

---

[95] In a famous study of the Haitian slave revolution of 1791 and its influence on the political history of sovereignty, Susan Buck-Morss offers a relevant observation: "rather than giving multiple, distinct cultures equal due, ... human universality emerges in the historical event at the point of rupture. It is in the discontinuities of history that people whose culture has been strained to the breaking point give expression to a humanity that goes beyond cultural limits." To use Buck-Morss's term, Arendt's implicit theory of human rights commitments in "We Refugees" is a "universalism from below." There is no need to regard all instances of domination as equal or to create an objectively valid hierarchy of wrongs. There is, however, a need to remember and stay in touch with the exclusion that is part of the particular history of one's own community. Susan Buck-Morss, *Hegel, Haiti, and Universal History* (Pittsburgh: University of Pittsburgh Press, 2009), 133.

[96] Gregor Noll focuses on credibility assessment in the realization of this right and argues that it is modeled on the Christian confession. See Gregor Noll, "Asylum Claims and the Translation of Culture into Politics," *Texas International Law Journal* 41 (2006): 491–502.

[97] Or, it may be enforced by third parties who also feel implicated by the encounter and can produce the effects of embarrassment (as discussed in Chapter 1 – and as will be discussed in Chapter 5). Koh's words can also read beyond the constitutionalist model and the notion of "We the People." According to this reading, when Koh says the Haitian

Note the emphasis in Blackmun's decision on both substance and process. While asserting the rule of *non-refoulement* substantively, he also inserts a procedural element, stressing the Haitians' *right to be heard*. A government could prevent *refoulement* even without providing a hearing. For significant parts of the Haitian refugee crisis that is precisely what the United States did, holding people in Guantánamo.[98] But that's not enough to meet the requirements of human rights. Neither aspect of this formulation is dispensable.

The distinction between the substantive and the procedural aspects of Blackmun's dissent tracks the analysis in the previous chapter, centered on survival and freedom. On its own, *non-refoulement* protects survival. As long as a government doesn't turn refugees back to persecution or imminent threat of life, it can still round them up and enclose them in a camp. But protecting human rights requires the dominant party in the encounter to recognize not only survival but also the freedom that is irrevocably tethered to it. Refugees must be able to do what Arendt invites them to do in "We Refugees": They must be able to speak who they are. In the spontaneity of speech, one takes the first step from the participation of *bare life* (discussed in the previous chapter) to the participation of (potential) membership. This, in other words, is the most rudimentary expression of freedom. But this also entails a duty: Blackmun's insight when he talks about a "right to be heard" is that speech cannot occur if no one's listening.[99]

Yet, reading this dissent does not provide a concrete notion of the result that would satisfy Blackmun, or the remedy he would issue if he were to win a majority. Presumably, he would require the government to allow the migrants to reach the US shores and enjoy access to asylum from within United States territory. Minimally, he would require an

---

narratives implicated him, he is in this borderline position of Arendt's Jew. He ties the case to his father's experience of exile, which requires him to recognize duties toward non-citizens. The effort to tie his commitment to "We Refugees" to his particular commitment to "We the People" fails because the source of such duties is not the American social contract. Rather, it is the Haitian refugees' own human rights claim.

[98] On the history of migrant detention and its relationship with war-on-terror detention, see Jeffrey Kahn, Islands of Sovereignty: Haitian Migration and the Borders of Empire (Dissertation, University of Chicago, 2013).

[99] Unlike Koh, Martin, and Robinson, no ruminations of violent interventions abroad are possible for Blackmun, who is after all (only) a judge. Such thoughts are beside the point. Human rights necessarily entail duties toward humans as such, and no one seriously thinks of intervention, including within the doctrine of "responsibility to protect" (R2P), as a duty. R2P has nothing to do with human rights. Robinson was right when he said, in his lecture discussed above, that there are no duties of rescue for non-citizens abroad.

asylum hearing for those migrants who demand it even from outside US territory, and importantly, before return to Haiti is initiated. Asylum requests would be decided under the substantive rule put forth by the Refugee Convention and its Protocol and by the 1981 Refugee Act. To be granted protection, an asylum seeker would have to show a well-founded fear of persecution on account of race, religion, nationality, membership in a particular social group, or political opinion.

A question remains, however, whether this would be a enforcement of human rights, as informed by the reading I suggested of "We Refugees." On the practical level, it may turn out that a hearing would be an exclusionary measure. First, the substantive rule could be interpreted narrowly, to require personalized political persecution that only few dissenters really suffer from. Second, the probative threshold for persecution could be set unrealistically high, excluding all asylum seekers due to lack of sufficient evidence. Third, and perhaps most importantly, people who suffer from economic human rights violations would still be excluded, even if they suffered from life-threatening abject poverty. Indeed, Blackmun reminds us of these options when he says that the refugees "do not demand a right of entry." Hearing asylum seekers, as Blackmun says, doesn't require granting access or providing a remedy.

The substantive human rights standard that emerges from "We Refugees" is not the rule codified in international or US law. According to the reading I suggested of Arendt's text, human rights are not only an ethical but, importantly, at the same time also a legal response to the constitutive violence that the foundation of sovereignty entails. Rather than focusing on persecution for a finite set of reasons, as positive law does, human rights require the powerful party to the encounter to imaginatively return to this foundational violence. Such an exercise can be formulated as a question: *If returned to the country she came from, would this asylum seeker be exposed to violence that cannot be justified by the need to exclude new members from my own polity? To operationalize this question means to enforce human rights.*

In previous chapters, I have focused on the imperative "thou shalt not kill" as the basic human rights prohibition. To understand the human rights commitment, this imperative must be contextualized in the political theory of the social contract. Social contract theory divides the world into members and non-members. Law is imagined as the mutual promises of members, while beyond membership there is no law (save for the international law stemming from a second layer of mutual promises between sovereigns).

This dichotomous division between law and non-law can be paraphrased, in the terms Carl Schmitt used, as a division between friends and enemies. A human rights commitment begins from the realization that not all non-members are enemies and that it is prohibited to kill those who are not. According to this understanding, it would be unjustified for one's own social contract to be premised on the annihilation of others. As mentioned above, such annihilation was often the plight of indigenous populations, which were massacred or displaced. Today, the existence of borders extends such annihilation to the present. While human rights do not require open borders, such annihilation is not something that a commitment to human rights can allow. The consequence is that no one can be excluded at the border, at the price of killing her.

While this prohibition of killing remains an important part of the human rights commitment, the legal imperative stemming from foundational violence cannot be reduced to it. Beyond "thou shalt not kill," "We Refugees" stands for a commitment not to expose humans to *any* kind of violence that one believes is unjustifiable by the need to close her social contract. Thus, for example, we may ask, is it justifiable to deport a person who would likely be exposed to the violence of hunger? One's answer to this question may be yes or no (depending among other things on the ability of one's polity to promise a protection from hunger to its own members). A human rights commitment can be observed *whatever one's final answer is*. The necessary condition, however, is that foundational violence is engaged with and not elided, and that one believes that *some* forms of foundational violence are beyond the pale.[100] This judgment differs from both the constitutionalist and the foreign policy models. It is not reducible to self-interest. It suspends the very existence of a bounded political community and assumes – momentarily – that it doesn't exist. From this position, it asks what kinds of violence would the need to found a political community not be able to justify.

Blackmun's opinion can be read as a human rights opinion, inasmuch as the Refugee Convention and the Refugee Act are understood as one kind of collective American response to the foundational violence of

---

[100] In most contexts, it would seem that this human rights standard is more expansive than the existing refugee definition, in the access it grants to non-members into one's polity. This, however, would not always be the case. For one thing, the conception of sovereignty as established upon violence toward non-members is only appropriate with regard to some of the world's sovereigns. If, as Antony Anghie has argued, sovereignty was basically imposed on some postcolonial countries as an act of violence from without, then for such countries the calculus may become different.

American sovereignty. More importantly, while judges can be the adjudicators coupling human rights claims with human rights remedies, this judgment does not require office. Executive decisions, legislative acts, and personal choices all count equally as such couplings. If we are convinced by Blackmun, the result he reached remains binding on those of us who are bound by human rights law, regardless of the Supreme Court's final decision. The question of what this entails in the world is an important one. A human rights commitment may, for example, lead one to civil disobedience, as some US citizens have indeed exercised in the immigration context.[101] In the final analysis, the task of responding to sovereignty's foundational violence falls on all those who enjoy its protection.

---

[101] See e.g. Allegra M. McLeod, "Immigration, Criminalization, and Disobedience" University of Miami Law Review 70 (2016): 556–584.

4

Between Moral Blackmail and Moral Risk

On Saturday, October 6, 2001, the *Adelaide* cruised the Indian Ocean – part of an Australian Navy operation aimed to prevent unauthorized migrants from accessing the country's territory. In the previous month or so, unauthorized migrants had kept the forces busy, several boatloads of people making attempts to enter Australia. It was presumably not a surprise when Commander Norman Banks received a signal alerting him that yet another boat was on its way. A patrol aircraft first detected the migrants shortly after 1 pm, 100 nautical miles north of Australia's Christmas Island. From his position in the sky, the pilot could see that the migrants had their brightly colored life jackets buckled on.

Half an hour later, Banks and the *Adelaide* edged closer to the migrant boat. Following their operational guidelines, they didn't approach it and stopped nine or ten nautical miles away. This brought the Navy vessel "just beyond the horizon," as a parliamentary report on "A Certain Maritime Incident" would later put it. They were as close as possible, without becoming visible from the migrants' perspective.[1] While the migrants couldn't see the Australian ship, this blindness was not mutual. Surveillance equipment allowed the navy to see while not being seen.[2]

Lurking beyond the curve of the planet in the afternoon sun, the image of the *Adelaide* might recall a predator waiting for its prey. But Banks and his crew did not intend any kind of ambush. As the Commander later explained, he intended to prevent the migrants from thrusting their bodies into the water in sight of the Australian ship. Under the law of the sea, this would force the Australians to initiate rescue, creating

---

[1] *Report of the Select Committee for an Inquiry into a Certain Maritime Incident* (Canberra: Commonwealth of Australia, 2002), 486, available at www.aph.gov.au/binaries/senate/committee/maritime_incident_ctte/report/report.pdf (hereinafter "A Certain Maritime Incident") (last accessed May 12, 2016).

[2] A Certain Maritime Incident, 495. For an analysis of surveillance and the construction of maritime space, see Chapter 5.

subsequent legal obligations toward the rescued party.[3] Such obligations were precisely what the guidelines from Canberra were designed to avoid: "moral blackmail" was what they called it.[4]

This stealthy positioning of the *Adelaide* with respect to the migrant boat is emblematic of an important moment in the history of human rights. It informs much of the policy debate in response to the contemporary refugee crisis. This chapter and the next explore what such practices of intervention in the staging of encounter might mean for human rights, as characterized so far. To recapitulate, Chapter 1 outlined the general structure of the human rights encounter; Chapter 2 focused on the nature of the human rights claim; and Chapter 3 developed a theory of the human rights commitment. In this and the next chapter, my objective will be to explain how both parties to the encounter deploy law in generating the event and in preventing it. I will do that by describing how the ambiguous conditions captured in this scene came to be.

Historically, the roots of the situation that developed off the Australian shores lie in Haitian-American cooperation described in Chapter 3, specifically in *Sale* v. *Haitian Centers Council*.[5] When the case was decided, *The New York Times* report on *Sale* foresaw the influence the decision would have. This influence has proven to be a global one and is still very much in the making. Back then, journalist Deborah Sontag asked the relevant questions: "Will this ruling by one of the most influential courts in the world set a tempting precedent, particularly for

---

[3] The duty of rescue is recognized as customary international law and has been codified in a number of international instruments, the most important of which is the United Nations Convention on the Law of the Sea, Article 98:

> (1) Every State shall require the master of a ship flying its flag, insofar as he can do so without serious danger to the ship, the crew, or the passengers: a) to render assistance to any person found at sea in danger of being lost; b) to proceed with all possible speed to the rescue of persons in distress, if informed of their need of assistance; insofar as such action may reasonably be excepted of him.
>
> *(hereinafter UNCLOS).*

See also the 1979 Search and Rescue Convention, which provides that "parties shall ensure that assistance be provided to any person in distress at sea. They shall do so regardless of the nationality or status of the people in distress, or the circumstances giving rise to that distress."

[4] "The reason Commander Banks took that course was, as he explained, because of his apprehension that, should the potential illegal immigrants see an Australian vessel, they might precipitate a safety of life at sea ('SOLAS') situation, thus compelling the Adelaide to effect a rescue." (A Certain Maritime Incident, 486)

[5] See Chapter 3.

developing nations? If the United States, with imprimatur of its highest court, appears to put the protection of its borders above its responsibilities under international law, will others be enticed to follow suit?"[6]

The processes that followed were not, however, initiated by developing countries. Italy first looked to the United States in 1997, when it attempted to control the movement of Albanian migrants and refugees.[7] Not until the 9/11 attacks did high-seas interdiction practices take the firm hold they now have in policies of countries other than the United States. The three branches of the Australian government, for example, attempted to eliminate the human rights encounter. First, the executive implemented emergency measures. Second, the judiciary upheld the policies carried out under emergency law, normalizing them within a particular conception of sovereignty. Third, the legislature streamlined the emergency measures through disaggregated cooperation with neighboring countries. The Haitian-American model of high seas interdictions was an important part of what led Commander Banks to the center of Australia's largest contemporary policy debate.[8]

When unauthorized migrants confronted the policies that emerged, they began to generate their own emergencies, which rendered the Australian government's efforts much more difficult. By adopting measures of self-harm, unauthorized migrants sought to compel encounters that would impose human rights duties on states that were doing

---

[6] Deborah Sontag, "Reneging the Refugee: The Haitian Precedent," *New York Times*, June 27, 1993, available at www.nytimes.com/1993/06/27/weekinreview/reneging-on-refuge-the-haitian-precedent.html?pagewanted=all&src=pm (last accessed May 12, 2016).

[7] The inspiration coming from the US arrangement was likely quite direct: in a 1999 treatise on the Rules of International Law on Illegal Immigration by Sea, Italian legal scholar Tullio Scovazzi specifically cites Reagan's Executive Order 12,324 as a precedent for the legality of the Italian-Albanian agreement. Scovazzi, a leading authority on maritime law, clarifies that the "freedom of the high seas" is merely a presumption of international law and can therefore be altered under bilateral agreements providing otherwise. See Tullio Scovazzi, "*Le Norme di Diritto Internazionale Sull'immigrazione Illegale via Mare Con Particolare Riferimento Ai Rapporti Tra Albania e Italia, in La Crisi Albanese Del 1997*" in *La crisi albanese del 1997. L'azione dell'Italia e delle organizzazioni internazionali: verso un nuovo modello di gestione delle crisi?*, ed. Andrea de Guttry and Fabrizio Pagani (Rome: Franco Angeli, 1999). See also Efthymios Papastavridis, "'Fortress Europe' and Frontex: Within of Without International Law?" *Nordic Journal of International Law* 87 (2010): 79, 75.

[8] One Australian newspaper described Banks as an "ambitious, a-political officer," forty-four-year old, who "boasts signing letters to superiors 'I have the honour to be, sir, your obedient servant.'" The title of the story reporting about the Senate's questioning of Captain Banks, asks why has the officer not been able to sleep. Mark Forbes, "Why Commander Norman Banks Has Sleepless Nights," *The Age*, March 30, 2002, available at www.theage.com.au/articles/2002/03/29/1017206151105.html (last accessed May 12, 2016).

everything they could to avoid them. Such measures of self-harm are a form of political action by which migrants seeking human rights remedies have utilized and engendered membership in humanity.

Building on insights from the previous one, this chapter will further characterize the inconsistent commitments that many of us have, both to (non-positive) human rights law and to the positive law of the social contract. When migrants challenge and strain the human rights commitments of personnel carrying border guard duties in the name of developed states, the basic characteristics of such commitments are highlighted.

The *Tampa* Encounter

Albert Blaustein, the self-proclaimed prophet featured in Chapter 3, predicted in his 1976 talk that incoming migrants would produce a perceived emergency in Australia come the year 2001: "The little old ladies in tennis shoes will bring them tea and toast – at first [But] What will the Australians do when the number reaches one million or two or three?"[9] These numbers would of course prove to be enormously exaggerated.[10] Little could Blaustein know, however, just how precise was the date he gave. Australian public support for refugee protection declined as early as 1977, when the first Vietnamese asylum seekers reached its shore. As the influx of Southeast Asian refugees continued into the 1990s and the *Orderly Departure Program* ended, popular demand for more stringent measures grew. The Australian government introduced mandatory detention in 1992. But the truly decisive and much-commented-upon policy change in Australia occurred in 2001, when the Norwegian MV *Tampa* sought to disembark 438 Afghan migrants it had saved.

On August 26, the 49,000-ton container ship received a signal from Australian authorities: Eighty people on board a fishing boat traveling from Indonesia were in need of rescue. When the *Tampa*, licensed to carry fifty, reached the boat about 140 kilometers north of Australia's Christmas Island Territory, it rescued the 438 Afghan migrants.

---

[9] Clyde Ferguson Jr., Albert Blaustein, John Thomas, James Wilson Jr., Dale de Haan, and Richard Plender, "Refugees: A New Dimension in International Human Rights," *Proceedings of the Annual Meeting (American Society of International Law)* 70 (1976): 63.

[10] Statistics covering 1976–2015 (updated September 11, 2015) are at the Australian Parliament's website, and the number is in fact quite low by international comparison. 2013 was the busiest year recorded, with 20,587 (including 644 counted as "crew"). Available at www.aph.gov.au/About_Parliament/Parliamentary_Departments/Parliamentary _Library/pubs/BN/2011-2012/BoatArrivals#_Toc285178607 (last accessed May 12, 2016).

The sixty-one-year old Norwegian Captain Arne Rinnan asked the Australian authorities where to disembark and was directed to an Indonesian port. But when the rescued migrants understood where the boat was headed, they immediately protested. Several threatened to commit suicide. Others refused to take food. The *Tampa* changed its course to the Australian Christmas Island.

Australian authorities informed the *Tampa* that entering Australian territorial water would now be illegal: "Australian Government at the highest level formally requests that you not approach Christmas Island and that you stand off at a distance at least equal to your current position – 13.5 nautical miles from the island."[11] They enforced a closure on the port of Flying Fish Cove pursuant to a law providing for "special powers of harbour master in emergencies" triggered when "the harbour master of a port is satisfied that a dangerous situation exists."[12] Canberra instructed boats from Christmas Island not to attempt reaching the *Tampa*: Physical contact with the rescuees stranded on board could mean jurisdiction over them, and legal obligations would follow. But Captain Rinnan, concerned for the rescued migrants as well as for his crew, called the Royal Flying Doctor Service. Several of the rescuees were now unconscious. One had broken a leg, and two pregnant women were "in distress."[13]

---

[11] *Minister for Immigration and Multicultural Affairs and Others* v. *Eric Vadarlis* (2001), FCA 1329, 59, available at www.austlii.edu.au/au/cases/cth/federal_ct/2001/1329.html (last accessed May 12, 2016) (hereinafter "Ruddock").

[12]   "(1) Where the harbour master of a port is satisfied that a dangerous situation exists in a port and that –

 (a) the presence of a vessel within the port constitutes a danger to the safety of persons, or to another vessel or to valuable property within the port; and

 (b) it is impossible to remove the vessel from the port or that the removal of the vessel from the port would itself create a danger to the safety of persons or to another vessel or to valuable property within the port, the harbour master may order the master of the vessel, the presence of which constitutes such a danger, to forthwith scuttle the vessel and, if the master fails to comply forthwith with that order, the harbour master may by any means that he thinks fit, cause the vessel to be scuttled.

 (2) An action shall not be brought against the Crown, the Minister, a harbour master or any person acting under the authority of a harbour master for loss or damage occasioned by any act done in good faith pursuant to the powers conferred by this section."

See Shipping and Pilotage Act, 1967, available at www.slp.wa.gov.au/legislation/sta tutes.nsf/main_mrtitle_894_homepage.html (last accessed May 12, 2016).

[13] This is the language the court uses, which is also (as reflected above) the language of Article 98 of UNCLOS.

Years later, Rinnan wryly recounted: "When I was looking down from the bridge, the people was listening into a radio they smuggle on board . . . and then they went on a hunger strike. The only man aboard the ship who was really happy was the cook" [*sic*].[14] On August 29, around 9 am – his own Mayday emergency signal having been ignored – Rinnan decided to proceed into Australian territorial waters. Within two hours, forty-five armed members of the Special Air Service Regiment Counterterrorism Squad boarded the *Tampa*. The emergency provision of the 1967 Shipping and Pilotage Act authorized the government to take over the ship and redirect it out of the port. But the operation stopped short of such a measure.[15]

Captain Rinnan was "not going anywhere." As he put it, *this was a humanitarian matter of saving life at sea, not a matter of politics.*[16] The next day the Norwegian ambassador visited the *Tampa*. "Afghan Refugees Now off the coast of Christmas Island" read the signature on the bottom of the letter he came back with. The Afghans appealed not only to morality but also to international law as the sources for their plea to be admitted into Australia.[17] But it was not clear how – or if at all – their

---

[14] See interview, available at www.youtube.com/watch?v=3c_phJsx1NE (last accessed May 12, 2016).

[15] Years later one of the commanders of the squad retold the events: "If we took this Norwegian flag vessel, and then decided to drive it into international waters by our own hand, is that not some form of piracy itself?" Available at www.youtube.com /watch?v=3c_phJsx1NE (18:45).

[16] Interestingly, duties of rescue at sea are recognized even with regard to an enemy at war, where the rescuees as well as any dead bodies must be protected against "pillage and ill-treatment." See sources in Robert Tucker, *The Law of War and Neutrality at Sea* (Clark: The Lawbook Exchange, 2006). Also, compare Rinnan's humanitarianism with Earl Harrison's, supporting the Zionist movement (discussed in Chapter 1).

[17]
> You know well about the long time war and its tragic human conse-quences, and you know about the genocide and massacres going on in our country and thousands of innocent men, women and children were put in public grieve yards . . . In this regard before this Australia has taken some real appreciable initiatives and has given asylum to a high number of refugees from our miserable people. This is why we are whole-heartedly and sincerely thankful to you . . .
>
> But your delay while we are in the worst conditions has hurt our feelings. We do not know why we have not been regarded as refugees and deprived from rights of refugees according to International Convention (1951).
>
> We request from Australian authorities and people, at first not to deprive us from the rights that all refugees enjoy in your country. And in the case of rejection due to not having anywhere to live on the earth and every moment death is threatening us. We request you to take mercy on the life of (438) men, women and children [*sic*]. See Ruddock, para. 137.

arguments could be voiced in an Australian court. Melbourne-based lawyer Eric Vadarlis was denied permission to meet the group. He and an Australian NGO, the Victorian Council of Civil Liberties, proceeded to submit a *habeas* application in their name. Phillip Ruddock, Minister of Immigration and Multicultural Affairs, was named primary respondent.

On September 3, the asylum seekers were transferred from the *Tampa* to an Australian military vessel under an agreement between the parties to litigation. Australia concluded two bilateral "arrangements" with neighboring countries, which would help the country deal with a legal conundrum generated by people that were perceived to be not yet *in*, but already not *out* of its jurisdiction.[18] One of the arrangements was with New Zealand, which agreed to take children and families. The Republic of Nauru would take the other less desirable migrants. The 21-square-kilometer Pacific island was on the verge of financial collapse and badly needed the US$20 million that Canberra tabled. On September 11, the trial Court accepted the asylum seekers' challenge and granted them the *habeas* injunction. But the government appealed to Australia's High Court. In *Ruddock v. Vadarlis*, the High Court rejected the asylum seekers' claims in a fascinating 2:1 decision. The emergency policy Prime Minister John Howard introduced was approved and subsequently normalized within a particular conception of sovereignty.

Why were the *Tampa* asylum seekers not granted access to asylum procedures in Australia under the Refugee Convention and Protocol? Things were clear enough politically: In early September, the government's stance with regard to the *Tampa* met with overwhelming bipartisan support.[19] As a legal matter, however, things seemed more difficult. The asylum seekers were in Australian territorial waters. Even if one were to follow the relatively restrictive principles laid out in Stevens's majority opinion in *Sale*, it would still seem they had a "right to be heard."[20]

---

[18] Compare this to Arendt's position writing "We Refugees." As I argued in Chapter 3, the essay is best understood in the context of her position as already part of American society, but only in the process of becoming a member.

[19] This support is reflected in the "special addition" of Q&A Adventures in Democracy, *Leaky Boats* (ABC, 2011), available at www.youtube.com/watch?v=3c_phJsx1NE (12:53) (hereinafter *Leaky Boats*).

[20] For the sake of comparison, remember that under the United States Supreme Court's (relatively narrow) interpretation of Convention obligations, they would now have access to asylum.

From *Ruddock* to "the Pacific Solution"

It was the executive rather than the judiciary that encapsulated in the most concise way the general message of the High Court of Australia in *Ruddock*. As Prime Minister John Howard put it, "*We* will decide on who comes to this country, and the circumstances in which they come." Just as deploying emergency measures against the *Tampa* implied, the underlying premise of the majority decision too was that the migrants challenged Australia's "independence, against attacks from without."[21] It was the judiciary, however, that expounded the theoretical premises behind this assertion. In doing so, the judges set forth the narrow terms in which human rights claims were to be cast.

Two principal issues were before the High Court on appeal. One was whether the executive power of the Commonwealth authorized the expulsion of the resucees. The other was whether the rescuees were subject to any restraint attributable to the Commonwealth, granting the Australian court *habeas* jurisdiction.[22] The majority, Justice Robert French and Justice Bryan Beaumont, answered the first question positively and the second negatively. They both held that the executive power to remove the rescued asylum seekers emanated from Australia's nature as a sovereign state. And they both believed that holding the asylum seekers on boats or transferring them to offshore facilities did not amount to grounds for *habeas*. Chief Justice Michael Black, on the other hand, upheld the trial court's decision: There was no statutory authorization for holding the refugees at sea or for expelling them. A writ of *habeas*, he thought, was warranted.

To understand the majority opinion, one must first recognize a rather peculiar fact: Australia's territory and its "migration zone" are not identical under Australian law. The Migration Act of 1958 only applies to what it designated as the Australian "Migration Zone" – a definition that excluded Australia's territorial waters outside the country's seaports.[23] As the *Tampa* entered territorial waters but did not enter the migration zone, the framework was understood to exclude those on board. The trial court judge (and Justice Black) held that the asylum seekers would have to be brought into the migration zone for deportation proceedings to be

---

[21] This is John Austin's paraphrase on Hobbes's definition of sovereignty. John Austin, *Lectures on Jurisprudence of the Philosophy of Positive Law* (New York: James Cockroft & Company, 1875), 129.

[22] Ruddock, para. 3.

[23] Section 5 of the 1958 Migration Act, available at www.austlii.edu.au/au/legis/cth/consol_act/ma1958118/s5.html (last accessed May 12, 2016).

ignited. But that was precisely what the government sought to *prevent*. Under the Migration Act, the Refugee Convention and its remedies would kick in. The rescuees would gain a "right to be heard," in Justice Blackmun's memorable formulation from *Sale*, discussed in Chapter 3.

Justice French explained that the matter was not one of *immigration* but one of *border control*. While the asylum seekers were not *outside* of Australia, they were not *inside* the country either. And the "gatekeeping function" was the prerogative of the executive branch. This understanding of expansive executive powers traces in his opinion back to the 1688 Glorious Revolution, and French discusses some of the relevant history. As the Justice explains, the power to protect borders flows from Queen Elizabeth's prerogative as monarch of Australia. This prerogative was never explicitly carved out of the executive's powers, neither by constitution nor by statute.[24] Great care, says French, is required in limiting this authority: "The greater the significance of a particular executive power to national sovereignty, the less likely it is that, absent clear words or inescapable implication, the parliament would have intended to extinguish the power."[25] The very first proposition provided in support of this view of sovereignty is grounded in "the general proposition of international law that: '. . . *the supreme power of every state has a right to make laws for the exclusion or expulsion of a foreigner . . .*'"[26] Furthermore, internationally wrongful acts are by definition against states, not against individuals. Afghan asylum seekers have no independent claim.[27] Offense to an individual asylum seeker under the Refugee Convention – or under human rights law – is not even contemplated.

---

[24] To quote Justic French's words:

> In my opinion, the executive power of the Commonwealth, absent statutory extinguishment or abridgement, would extend to a power to prevent the entry of non-citizens and to do such things as are necessary to effect such exclusion. This does not involve any conclusion about whether the Executive would, in the absence of statutory authority, have a power to expel non-citizens other than as an incident of the power to exclude. The power to determine who may come into Australia is so central to its sovereignty that it is not to be supposed that the Government of the nation would lack under the power conferred upon it directly by the Constitution, the ability to prevent people not part of the Australia community, from entering. Ruddock, para. 193.

[25] Ruddock, para. 185.

[26] Ruddock, para. 186. Quoting *In Re Adam* [1837] 1 Moo PC; 12 ER 889.

[27] French quotes *Musgrove* v. *Toy* [1891]: "it seems beyond question that every nation may exercise the right of excluding aliens without giving offence to *the country* to which those aliens belong" (emphasis added).

Though more protective of asylum seeker's rights in its general tenor, Chief Justice Black's dissent is not grounded on their individual rights either. It too is based on a notion of sovereignty, fashioned this time in the British tradition of parliamentary supremacy. Black rejects the majority's expansive concept of executive powers and emphasizes the *legislature* as the locus of sovereignty instead. While the prerogative of executive power to protect borders has been recognized in both common and international law, he says, it has long been superseded. Black goes into a little bit more detail than French in the relevant history. This prerogative, he explains, was used for political ends, surely no longer appropriate. One such end was to prevent the infiltration of revolutionary ideas from France across the English Channel. Its most recent application was in 1771, when it aimed to keep Jews out of England.[28] Already in the eighteenth century it had been overridden by demands that it be replaced by legislation. A fundamental tenet of the British tradition of parliamentary supremacy is that the monarch requires direct authorization by statute for all authorities that are beyond "Royal Prerogative." But Black's dissent can be understood in two rather different ways. By one account, it utilizes the instruments of British constitutional law to protect the rights of migrants like those of the *Tampa*. By another, it is an invitation for the legislature to provide statutory authorization and normalize their exclusion, instead of relying on executive fiat. The latter option was taken up quite adamantly by the legislature, with the adoption of the "Pacific Solution," described below.

Moving to the second question, Justice French explained that extending a writ of *habeas corpus* requires a restraint upon the freedom of movement, which must be attributable to the Australian government. The asylum seekers on the *Tampa*, however, have no right to enter Australia's territory. The only restraint upon their movement is the closure of Australia's port. "The Nauru/NZ [New Zealand] arrangements of themselves provided the only practical exit from the situation." However, "Those arrangements did not constitute a restraint upon freedom attributable to the Commonwealth given the fact that the Captain of the Tampa would not sail out of Australia while the rescuees were on board."[29] The Tampa was free to travel anywhere it wanted in the world, but Australia. The fact that Rinnan would not leave

---

[28] Ruddock, para. 22–23.
[29] Ruddock, para. 213.

presented "no restraint on their liberty which could be attributed to the Commonwealth."[30] By the same token, if all countries were to adopt the Australian policy – the asylum seekers would still be free to roam the oceans.[31]

Here Black's dissent takes a markedly different approach, adopting a construction of the writ that realizes the "rights of encounter," the "right to be heard," or simply *human rights*. Referring to persuasive precedent from a number of foreign courts, Black asks what options the asylum seekers had *in reality*. "The question should not be, 'Would the person be free if they went somewhere else?' but rather 'Is the person detained here and now?'"[32] To mention only one of the cases cited, consider *Amuur v. France* (1992). The European Court of Human Rights found that four Somali asylum seekers confined for twenty days in the transit zone in Orly Airport in Paris were indeed detained.[33] They were offered return to Syria where they had come from. Black quotes the European Court of Human Rights (ECtHR): "The mere fact that it is possible for asylum seekers to leave voluntarily the country where they wish to take refuge cannot exclude a restriction on liberty . . ."[34] Black therefore follows the trial court judge in saying that the arrangements with Nauru and New Zealand are "merely a continuation of control or custody by the appellants in another form." Implementing a policy by proxy does not change the underlying power structure.[35]

The majority and minority opinions do not simply differ with respect to the result. More importantly, they are grounded in two different ways of understanding law. Emphasizing robust executive competences to guard borders, the majority followed the Australian government in framing the *Tampa* as a national security threat. The dissent, on the other hand, rests on a theory of representation: Executive powers can

---

[30] Ruddock, para. 213.

[31] Jessica Tauman, "Rescued at Sea, but Nowhere to Go: The Cloudy Legal Waters of the Tampa Crisis," *Pacific Rim Law and Policy Journal* 11, no. 2 (2002): 461–496.

[32] One may recall Anatole France's famous formulation, according to which the rich and the poor are equally free to sleep under the bridge. Conceptually, it is indeed its counterpart.

[33] *Amuur* v. *France* (1992) 22 EHRR 533.

[34] The Australian court also cites *Chin Yow* v. *United States of America*, where the United States Supreme Court decided a case where a Chinese man was held by the San Francisco Commissioner of Immigration. The Court held that the question whether the detainee had a right to enter was not relevant to whether he was wrongly imprisoned. As the Court found, the Chinese man was imprisoned.

[35] On this notion of jurisdiction, see Chapter 5.

only be authorized by democratic will.[36] In more abstract terms, one might say that the majority imagines a transcendent sovereignty, which is entrusted with securing its citizens by being beyond "The People." The dissent imagines an *immanent* sovereignty that *is* "The People." The People must decide by statute when they want or do not want to open the border. For the judiciary, there is no second-guessing that decision.[37] From the perspective of a non-citizen, however, the distinction between expansive executive powers and parliamentary supremacy doesn't make a difference. Under both theories, sovereignty is hermetically closed to her.[38] Neither theory assumes that humans as such have legal protection, derivable from an independent source of law. There are no politics and no rights beyond state sovereignty. There is no space for the iteration "We Refugees," which is discussed in Chapter 3.

Yet, the dissent's understanding of *habeas* still institutionalizes certain responsiveness to human rights claims. Crucially, Justice Black emphasizes that it does not matter if a migrant is passively thrust on an Australian authority or thrusts herself upon that authority. What is important is that when her life is placed in the hands of Australian agents, it demands consideration.[39] A human can thrust herself or be thrust upon sovereignty, extending jurisdiction as well as accountability toward her. More generally speaking, for Black, sovereignty cannot be understood merely on its own terms, as a self-contained source of authority.

On the day the trial court handed down its decision upholding the rights of the *Tampa* asylum seekers to enter the Commonwealth, terrorists attacked the World Trade Center. "It's big and it's bad," said Farid Abdullah, recalling what the Australian guards on the *Tampa* said

---

[36] The British Parliament was not in fact structured to represent the popular will, and its theory of representation is more complicated than that. But that is how the argument function is understood in *Ruddock*, which is my concern here.

[37] Compare with the discussion of the scope of presidential powers, in relation to the Constitution and to statutory limitations, in *Youngstown Sheet and Tube Co. v. Sawyer* – 343 U.S. 579 (1952). In *Youngstown*, the US Supreme Court famously struck down an Executive Order in which President Harry Truman ordered that the Secretary of Commerce seize and operate most American steel mills in the interest of national defense.

[38] Compare with last lines of Chapter 3.

[39] In other words, Black understands the question whether a condition is "self-inflicted" as a formal one. As he explains, the asylum seekers' position simply cannot be self-inflicted. Saying otherwise would confuse this area of *habeas* jurisprudence with tort jurisprudence. In tort, when a party *voluntarily* assumed a risk, it will not be able to sue for the damages that follow. But the same principle cannot be applied here: "notions of fault and defences such as *volenti non-fit injuria*, which are significant in tort law, have no place in the law with respect to *habeas corpus*." Ruddock, para. 88.

when they delivered the news.[40] The attack sparked a US-led military campaign, sending Australian troops to Abduallah's home country of Afghanistan as part of the coalition forces. This, in turn, further displaced Afghanistan's population.[41] One may speculate on the question of how the High Court would have decided the government's appeal were it not for the 9/11 attacks. The influence the attacks had on the legislature was far more apparent.

The Parliament advanced legislation that solidified and immensely broadened the framework that the ad hoc arrangements with Nauru and New Zealand first introduced.[42] Through six legislative amendments, Australia removed numerous Pacific islands from its migration zone. Further amendments in coming years gradually resulted in almost 5,000 Australian islands being deemed "excised off-shore places."[43] The islands were redefined so as not to be part of Australian sovereign territory for the purpose of refugee protection. An asylum seeker who first arrived at such a place was deemed an "offshore entry person" – a neologism peculiar to Australian law. Thus, she would be prohibited from access to protection under the Refugee Convention, unless the Minister for Immigration decided upon an exception.[44]

The Howard government relied on Section 198A[45] of the Migration Act in advancing the Pacific Solution, which involved the transfer

---

[40] Leaky Boats, 13:52–14:29.

[41] As statistics collected by the Australian government show, during the years 2010–2012 the largest group of asylum seekers with respect to which refugee status determination procedures were initiated were Afghans. See "Asylum Statistics – Australia: Quarterly Tables – March Quarter 2013" (Canberra, Government of Australia, 2013), 10. Available at www.immi.gov.au/media/publications/statistics/asylum/_files/asylum-stats-march-quarter-2013.pdf (last accessed May 12, 2016).

[42] In doing so, it followed Black's minority opinion, emphasizing the lack of Parliamentary consent to offshoring policies.

[43] Michelle Foster, "The Implications of the Failed 'Malaysian Solution': The Australian High Court and Refugee Responsibility Sharing at International Law," *Melbourne Journal of International Law* 13 (2012): 1, 5.

[44] Rather than being required to process an application for Convention protection, the government could *choose* to determine asylum seekers' refugee status on Christmas Island. Alternatively, it could transfer asylum seekers to another country. Foster, "The Implications of the Failed 'Malaysian Solution'," 1, 4.

[45] Section 198A was inserted into the Migration Act in 2001 to provide that "[a]n officer may take an offshore entry person from Australia to a country in respect of which a declaration is in force under subsection (3)." Section 198A(3) in turn provided that the minister could declare that a particular country meets the requirements of the Refugee Convention.

(3) The Minister may:

of more than 1,500 asylum seekers from Australia to Nauru. The legislative amendments, which began late in September, created a mechanism through which the government responded to those who sought to impose on Australia duties that could fulfill their own rights. As part of the Parliamentary debates, Australian government lawyers provided legal justification for this measure. One comment is particularly illuminating: "Support for this conclusion [that the policy is legal] is to be found in the U.S. Supreme Court case of *Sale* v. *Haitian Centers Council Inc. . . .* [I]n an 8:1 decision the Court . . . concluded that the Convention did not place any limits on the President's authority to repatriate aliens interdicted beyond the territorial seas of the United States."[46]

Eliminating the Encounter

Ruddock and the Pacific Solution illuminate two different though complementary aspects of sovereignty. In understanding Australia's attempts to eliminate the human rights encounter, the two must be analytically separated, but also understood in tandem. In constructing its decision around the idea of "gatekeeping" at the border, the judiciary emphasized unilateral executive power. There are certain policies, we are told, with respect to which the executive has absolute discretion. Border enforcement is one of them. It is not merely by chance that the judiciary embraces so fully the government's security argument in this context. The emergency the Australian executive branch declared may have sought to create a temporal suspension of ordinary law. This, the judiciary explained, was largely redundant: The border achieves the same suspension, though in spatial rather than temporal form.[47] The concept

(a) declare in writing that a specified country:
   (i) provides access, for persons seeking asylum, to effective procedures for assessing their need for protection; and
   (ii) provides protection for persons seeking asylum, pending determination of their refugee status; and
   (iii) provides protection to persons who are given refugee status, pending their voluntary repatriation to their country of origin or resettlement in another country; and
   (iv) meets relevant human rights standards in providing that protection.

[46] *Article 31 – Refugees Unlawfully in the Country of Refuge – An Australian Perspective* (Canberra: Refugee and Humanitarian Division Department of Immigration and Multicultural and Indigenous Affairs, 2002), 129.

[47] Compare with Paul Kahn, *The Cultural Study of Law* (Chicago: University of Chicago Press, 2009), 36 (explaining that "The imagination of political space . . . exists prior to

of sovereignty that emerges from the judiciary's decision highlights the exceptionalist, self-referential, aspect of sovereignty. It does not so much matter if closing the border demanded the use of force in the form of an anti-terrorism commando operation, and it doesn't matter if closing the border frustrated the sole opportunity that a particular individual may have had to build a life worth living. Sovereignty is defined here by its capacity to take a life with impunity: Strictly speaking, this is neither warfare, nor punishment.[48]

The legislature, on the other hand, advanced a seemingly alternative concept, in which sovereignty is operationalized and realized through a cooperative transnational network. The Pacific Solution relied on galvanized popular opinion, but the policy could not have been achieved were it not for the cooperation of fellow governments.[49] Casting the problem of unauthorized migrants as regional, the policies of the Pacific Solution demanded partnership, rather than exceptionalism. Instead of the unilateral model of sovereignty the judiciary talked about, here the emphasis is on multilateralism and mutual benefit.

Rather than being opposing orientations, unilateralism and multilateralism figure as two complementary aspects of the transnational political environment.[50] The former generates an emergency and seemingly suspends ordinary law; the latter streamlines and facilitates the policies that the emergency introduces through international arrangements and the necessary allocation of funds. "Transnational" and "sovereign" authorities, contrasted in the previous chapters,

---

efforts to justify the geographical reach of law"). In that respect, one might argue that a border is to space what a state of emergency is to law.

[48] Giorgio Agamben, *Homo Sacer: Sovereign Power and Bare Life*, trans. Daniel Heller-Roazen, 1st edition (Stanford: Stanford University Press, 1998).

[49] This was not achieved without domestic opposition. Read for example the words of Anthony Audoa, member of the Nauruan parliament:

> I don't know what is behind the mentality of the Australian leaders but I don't think it is right. A country that is desperate with its economy, and you try to dangle a carrot in front of them, of course, just like a prostitute ... if you dangle money in front of her, you think she will not accept it. Of course she will, because she's desperate.

A Certain Maritime Incident, 295–299.

[50] David Kennedy makes this point in James Der Derian, Michael W. Doyle, Jack L. Snyder, and David Kennedy, "How Should Sovereignty be Defended?" in Christopher J. Bickerton, Philip Cunliffe, and Alexander Gourevitch (eds.), *Politics Without Sovereignty: A Critique of Contemporary International Relations* (Oxon and New York: UCL Press, 2007), 188.

increasingly figure as two different aspects of the same political and economic structure.

In the present context, the different capacities of the Australian government play complementary roles in eliminating the human rights encounter. Now, when the navy would stop a migrant boat beyond Australia's migration zone, it would no longer be violating age-old rules such as the freedom of the high seas; and no longer exposing a migrant to potential death. Offshore processing in Nauru or New Zealand would transfer jurisdiction over the migrants to those countries, and those countries would have to confront the migrants' human rights claims. Within this scheme, there is no room for a migrant to address herself to a particular person with the universal boatperson's message: "it is you, and no one else, who must decide upon my fate."[51] The Australian population conceals from itself the role it plays in the allocation of death and unlivable life on the planet.[52] The events that unfolded at sea during the months following September should be understood within this context. They were attempts to reinstitute the moment in which one person can impose the duties that correspond to her rights on another.

From Self-Help to Self-Harm

Commander Banks was sent out to sea with guidelines charging The Royal Australian Navy with implementing the Pacific Solution. "Operation Relex" involved ships and amphibious vessels, as well as customs and coastguard boats. Aircraft and helicopters supported the Navy's interdiction efforts by providing "layered surveillance."[53] The idea was to prevent the migrants from submitting asylum requests in Australia's "Migration Zone." Looking back at what turned out to be a complicated mission, The "Senate Select Committee on a Certain Maritime Incident" summarized the events that ensued:

> Under Operation Relex, twelve Suspected Illegal Entry Vessels were intercepted between 7 September and 16 December 2001. Where previously the Navy's role had been to escort unauthorised arrivals to an Australian port for reception and processing by relevant agencies, the new ADF role was to thwart their objective of reaching Australian territory.

[51] This is a paraphrase of Max Weber's famous definition of ethics of conviction formulated in Chapter 1.

[52] I will interrogate further the assumptions implicit in such self-concealment in the next chapter.

[53] A Certain Maritime Incident, xx.

The new Australian response led to a corresponding change in the behaviour of the asylum seekers. From being cooperative and compliant, their
behaviour changed to include threatened acts of violence, sabotage and
self-harm, designed to counter the Navy's strategies.[54]

The Committee was composed to investigate what became known as
the "Children Overboard" affair. On October 7, 2001, as the Navy
ratcheted up operation Relex, Phillip Ruddock announced that
a number of children had been thrown overboard from an asylum
seekers' boat that had just been intercepted. The "children overboard"
story originated in a report from Banks' *Adelaide*. Senior government
ministers, including the Minister for Defence, and Prime Minister
Howard reiterated it numerous times in subsequent days and weeks.
But as high-level Navy officials admitted and as the Committee found,
"the story was in fact untrue." The Committee's primary purpose was to
find out how false information was disseminated to the Australian public.
It claimed to expose prevarication by high-ranking officials, including
Howard. The government, for its own part, responded that the committee proceedings were a show trial: After being defeated at the ballot,
Labor Senators were out to seek revenge.[55] The Pacific Solution after all
proved a resonating electoral success.

When one of the boats that Relex forces encountered arrived at
Australian territorial waters, the rumor that a child was thrown into
the water caught on. Officials deployed on *Adelaide* later explained that
the boat communicated that a child was held overboard. Zaynab
Hassan, a young Iraqi woman who was among the migrants on the
boat, confirmed this claim: "We didn't know the language and this was
the only way to communicate to these people, so he was holding his
child to tell them, look we have children, if you don't care about me care
about my child."[56] But what the authorities heard and wrote down was
that the children were thrown. The next morning a picture of a child
and his mother – a female Australian Navy soldier swimming beside
them – spread across newspapers. The Australian Navy had allegedly

---

[54] A Certain Maritime Incident, xx–xxi
[55] According to this account, "The most strident critics of the public servants concerned
were the predictable parade of professors who, as is their wont, offered the Committee
counsels of perfection which appeared to owe more to the ideals of Plato's Republic than
to familiarity with the vicissitudes of public administration in the real world." A Certain
Maritime Incident, 531.
[56] Leaky Boats, 31:07.

saved the Afghan boy from the migrants he was with – and from his own family.

In reality, the encounter was rather different. After not having been able to turn previous boats back, the *Adelaide* fired across the asylum seekers' bow. A dozen asylum seekers immediately jumped into the ocean. Under instructions from Canberra, Commander Banks decided not to pursue rescue. In the next hours, asylum seekers tore a hole in their boat's body and water began flooding in. The Captain and the crew waited and watched until the asylum seekers' boat sunk. Only then came the permission to begin rescue. The pictures presented as those of the "children overboard" were pictures of this late rescue operation, after the group of asylum seekers dispersed in the water. In the course of the operation, the crew was given instructions not to let images that would "humanize" the asylum seekers reach the public. "They didn't want to have any kind of connection between our values, and the values these people may well have presented ... They wanted to portray that these were not normal people," said Able Seaman Bec Lynd.[57] But with the right framing, the picture of Laura Whittle swimming in the ocean beside drifting men, women, and children, lifting them from the water, could be politically beneficial.

Whatever the reasons for the misinformation, the government took the report about a child overboard as an opportunity to fuel its campaign against boat people. Prime Minister Howard was clear about the stakes involved: "I don't want here in Australia people who would throw their own children into the sea ..." The issue was boiled down to a statement about the range of acceptable human behavior: "There's something incompatible, to me, between someone who claims to be a refugee and someone who would throw their own child into the sea. It offends the natural instinct of protection, and delivering security and safety to your children."[58] Phillip Rudock, for his own part, said that throwing a child overboard was "clearly planned and premeditated ... I imagine the sorts of children who would be thrown would be those who can be tossed and can be lifted without any objection from them."[59]

A dozen boats were detected during Operation Relex from early September to late December. Only one of the boats was turned back, in a case in which the Australian Navy boarded it and drove it

---

[57] Leaky Boats, 26:12.
[58] www.youtube.com/watch?v=E3WJ10xGkas (0:15) Leaky Boats, 31:00.
[59] www.youtube.com/watch?v=E3WJ10xGkas (0:30) Leaky Boats, 31:50.

back to Indonesia on its own. One boat sank, drowning 350. In the course of the Committee's investigation some fascinating things were revealed.

On September 7, operation Relex encountered the first boat. The *Aceng* was warned not to enter Australian water. When it did, the Navy boarded it and tried to turn it back toward Indonesia. *Aceng* recommenced its journey toward Australia every time the boarding party left. "When the Master realised that again he was heading North towards Indonesia he became nervous and, pointing to himself, made slashing motions at his neck, and said 'Indonesia'."[60]

> On the third occasion that the boarding party was put aboard to direct the boat out of Australian waters, the behaviour of those on board became abusive, with threats of harm to the boarding party, smashing of windows in the wheelhouse, and objects thrown at the boarding personnel.[61]

Wary of killing one of the asylum seekers in the event of a more aggressive attempt to redirect the boat, the Navy gave up. At sunrise all 237 asylum-seekers were transferred to an Australian flag vessel that took them to Nauru for offshore processing. The next boat provoked a similar scenario. Once again there was a standoff, and one of the English-speaking passengers "indicated that his people would 'throw themselves overboard if they were taken back to Indonesia.'"[62] On September 12, four or five young men started a hunger strike on this boat too. By the next day, the group was transported to Nauru. The migrants had intended to reach Australia.

The Australian government's narrative presented to the Committee was one of gradual escalation in measures of "self-harm." Migrant and smuggler networks quickly spread the lessons of experience. Every new boat learned from the previous one, better prepared for intensifying the confrontation. There were sit-ins and hunger strikes; threats of self-harm and threats of harm to others; "intimidating behavior" toward Australian forces, protests, and riots. In some cases, asylum seekers sabotaged the boats they were in, and sometimes the Navy attempted to deploy engineers to repair the boats while still at sea. Migrants immolated their own boats or threw litter or excrement on the Australian forces.[63] In yet other cases, the Navy teams felt they

---

[60] A Certain Maritime Incident, 537.
[61] Report on a Certain Maritime Incident, 537.
[62] Report on a Certain Maritime Incident, 538.
[63] On one boat:

were charged with a mission they simply could not perform and had to withdraw.[64]

One testimony about a boat that arrived in late October includes an account of a young girl held overboard by an older woman. The child "appeared to be aged 4–5 years and had a cast on one arm. She was noticeably distressed," recalled an Australian member of the Navy.[65] A child was thrown overboard, yet it remains unclear if that was the girl with the injured arm. The only thing it seems fair to conclude is that the ambiguity of the report reflected general mayhem. As some asylum seekers jumped into the ocean, others started a fire in the hold and poured fuel on the deck. The boarding team counterattacked using pepper spray. Yet another report included testimony about a child being strangled. The confusion of the Australian forces is reflected by their accounts. The "strangulation" is described as a "family domestic incident, as a father prevented his daughter from joining in a riot by grabbing her near the throat region, pushing her to the ground and making her sit down."[66] At times the prevalent measures looked more like passive resistance in the tradition of anti-colonial and civil rights struggles.[67] As one Lieutenant put it: "During the riots, self harm and

> Extensive sabotage of the SIEV's [suspected irregular entry vessel] engineering plant was discovered and efforts were made by the Warramunga engineers to repair the boat. Those aboard the SIEV responded aggressively, starting fires, tearing up duckboards, attempting to kick out hull planks and ripping the bilge area apart. The situation was serious enough to cause the Warramunga to go to action stations in readiness for a potential safety of life at sea situation and only resolved when the potential illegal immigrants were shown that they were being videotaped and told that their actions would not assist their case with the Australian government.

A Certain Maritime Incident, 542.

[64] "The situation continued to worsen with all male PIIs [potential illegal immigrants] starting to riot and threaten the BP [boarding party] as a mass. I assessed that the situation could not be controlled without the use of high force and possibly lethal force. Having two unarmed BP [boarding party] members (the doctor and the interpreter) and no sign of the situation de-escalating without casualties I informed the Commanding Officer that I was conducting an emergency extraction" (insertions in the original). A Certain Maritime Incident, 540.

[65] Report on a Certain Maritime Incident, 543.

[66] A Certain Maritime Incident, 545.

[67] One Navy commander described the protest he encountered as "passive," even if angry:

> At approximately 1415, the [unauthorised arrivals] began staging passive protest by de-rigging their awning in the heat of the afternoon sun, sitting on the awning with children and refusing to allow holding party to re-rig the awning. Steaming party reported to me that [unauthorised arrivals]

threats to children became common place and were not seen to be out of the ordinary, almost a 'modus operandi'."[68]

More than a decade after the events, the philosophical challenge these cases present is still powerful.

Moral Risk and Moral Blackmail

Positive international law saturated the chaotic events that unfolded at Australia's maritime frontier between September and December 2001. It not only choreographed the moves of the Australian Navy. It also spelled out the modes of action that asylum seekers employed. In declaring an emergency, the executive branch rejected the idea that it owed legal duties to those who chose to enter Australia without authorization. The country's High Court endorsed this position. With Justice French deeming it irrelevant – and Justice Black ignoring it altogether – the justices disregarded the Refugee Convention almost completely.[69] The legislature immediately followed suit by normalizing the emergency policies, couching them in the web of transnational governance. But *Ruddock* still left intact an extremely limited positive

> had become angry, were ripping clothes, shouting at the steaming party and gesticulating in a threatening manner.

A Certain Maritime Incident, 544.
[68] A Certain Maritime Incident, 545.
[69] Justice French explained:

> Australia has obligations under international law by virtue of treaties to which it is a party, including the Refugee Convention of 1951 and the 1967 Protocol. Treaties are entered into by the Executive on behalf of the nation. They do not, except to the extent provided by statute, become part of the domestic law of Australia. The primary obligation which Australia has to refugees to whom the Convention applies is the obligation under Article 33 not to expel or return them to the frontiers of territories where their lives or freedoms would be threatened on account of their race, religion, nationality, or membership of a particular social group or their political opinions. The question whether all or any of the rescuees are refugees has not been determined. It is questionable whether entry by the Executive into a convention thereby fetters the executive power under the Constitution, albeit there may be consequences in relation to the processes to be applied in the exercise of that power or relevant statutory powers – Minister of State for Immigration and Ethnic Affairs v. Teoh (1995) 183 CLR 273. In this case, in my opinion, the question is moot because nothing done by the Executive on the face of it amounts to a breach of Australia's obligations in respect of *non-refoulement* under the Refugee Convention. (Ruddock, para. 203)

legal duty toward all human beings, regardless of membership in a polity: the duty to rescue humans drowning at sea. Two brief dicta explain this in the text of *Ruddock.*

The first point is the High Court's unanimous rejection of one of the Australian government's arguments on appeal. The government demanded that the court pronounce the asylum seekers' circumstances "self-inflicted" (the trial court had rejected that formulation). "There is nothing to be gained by the use of such pejorative terms as 'self-inflicted',"[70] wrote Justice French. The message is that if a person is drowning and calling for help there is a duty to save her even if she's the one who jumped. The second and more important point appears in a passage from Justice Beaumont's concurring opinion, in which he explains there is no obligation under international law to allow refugees into a sovereign state. Notice Beaumont's "postscript":

> Finally it should be added that this is a municipal, and not an international, court. Even if it were, whilst customary international law imposes an obligation upon a coastal state to provide humanitarian assistance to vessels in distress, international law imposes no obligation upon the coastal state to resettle those rescued in the coastal state's territory. This accords with the principles of the Refugee Convention. By Art 33, a person who has established refugee status may not be expelled to a territory where his life and freedom would be threatened for a Convention reason.[71]

Although the Australian government sought to eliminate the rights of encounter, Beaumont recognized a (limited) universal obligation that states have toward all humans as such. This is the humanitarian obligation to assist vessels in distress. The government never denied this obligation, though by claiming that the condition was self-inflicted it did suggest that it was being exploited in an objectionable way. This obligation's positive sources rest both upon treaty and upon custom.[72] This

---

[70] Ruddock, para. 212.
[71] Ruddock, para. 126.
[72] See Regulation 7, Chapter 5 of the Safety of Life at Sea Convention (1974):

> Each Contracting Government undertakes to ensure that necessary arrangements are made for distress communication and co-ordination in their area of responsibility and for the rescue of persons in distress at sea around its coasts. These arrangements shall include the establishment, operation, and maintenance of such search and rescue facilities as are deemed practicable and necessary, having regard to the density of the seagoing traffic and the navigational dangers and shall, so far as possible, provide adequate means of locating and rescuing such persons.

obligation is what Captain Rinnan talked about, when he said the fate of the Tampa asylum seekers was a humanitarian issue, not one of politics.

By assuming volition on the part of the migrants on *Tampa*, the government's argument that their situation was "self-inflicted" supported the Afghan migrants' own view that freedom, not just survival, was at stake. It was not only about demanding a life that is better than death. Ultimately, it was about membership. Ms. Hassan, who was a passenger on one of the migrant boats and whom I quoted above, obtained both refugee status and Australian citizenship. Would she have obtained this status but for the encounter the migrants generated? In a televised interview, she said that she feels part of Australian society. Her story thus illustrated in the most concrete way that a claim of survival as a human can be transformed into a claim of freedom as a citizen.[73] Recall, in this context, the argument of Chapter 2 concerning the question what is a human rights claim.

The political nature of the migrants' actions is reflected by the means they used in order to achieve their ends: their resistance to return to Indonesia, their demonstrations and riots, and their appeal to the Norwegian Ambassador. All these are traditional ways of collectively participating in powerful institutions. But the court refused to follow the government's attempt to cast them as *merely* political. That would presumably have canceled out any legal obligation toward these non-citizens. In the final analysis, the Australian court could not simply discard Captain Reenan's conviction that this was (also) a humanitarian matter.

To be sure, the arguments about self-inflicted circumstances, though rejected by the High Court, had enormous influence on the public debate on asylum seekers in the years to come. Ever since the "modus operandi" during "Relex" was exposed, this idea of self-harm has preoccupied the political imagination of Australians: politicians, administrators, lawyers, and laypeople. The same allegations crop up virtually everywhere significant numbers of asylum seekers appear.[74] "Moral Blackmail" was the

---

[73] See also, Cindy Wockner, "These are the people Australia didn't want - the controversial Tampa refugees reveal life now, news.com.au, June 11, 2015, available at http://www.news .com.au/national/these-are-the-people-australia-didnt-want-the-controversial-tampa- refugees-reveal-life-now/news-story/fa596f8167daf7e2641694c4b975f6bc (last accessed June 16, 2016).

[74] See, e.g., on May 31, 2012, British Member of the European Parliament Andrew Brons asked: "Who is to blame if seventy-two – Yes 72! – people set off across a dangerous sea route in a small – Yes Small! – rubber dingy?" and the answer: "The blame belongs first and foremost to those who travel to Europe for economic reasons and impose moral blackmail on their rescuers to grant them asylum." Available at http://andrewbrons.eu/index.php?

catchphrase coined to express the idea that such political "exploitation" of humanitarian duties was illegitimate. The phenomenon is not only moral, however, but political and legal as well.

The statements quoted above by John Howard and Phillip Ruddock may seem to have a family resemblance with the idea of "moral blackmail." They are, however, of a different register. Portraying the disturbing events of Relex as they did, they suggested a distinction between members of humanity and enemies of humanity. Ruddock suggested migrants were guilty of premeditated acts of murder, victimizing the most helpless members of their own families. Such an allegation is intended, first, to deny the political nature of the migrants' confrontation. This is a crime, not a way of challenging the existing world order. Such a heinous crime is supposed to render the criminal unworthy of compassion. The narrative of infanticide in effect banishes the parents beyond the pale of rationality, where they become the psychopathic protagonists of a blood libel. Howard went even further, suggesting that throwing children overboard was not merely murder. Migrants did not follow an *instinct* telling them to protect and love their children. They were guilty of violating the laws of nature, laws that humans are supposed to follow by their biological making. Their role is no longer psychopathic – it is monstrous. Unlike Arendt, for Howard unauthorized migrants were freaks of nature, not of law.[75]

On the other hand, there is an internal tension in the idea of "moral blackmail." The self is divided before the demand of the other.[76] The charge is introduced as an argument against migrants' measures of self-harm. But Australians (or members of any other polity) cannot be morally blackmailed, if the moral values that are appealed to by a party that engages in "blackmail" are not *their own*. If the bodies in the water really generated no claim upon the self, they would be morally irrelevant. Tearing apart their own boats and relying on duties of rescue, asylum seekers ostensibly exploited the law of rescue for ends foreign to its original meaning. A straightforwardly positivist understanding of the international law of rescue at sea would not suffice to explain this feat. Without a human rights

---

option=com_k2&view=item&id=538:if-illegal-immigrants-were-returned-home-immedi ately-their-relentless-flow-would-dry-up. See also: Donna Rachel Edmunds, "Watch: The Moment A Migrant Threatens to Throw A Newborn Baby at Greek Harbor Officers," Breitbart, April 7, 2016 available at http://www.breitbart.com/london/2016/04/07/watch-moment-migrant-threatens-throw-newborn-baby-greek-harbour-officers/ (last accessed June 16, 2016).

[75] Hannah Arendt, *The Origins of Totalitarianism* (New York: Harcourt, 1973), 278 (calling the stateless, or *apatride*, a "legal freak").

[76] See Simon Critchley, *Infinitely Demanding* (London and New York: Verso, 2007), 38–68.

commitment, a re-interpretation of the law as inapplicable to these cases would be readily available. Australian government lawyers could have simply said that the duty of rescue's purpose was to provide for mutual assistance between seafarers. Under a purposive interpretation, unauthorized migrants could simply be excluded from that category. If such an interpretation doesn't sound possible, it's not because it *contradicts* positive law. It is because we find ourselves bound by another, non-positive source of law: human rights law.

When someone provokes another to rescue her by employing self-harm, she *is* "exploiting" the other's convictions for her own political ends. But such convictions, both legal and ethical at the same time, can only be realized inasmuch as they are put to action. The very idea of "moral blackmail" thus runs in the opposite direction from the dehumanizing rhetoric of Howard and Ruddock. Its condition of possibility is that this form of "blackmail" morally implicates its addressee.

The idea of "moral blackmail" points to a duality of commitments within the same individual.[77] Explaining Emmanuel Lévinas's understanding of ethics, philosopher Simon Critchley opposes it to that of Kant. For Kant, the moral imperative follows from reason. Acting morally, we give ourselves the law. But when we respond to the temptations our senses expose us to, or seek our own pleasure, we are not following the dictates of reason but are subject to causation. In such moments, says Kant, we are not acting ethically, just as natural phenomena do not act ethically. Unlike Kant, Critchley explains, Lévinas does not banish desire from ethics. For Lévinas, the ethical imperative is something that is experienced in the world – paradigmatically in the encounter with the other. But, of course, not all temptations are ethical imperatives. Indeed, Lévinas believes that in the encounter with the other we also experience the temptation of violence. The vulnerability of the face of the other can make us want to destroy the face. As Critchley explains, at issue is a division within the individual between experiencing pleasure, which may include but is not limited to the pleasure of violence; and the ethical command. There is no attempt to say – as one may understand Kant to be saying – that ethics should overcome the temptation of pleasure seeking. Rather, both an ethical response to the other and unjustifiable violence toward the other are bound up with desire and neither can be extinguished.

---

[77] It thus recalls philosopher Simon Critchley's discussion of "dividualism." *See* Critchley, *Infinitely Demanding*, 38–68.

The division here is different but not unrelated. The agent wants to perform a task, in this case carrying out her duty as a border enforcement agent. But she also wants to perform another task, namely, to rescue human beings that are drowning at sea. Both tasks are inscribed in positive law. Closing the border is provided for by one's operational guidelines and is supported by a decision like *Ruddock*. Saving at sea is provided for in treaty and customary law of the sea. The migrants' strategy is to push state agents to decide which task reflects a more fundamental commitment. Such a strategy is absolutely absent from Lévinas's work. The actions of the *Other* (now capitalized) are strangely not accounted for. To amend this shortcoming in Lévinas's philosophy, I have proposed to talk about the *universal boatperson* (who is an agent) as opposed to the *Other* (who is not). In other words, we must talk about the other in lowercase: The other who can also be myself. As long as this lowercase other doesn't position herself as one's enemy, those committed to human rights cannot simply set aside the ethical-legal command the universal boatperson imposes. To use Critchley's lanaguage, this "dividualism" of positive-law and human rights commitments might characterize not only an individual but also a polity. Confronting the universal boatperson, an individual or a group is required to judge and make its own normative determination.

Able Seaman Bec Lynd of the Australian Navy gave a relevant assessment of the sentiments involved. Lynd was a member of the *Adelaide*'s crew and was posted under Banks' command during the events that came to be known as the "Children Overboard Affair." Rather than accusing the migrants of moral blackmail, Lynd spoke of her own *moral risk*. By sending her out to sea with a team that received guidelines on how to avoid engaging in rescue operations, the government not only exposed migrants to risks of drowning. It also put *her* in harm's way – potentially implicating her in the responsibility for unnecessary death. Lynd describes the avoidance of encounter strikingly: "If that had been the Manly Ferry in Sydney Harbor we would have rushed over there and gotten everyone off as quickly as possible. But we were to do whatever we could in order to avoid these people entering into Australian territory. And that would mean, if they came onto the boat, then they're in Australian territory."[78]

Lynd felt the government did not want to portray the boat people as connected with Australian values. Putting her at moral risk meant

---

[78] Leaky Boats, 33:55.

putting her at risk of having to violate precisely those values. Her resentment toward the operational instructions she received made it an intense
relief when the team finally raised living migrant bodies from the ocean.
The moment is described as nothing short of *catharsis*, leading to
newfound self-knowledge. Considered from a distance, the way she
described this encounter may sound somewhat banal. But the mere fact
that this could be experienced as a kind of revelation goes a considerable
way in explaining what it means to make the normative determination in
question: "I certainly had an overwhelming sense that these were
humans . . . they were not dogs, they were not animals. For me personally
that was a sort of *turning point*"[79] (emphasis added). Lynd's "turning
point" was when the human rights encounter – which the three branches
of government sought to eliminate – had resurfaced after all.

Both the cruelty and the hope of human rights are framed between the
two conceptions of moral blackmail and moral risk. *Precisely because
a demand to ignore a drowning person puts a sailor at moral risk, she is
amenable to moral blackmail.* Only someone who cannot be put at moral
risk is absolutely immune from such blackmail. Such immunity would
mean stepping out of the group that self-defines through human rights.
It would also mean defining some persons or groups as less than human.

Lynd's experience captures how as morally committed political actors
we can be bound to human rights, while still remaining members of an
exclusive community of *citizens*. As explained in Chapter 3, the experience figures as one of being bound simultaneously by two spheres of
obligation: the obligation to one's state, which in this case is represented
by the operational guidelines, and the duties that emanate from the
presence of another person. While Lynd's dissatisfaction upon being
exposed to moral risk is understandable, it might very well refer to an
inevitable condition of political life. For what it means to be acting in the
name of a government – and indeed what it means to be obeying the
positive law of one's country – is precisely to *assume* such a moral risk.
Positive law may contradict one's judgment or one's own self-defining
convictions. Far from banal, Lynd's account is poignant because she
stretched both normative commitments – to citizenship and to humanity – to the very limit of where they could still coexist.[80]

---

[79] Leaky Boats, 35:32.
[80] But one set of commitments can also collapse and give way to action exclusively according
to the other, in which cases, in retrospect, the actor will either be venerated as a hero or
accused as a villain.

Thus, engaging in moral blackmail is not about bringing your addressee to submission or about somehow defeating the addressee of your claim. The revelation or catharsis that Lynd expressed occurred only upon such moral blackmail. Rather than being *defeated*, her narrative is about a self that was discovered and prevailed. Taken together, the experiences of moral risk and moral blackmail constitute the citizen who claims to be bound by human rights.

Since antiquity, political membership and political freedom have been associated with the capacity for discourse.[81] But today migrants who make human rights demands do so, at least initially, with their bodies.[82] Their actions suggest a form of political participation that demands recognition as a human being who must not be killed. The duty a person overboard imposes on a vessel that encounters her is an embodied and radicalized claim of survival. It is a minimal duty toward all human beings that remains intact even under some perceived risk to the polity. Such a duty creates a concrete remedy of rescue, where no claim of freedom would do the same. The basis for such a claim is reflected in positive law but is not reducible to it. Making a claim with respect to this remedy requires no words: The body in the water performs it. Providing a remedy for a drowning individual falls on both private and public actors alike. A call of distress is comparable to a declaration of emergency. It is not however generated by a sovereign authority but rather by the seemingly powerless party in the human rights encounter.[83] When overboard, citizens and non-citizens are all in the position of *bare life*.

Lingering beyond the horizon of Banks's ship is a good metaphor for the contemporary state of human rights. While remaining nominally committed to human rights, governments of relatively well-off countries pursue policies designed to avoid the encounter in which human rights are enforced. When these policies are successful, no human rights remedies are provided. Human rights remain a dead letter on the books or empty rhetoric in the media.

Under these conditions, unauthorized migrants pursue various methods designed to press human rights remedies back into existence.

[81] See Hannah Arendt, *The Human Condition* (Chicago: University of Chicago Press, 1998).
[82] Compare with Judith Butler, "Bodies in Alliance and the Politics of the Street," September 2011, available at www.eipcp.net/transversal/1011/butler/en (last accessed May 12, 2016).
[83] Compare with Ariella Azoulay's conception of an emergency claim. Ariella Azoulay, *The Civil Contract of Photography* (Cambridge: MIT Press, 2008), 27.

They cabin state authorities in the limited space that exists between moral risk and moral blackmail. Employing measures of self-harm, they stretch the notion of the rights of encounter to its conceptual limits. They make political use of the meager legal categories that apply to all humans and demonstrate that these categories are not reducible to positive law. An ethical force field surrounds the unauthorized migrant boat. The Navy stays away, precisely *because* the felt duty within that field demands of members of the crew that they exercise judgment that will, in some way, implicate and define them as well.

What will happen to these migrants after the encounter remains a question. The best-case scenario from the perspective of the migrant is the granting of access to asylum, which may ultimately lead to a grant of citizenship. This does not necessarily have to be citizenship in a particular polity. Resettlement may send a refugee far away, as described in Chapter 2. What matters is that citizenship is realized as a functioning social contract and does not simply become an empty placeholder that serves to eliminate a refugee's presence. In the particular instances examined above, it might be either Australian citizenship or resettlement elsewhere. The label of the universal boatperson aims to capture and call attention to a moment in which the particular social contract has not been determined. Her action is a condition for access to any polity. For this reason, such action is so important for the understanding of law.

5

The Place Where We Stand

There may be something disturbingly incomplete, perhaps even misleading, in comparing "a refugee" to "a vessel on the open sea, not sailing under any flag."[1] This analogy, introduced at the opening of Chapter 1, may suggest that the human rights encounter happens fortuitously. But it would be a mistake to imagine the self suddenly struck by a duty that is both ethical and legal. A crucial question is how power struggles shape the conditions that allow such an encounter to occur or prevent it from occurring in the first place. Previous chapters address this question, though indirectly. Taking on this question requires quite a different analysis from what I offered so far. Such analysis is about the transformations of the environment in which encounters appear or disappear. And it is about the possibility of influencing such transformations. The place where we stand when the human rights encounter occurs is not naturally given. It is manufactured by political and economic power, history, culture, and technology. Fortunes are spent in reshaping it and lives are lost in attempts to reconfigure it. Addressing these structural conditions requires a shift in focus. It cannot be done by considering the human rights encounter from the internal point of view of one of its two parties. The position of an implicated third-party observer, responding to the human rights encounter after it occurred, is also not helpful. To discuss the space where the human rights encounter occurs, it is necessary to try to think of the human rights encounter from an external point of view. Attention must be granted not only to such encounters after they had already occurred. Equally important are those that have not yet taken place or that are yet to take place.

This chapter focuses on two journeys that embarked from Libya and aimed to reach Italy, one in 2009 and the other in 2011. By revisiting these

---

[1] See Paul Weis, "The International Protection of Refugees," *American Journal of International Law* 48, no. 2 (1954): 193–221. See the same assertion in Erwin Loewenfeld, "Status of Statless Persons," *Transactions of the Grotius Society* 27 (1941): 59–112.

much-discussed cases, the chapter explores the ways in which various actors have in recent years partaken in manufacturing the place where the human rights encounter occurs. This is the place in which the relatively powerless party addresses the relatively powerful one. Think once again of Max Weber's implicit reference to place in his famous formulation of an ethics of conviction: "Here I stand, I can do no other."[2] When the human rights encounter occurs, the universal boatperson aims to evoke such a response by projecting the message: here you stand. You, and no one else, will decide if I will live or die.[3] But where do I stand, when I say that I can do no other? An account of the active construction of the space in which the human rights encounter occurs is a necessary aspect of a larger theory of the human rights encounter at the foundations of international law.

The discussion begins with a brief look at the European Court of Human Rights (ECtHR) judgment in *Hirsi Jamaa and Others* v. *Italy*.[4] The Court conceptualizes state jurisdiction in a way that reflects the notion of the human rights encounter as developed thus far. The Court recognizes that an asymmetric encounter, in which a state party takes control over the fate of non-members of its own polity, creates duties toward those people. What are the forces, political, economic, and other, that constructed this encounter? What are the forces that are ignored or taken for granted in this particular construction of the human rights encounter? And how will the judgment itself become a force constructing encounters yet to come? One main way in which the human rights encounter has been manufactured anew in recent years was through the use of technology. Border-enforcement agencies at the margins of Europe pioneered the transformation of encounter using advanced surveillance systems. States have often been able to carry out policies that likely fall beyond their own jurisdiction and beyond the jurisdiction of ECtHR. But unauthorized migrants and activists supporting them have also used technologies to manufacture the jurisdictional conditions in which they make their own human rights claims.

The two groups may seem to be struggling against each other – each aiming to utilize jurisdiction for its own needs.[5] It is no doubt true that their purposes are different. Yet from the perspective of an inquiry into the

---

[2] Max Weber, *The Vocation Lectures* (Hacket Publishing, 2004), 92.
[3] See Chapter 1.
[4] *Hirsi Jamaa and Others* v. *Italy*, Application No. 27765/09.
[5] Lorenzo Pezzani and Charles Heller, "A Disobedient Gaze: Strategic Interventions in the Knowledge(s) of Maritime Borders," *Postcolonial Studies* 16, no. 3 (2013): 289–298, 191.

ways in which the space of the human rights encounter is transformed, this opposition is of secondary importance. In and around the Mediterranean Sea, both border-enforcement authorities and migrants have simultaneously ushered in new patterns of jurisdiction. In the Mediterranean perhaps even more than elsewhere, "borders are not stable and 'univocal', but instead, 'multiple', shifting in meaning and function from group to group."[6]

We will have to consider the possibility that the human rights encounter – at least as a label denoting an actual physical event – is no longer possible. But is the theory of the non-positive foundations of human rights law really about the physical event? Ultimately, I invoke these events in order to illuminate an imagination at the basis of international law alongside the social contract as the imaginary basis of sovereignty. The next chapter thus turns to imagination.

The Human Rights Encounter Enforced in Court

In *Hirsi Jamma et al.* v. *Italy*,[7] ECtHR discussed the plight of migrants and refugees that left Libya for Italy in 2009. In this judgment (from February 2012), we find what seems to be a positive legal recognition of the non-positive law of the human rights encounter. Law traditionally applies to anyone within the territory of a state and to any citizen of the state. These are the bounds of the social contract, delineated by what Arendt described as "the holy trinity between people-territory-state."[8] *Hirsi* recognizes that a physical, embodied meeting between state agents and non-members of the polity, in which the latter come within the state's control, triggers the state's human rights duties. As others have explained, this happens when a state party to this encounter has "factual authority" over individuals.[9] To be sure, *Hirsi* does not advance an entirely new doctrine of personal jurisdiction. The Court has developed this doctrine of personal jurisdiction over time, in a number of important cases that have generated considerable commentary both in

[6] Alison Kesby, "The Shifting and Multiple Border and International Law," *Oxford Journal of Legal Studies* 27, no. 1 (2007): 101.

[7] Hirsi, Eur. Ct. H.R. (Grand Chamber No. 27765/09) (hereinafter Hirsi).

[8] Hannah Arendt, *The Origins of Totalitarianism*, New edition (New York: Harcourt, Brace, Jovanovich, 1973), 232.

[9] Samatha Besson, "The Extraterritoriality of the European Convention on Human Rights: Why Human Rights Depend on Jurisdiction and What Jurisdiction Amounts to," *Leiden Journal of International Law* 25 (2012): 864.

academia and in the legal profession.[10] Through this doctrine, the court has gradually expanded the notion of jurisdiction for the purposes of human rights based judicial review. Responses have varied from considerable enthusiasm to a measure of skepticism.[11]

The Court reviewed Italian–Libyan cooperation in enforcing maritime borders. Judge Pinto De Albuquerque's concurrence begins with the recognition that "The ultimate question in this case is how Europe should recognise that refugees have 'the right to have rights', to quote Hannah Arendt."[12] Appropriately, his answer to this question appears in the final lines of his opinion. Here, he embraces Justice Harry Blackmun's dissent in *Sale* v. *Haitian Centers Council*.[13] *Hirsi* thus seems to demonstrate what an institutional enforcement of the non-positive human rights constituted by the human rights encounter may look like. If securing or solidifying these rights advances us toward a better world, *Hirsi* is a historic judgment.[14] An institution lauded as the world's leading human rights court says that freedom cannot be decoupled from survival. Rescuing lives is bound up with granting "the right to be heard" – to use Blackmun's memorable language.

The case may thus be read as a firm recognition of the non-positive character of human rights law. From now on, migrants and refugees making human rights claims will no longer have to rely on the command

[10] See, e.g., *Drozd and Janousek* v. *France and Spain*, June 26, 1992, § 91, Series A no. 240; *Banković and Others* v. *Belgium and Others* (Dec.), [GC], no. 52207/99, § 66, ECHR 2001–XII) § 67; *Ilaşcu and Others* v. *Moldova and Russia* [GC], no. 48787/99, § 311, ECHR 2004–VII) § 314).

[11] Tom De Boer, "Closing Legal Black Holes: The Role of Extraterritorial Jurisdiction in Refugee Rights Protection," *Journal of Refugee Studies* 28, no. 1 (2014): 1–17; Maarten Den Heijer, "Reflections on Refoulement and Collective Expulsion in the Hirsi Case," *International Journal of Refugee Law* 25, no. 2 (2012): 265–290 (on the enthusiastic side); David A. Martin, *Interdiction of Asylum Seekers: The Realms of Policy and Law in Refugee Protection*, SSRN Scholarly Paper (Rochester, NY: Social Science Research Network, September 1, 2014), available at http://papers.ssrn.com/abstract=2500469 (last accessed May 12, 2016); Itamar Mann, "Dialectic of Transnationalism: Unauthorized Migration and Human Rights, 1993-2013," *Harvard International Law Journal* 54, no. 2 (2013): 315 (on the skeptical side).

[12] Hirsi, p. 59. See also footnote 1 on the same page, where De Albuquerque quotes "We Refugees," the text that has also been discussed in Chapter 3.

[13] See Chapter 3.

[14] See Simon Cox, "Case Watch: European Ruling Affirms the Right of Migrants at Sea," Open Society Justice Initiative, February 27, 2012. Available at www .opensocietyfoundations.org/voices/case-watch-european-ruling-affirms-the-rights-of -migrants-at-sea (last accessed May 12, 2016).

of the conscience (as explained in Chapter 3). The European Convention on Human Rights and International Refugee Law limit state action extraterritorially. According to the court's view, jurisdiction stems from effective control rather than territoriality.[15] As reflected by the Court's words in a previous famous case, Al-Skeini, the doctrine of effective control imagines jurisdiction as an encounter in conditions of radical power asymmetry: "Jurisdiction flows not only from the exercise of democratic governance, not only from ruthless tyranny, not only from colonial usurpation. It also hangs from the mouth of a firearm. In non-combat situations, everyone in the line of fire of a gun is within the authority and control of whoever is wielding it."[16] For ECtHR, this imperative to protect the human rights of those under state jurisdiction is also grounded in a treaty, the European Convention on Human Rights (ECHR). Article 1 ECHR provides that "The High contracting Parties shall secure to everyone within their jurisdiction the rights and freedoms" defined in the Convention.

The applicants to the Court in *Hirsi*, eleven Somali and thirteen Eritrean nationals, were part of a group of about 200 men and women that left Libya in three vessels, aiming to reach Italy. On May 6, 2009, three Italian coastguard ships intercepted them on the high seas. The passengers of the vessels were transferred onto Italian military ships and returned to Tripoli. Upon arrival at the Port of Tripoli, a mixed Italian–Libyan crew handed the migrants over to the Libyan authorities. As the applicants to the Court testified, they requested refugee protection and initially refused to disembark. They were forced to leave the Italian ships and were transferred back to Libyan custody.[17] The Italian authorities announced the operation was performed under bilateral

---

[15] This doctrine is in stark distinction to the United States' position, according to which human rights treaties do not apply extraterritorially. For a study of this doctrine in the United States, see Kal Raustalia, *Does the Constitution Follow the Flag?: The Evolution of Territoriality in American Law* (New York: Oxford University Press, 2009). See also Charlie Savage, "U.S. Seems Unlikely to Accept That Rights Treaty Applies to Its Actions Abroad," *New York Times*, March 6, 2014, available at www.nytimes.com /2014/03/07/world/us-seems-unlikely-to-accept-that-rights-treaty-applies-to-its-actions -abroad.html (last accessed May 12, 2016).

[16] *Al-Skeini* v. *United Kingdom*, App. No. 55721/07, Eur. Ct. H.R. (2011), available at www .unhcr.org/refworld/docid/4e2545502.html (last accessed May 12, 2016). Compare this to Arendt's reference to throwing a stone in "We Refugees," as explained in Chapter 3, and to the reading of Rousseau at the end of the Conclusion.

[17] Hirsi, para. 11. Like the deportees of the 1947 Exodus ship (described in Chapter 1).

agreements with Libya and "represented an important turning point in the fight against clandestine immigration."[18]

The applicants' principal argument was that Italy violated their rights under Article 3 ECHR – prohibiting torture and inhuman and degrading treatment. Protections under Article 3 are conceived of as absolute. Italian enforcement authorities, the applicants argued, realized that transferring them to Libya would result in violation of their most fundamental of fundamental rights. In doing so, they did what Italians, as members of the Council of Europe who are thus bound to the ECHR, must never do. In its judgment, ECtHR goes into some detail regarding the relevant agreements between Italy and Libya. These agreements illustrate that what I have called the human rights encounter is always constructed by power. Needless to say, these agreements have not been in place since the fall of Muamar Qadaffi's government. But they are the legal framework that was before the ECtHR in *Hirsi*, and they remain relevant as examples of particular genre of transnational policymaking. Particularly relevant is Article 2 of a bilateral cooperation agreement, dated December 29, 2007:

> Italy and the "Great Socialist People's Libyan Arab Jamahiriya" undertake to organise maritime patrols using six ships made available on a temporary basis by Italy. Mixed crews shall be present on ships, made up of Libyan personnel and Italian police officers, who shall provide training, guidance and technical assistance on the use and handling of the ships. Surveillance, search and rescue operations shall be conducted in the departure and transit areas of vessels used to transport clandestine immigrants, both in Libyan territorial waters and in international waters, in compliance with the international conventions in force and in accordance with the operational arrangements to be decided by the two countries.[19]

In a following agreement dated February 4, 2009, the Italian–Libyan cooperation was expanded. As part of their mutual commitment, the countries specified that the ships would become Libyan property and that "The two countries undertake to repatriate clandestine immigrants and to conclude agreements with the countries of origin in order to limit

---

[18] Hirsi, para. 13. The basic model is one already analyzed above, in the context of Haitian–American cooperation (Chapter 3) and Australia's cooperation with its Pacific partners (Chapter 4). The Minister of Interior told the country's Senate that between May 6 and 10, 471 migrants had been similarly intercepted on the high seas and transferred to Libya.

[19] Hirsi, para. 19.

clandestine immigration."[20] When the United States Supreme Court examined a comparable policy in *Sale*, it upheld it (see Chapter 3). In *Ruddock*, the Australian High Court gave a similar answer (see Chapter 4). ECtHR considered the case not only under the 1951 Refugee Convention but also under the European Convention on Human Rights, which neither the US nor Australian courts are bound by. But advocates believed this case could provide persuasive precedent also for courts outside the gamut of the European Convention on Human Rights. The most important part of the ECtHR's opinion in this context is its discussion of jurisdiction.

The Italian government argued that the interdiction of the migrant boat was a rescue operation. Italian military ships intervened under the United Nations Convention on the Law of the Sea (UNCLOS) and the International Convention on Maritime Search and Rescue, in order to "deal with a situation of immediate danger that the vessels had been in and to save the lives" of the migrants.[21] This wasn't border control, and therefore Italy had no obligation toward the migrants beyond saving them from the threat of drowning.[22] But the Court rejected this argument. It noted that a ship sailing under a state's flag is under the jurisdiction of that state. Italy had an obligation to grant asylum seekers access to human rights protections, most importantly from *refoulement*. The court identifies how Italy manipulated jurisdiction: "Italy cannot circumvent its 'jurisdiction' . . . by describing the events at issue as rescue operations on the high seas."[23] The Italian manipulation here was intended precisely to avoid the human rights encounter.

The fact that the removal of the migrants to Libyan territory took place entirely on board boats carrying the Italian flag signaled that "the applicants were under the continuous and exclusive de jure and de facto

---

[20] The cooperative framework the two countries put in place went further than what the court specified in its judgment. Among other provisions that dealt with Libyan development and oil sales, it included an Italian apology for the country's policies during Libya's colonization. Although other interests came into play in this area of Italian foreign policy, assigning border-enforcement tasks to its neighbor on the Southern Mediterranean coast was high on Italy's priority list.

[21] Hirsi, para. 95.

[22] Compare to similar arguments voiced both in Chapter 3 and in Chapter 4. Indeed "Protecting people from harming themselves" is a globally-pervasive "justification for regulation" of borders. See Chantal Thomas, "Undocumented Migrant Workers in a Fragmented International Order," *Maryland Journal of International Law* 25 (2010): 187–229, 193.

[23] Hirsi, para. 79.

control of the Italian authorities." The court goes further than just considering if Italian or Libyan forces physically held the migrants.[24] Migrants, the court observed, are regularly maltreated in Libya. Once in Libya, they are at risk of being sent back to dangerous countries such as Eritrea and Somalia, with no access to asylum granted. Italian authorities knew this and therefore violated the absolute prohibitions of inhuman and degrading treatment and *refoulement* under Article 3 of ECHR. These prohibitions are uncompromising, even "In time of war or other public emergency threatening the life of the nation . . ."[25] The underlying question in determining de facto jurisdiction is one about power: when the migrants met with the boat that returned them to Libya, which authority had power over their bodies, as well as the ability to hear their demands?

Judge Pinto De Albuquerque of ECtHR symbolically "overturned" the historical decision in *Sale*. As mentioned above, the final words of his opinion are a heartfelt tribute to Blackmun's dissent. Like Blackmun, ECtHR asserts "a right to be heard." Like Blackmun, De Albuquerque too went beyond positive or natural law to ground this assertion. The judge appealed to a narrative about identity.[26] This time the story is about "We Europeans," not about "We the People." Implicitly, De Albuquerque acknowledges that human rights commitments are not only a matter of treaty law. They are deeply connected to a particular imagination of the self (whether in singular or in plural form) and to a view about what the self should stand for:[27]

> The words of Justice Blackmun are so inspiring that they should not be forgotten. Refugees attempting to escape Africa do not claim a right of admission to Europe. They demand only that Europe, the cradle of human rights idealism and the birthplace of the rule of law, cease closing its doors to people in despair who have fled from arbitrariness and brutality. That is a very modest plea, vindicated by the European Convention on Human Rights. We should not close our ears to it.[28]

---

[24] Compare this with the case of the Salamis, Niels Frenzen, "Italy Conducted De Facto Push-Back of Migrants by Ordering Cargo Ship to Rescue and Transport Migrants to Libya," *Migrants at Sea*, August 13, 2013, available at http://migrantsatsea.wordpress.com /2013/08/13/italy-conducted-de-facto-push-back-of-migrants-by-ordering-cargo-ship-to-rescue-and-transport-migrants-to-libya/ (last accessed May 12, 2016).

[25] The European Convention on Human Rights, Article 15.1.

[26] In what I have called in Chapter 3 "the constitutionalist model." Compare also to the discussion of Jean-Claude Juncker's State of the Union speech in Chapter 6.

[27] This imaginary aspect of human rights commitments is taken on directly in the next chapter.

[28] Hirsi, para. 82.

With *Hirsi*, it may seem international human rights law found a doctrinal toolbox to protect individuals that have lost de facto or de jure membership in a polity. This conclusion is what De Albuquerque's return to the problem of the "right to have rights" amounts to. As De Albuquerque writes, "The ultimate question in this case is how Europe should recognise that refugees have 'the right to have rights' to quote Hannah Arendt." Italy had restructured the encounter in a corrupted, potentially harmful way through its bilateral agreements with Libya. The Court strips away that added layer. Scratching the surface, it purportedly finds an authentic encounter: the real place where Italian agents under the Court's own jurisdiction stood and took their action.[29] Simon Cox, one of the lawyers involved in this case, traced the thread leading from *Sale* to *Hirsi*. This new precedent, he explained, may help counter anti-migrant developments in Australian policies (which directly continued those described in the previous chapter):

> The clear and far-reaching opinion of Judge Pinto de Albuquerque shows the stark contrast between this result in Strasbourg and the much criticized ruling of the US Supreme Court in Sale v. Haitian Centers Council, which upheld the action of US coast-guard vessels in intercepting and repatriating Haitian migrant boats. The judgment is already being cited in Australia's debate over migrant boats, as the country's opposition coalition argues for the adoption of a similar "push-back" policy. By requiring states to guarantee human rights beyond their state's territorial boundaries, Europe's human rights court has upheld the primacy of fundamental rights and the rule of law.[30]

But is this particular notion of an encounter really more natural, or authentic, than other alternative understandings? And what effect does the *positive* recognition of the encounter have on a general field of power, in which actors with differing interests are often in a struggle against each other?

Restructuring the Encounter

Around the time the migrant boats discussed in *Hirsi* embarked, surveillance technologies transformed the maritime space of the

---

[29] To illustrate through an example from an entirely different area of law, the question the court confronts here is not dissimilar to the kind of question tax courts often confront. Did a particular transaction have a business purpose or was it artificially designed to reduce tax? Just as such a court must have an idea what a real transaction is, the human rights court must have an idea what a real encounter is. On this tax law analogy, see also: Thomas Gammeltoft-Hansen, "International Refugee Law and Refugee Policy: The Case of Deterrence Policies," *Journal of Refugee Studies* 27, no. 4 (2014): 14.

[30] Cox, "Case Watch."

Mediterranean.[31] Similar technological restructuring in another part of the world was suggested in Chapter 4: remember how Norman Banks and the *Adelaide* waited beyond the horizon. Thanks to surveillance technologies that were available to them, coastguard authorities could take a bird's-eye view and inspect the migrants' behavior from afar. The migrants couldn't make a human rights claim when only one side encountered the other. The parties to the human rights encounter were not standing in the same place. Comparable dynamics have also developed on the US–Mexican border, where drones and other surveillance technologies have transformed the border into a much wider "borderland."[32] On the outskirts of Europe, this restructuring of space reached a new extreme in the beginning of the second decade of the twenty-first century.

In the first decade of the twenty-first century, the enforcement of European borders further developed the disaggregated form that the United States pioneered in its relations with Haiti in the 1980s. The fingerprints of this kind of enforcement are discernible, for example, in the provisions of the Italian–Libyan agreement quoted above. But here, an added layer of surveillance technologies facilitated new forms of police cooperation, further augmenting the model. The idea was to detect unauthorized migrant boats before they left territorial waters belonging to African countries. Partner police forces in relevant non-European countries were to be informed and were expected to intercept the boats under their own authority to control seaports. Similar to the relationship between Australia and Nauru, developing countries took this role for compensation: foreign aid, military assistance, services, and training were all on the table. Consider some of the techniques applied by Frontex – an EU agency based in Warsaw – tasked with the mandate to coordinate member-state border police forces.[33] Since 2006, Frontex has facilitated "joint operations," in which the forces of different

---

[31] There is a large European "critical security studies" literature on this. Vaughan-Williams surveys this academic terrain in Nick Vaughan-Williams, "Borderwork beyond Inside/Outside? Frontex, the Citizen-Detective and the War on Terror," *Space and Polity* 12, no. 1 (2008): 63–79. For background, see also Lori Nessel, "Externalized Borders and the Invisible Refugee," *Columbia Human Rights Law Review* 40 (2009): 625–629.

[32] Derek Gregory, "The Everywhere War," *The Geographical Journal* 177, no. 3 (2011): 238–250.

[33] See, e.g., Apostolis Fotiadis, "Drones May Track Migrants," *Inter Press Service*, November 1, 2010, available at www.ipsnews.net/2010/11/europe-drones-may-track-migrants/ (last accessed May 12, 2016; discussing "win–win" solutions for border enforcement and the technology industry).

European member states acted together to enforce borders. Their operations sent ships as far as Senegal to monitor migrant boats that left Africa
for Europe. Once they were spotted by "joint operations," the coast
authorities of countries like Mauritania and Senegal were summoned to
intercept them – with no violation of the Refugee Convention.[34] While
European states were clearly projecting power, their jurisdiction was
avoided.

A form of knowledge called "risk analysis" employs patterns of migration detected inside and outside of Europe in order to predict where
"migration pressures" will emerge next.[35] Ilkka Laitinen, Frontex's
Finnish Executive Director, speaking after *Hirsi*, described the organization's strategy as a "common pre-frontier intelligence picture."[36]
By using drones and satellite images, Frontex recorded a "real-time
image" of areas outside EU's borders, including the Mediterranean Sea
and North African countries. Surveillance equipment would detect the
movement of migrants in these "pre-frontier" areas. Part of their success,
explained Laitinen, is due to the organization's partnership with the
technology industry. Industry actors "have been able to make border
guards think things in a new way."

At the end of April 2013, Spain launched the (ironically named)
CLOSEYE,[37] a project aimed to provide the EU "with an operational
and technical framework that increases situational awareness and
improves the reaction capability of authorities surveying the external
borders of the EU." Arsenio Fernandez de Mesa, head of Spain's

---

[34] See Seline Trevisanut, "Maritime Border Control and the Protection of Asylum-Seekers in
the Eurpean Union," *Touro International Law Review* 12 (2009): 157–161, 159.

[35] In its annual risk reports, Frontex "combines an assessment of threats and vulnerabilities
at the EU external borders, with an estimation of their impacts and consequences to
enable the Agency to effectively balance and prioritize the allocation of resources against
identified risks." These reports are formulated as forecasts. By studying the flows of
migration over time (to use the agency's own terminology) and the factors that influence
it, Frontex predicts where pressures at the border will appear next. According to these
predictions, the agency issues its offers to member states – recommendations where to
deploy "joint operations." All recommendations are couched in the language of
cost–benefit analysis, making the decision where and how to send ships to conduct
enforcement a technical one, quite similar to administrative decisions on preparing for
a natural catastrophe, for example. This allows the EU to allocate funds for border
enforcement accordingly, spatially reshaping the maritime border according to the ebbs
and flows of destitute populations washed upon its beaches.

[36] http://euobserver.com/fortress-eu/118471. See also www.statewatch.org/news/2013/
may/09eu-frontex-opa.html (both last accessed May 12, 2016).

[37] The acronym stands for "collaborative evaluation of border surveillance technologies in
maritime environment by pre-operational validation of innovative solutions."

Guardia Civil, reportedly said at the CLOSEYE launch meeting that "The Guardia Civil aims to protect the Spanish and Europeans as well as helping those who risk their lives at sea for a better future in Europe." According to research by the EU monitor organization Statewatch, the Moroccan paper *Ya Biladi* quoted a Spanish official explaining that CLOSEYE would "quickly send alerts on what's going on without waiting for migrants or mafia to reach the Spanish coast."[38] In this configuration, there is no place for a powerful party committed to human rights and a disempowered party seeking protection to meet each other. The story that came to be known as that of the left-to-die boat illustrates the construction of a space in which the human rights encounter is no longer possible.

The Elimination of Encounter

Late in November 2013, contradictory reports by both Libyan and international sources emerged about the interception of 300 Europe-bound migrants. As the reports had it, this group of Africans left Libya's shores for Europe but were detected and returned to Libya where they were transferred to immigration detention. While one Libyan source said that Libyan forces were involved, *Reuters* reported that the intercepting vessels were registered as Libyan but staffed by a Maltese crew. The *Reuters* report was initially reprinted by *The Times of Malta*.[39] Within a few days, the newspaper published a clarification by the Maltese government: "no Malta-registered boats or Maltese citizens were involved in transporting 300 migrants stopped by the Libyan coastguard."[40]

As long as jurisdiction is associated with encounter, surveillance technologies open possibilities for conducting policy beyond jurisdiction. They reintroduce the scenario the Court struck down in *Hirsi* yet embed it in a different transnational institutional structure. The perfection of such a model means that it would no longer be necessary for Europe to enforce its border at all. From the perspectives of would-be asylum seekers and migrants, however, such a situation wouldn't be any better than a situation in which European vessels push them back to

---

[38] http://database.statewatch.org/article.asp?aid=32328 (last accessed May 12, 2016).

[39] www.timesofmalta.com/articles/view/20131129/local/libyas-coastguard-picks-up-almost-300-african-migrants.496840#.UpmckX-9KSM (last accessed May 12, 2016).

[40] www.timesofmalta.com/articles/view/20131208/local/No-Maltese-boats-in-Libya-incident.498016 (last accessed May 12, 2016).

where they came from. European border enforcement would thus be able to achieve the goals Italy achieved in *Hirsi*, without violating the Court's judgment. While more people's lives might be saved from drowning, the human rights encounter would cease to occur. Saving lives in this vision is strictly and exclusively about survival. Inasmuch as one understands the human rights claims and commitments in the framework I proposed in Chapters 2 and 3, access to human rights remedies is shut off.

When Europe and the United States assisted the rebellion against Qadaffi in 2011, the dictator exploited migration for political ends.[41] On March 27, 2011, at the height of the NATO-backed uprising against Qadaffi, a migrant boat provided by the Libyan military embarked for Lampedusa with seventy-two people on board. Among its passengers were forty-seven Ethiopians, seven Nigerians, seven Eritreans, six Ghanaians, and five Sudanese migrants. Twenty were women and two were children – the youngest of them one year old. They lost their way at sea and finally landed on April 10 in Zlitan, Southeast Libya. Eleven disembarked and two died upon landing. If *Hirsi* appears as a realization of the law of encounter, the left-to-die boat demonstrates what it means for this kind of encounter to become impossible.[42]

The migrants sent distress signals that reached the Italian Maritime Rescue Coordination Center (MRCC). According to their testimonies, they encountered military authorities and civilian boats several times, but no one would help. Several NGOs documented the migrants' trajectories and filed a lawsuit in their name against authorities that allegedly ignored them.[43]

The vessel first came to the attention of MRCC shortly after embarkation. When the migrants saw a military helicopter approaching a few

---

[41] "Gaddafi Wants EU Cash to Stop African Migrants," *BBC News*, available at www.bbc.com/news/world-europe-11139345 (last accessed May 12, 2016). Compare with the Vietnamese government's strategy, explained in Chapter 2; and also with the more recent strategies of the Islamic State (IS): "ISIS Threatens to Send 500,000 Migrants to Europe As a 'Weapon'," *Mail Online*, February 18, 2015, available at www.dailymail.co.uk/news/article-2958517/The-Mediterranean-sea-chaos-Gaddafi-s-chilling-prophecy-interview-ISIS-threatens-send-500-000-migrants-Europe-psychological-weapon-bombed.html.

[42] And it is perhaps not by chance that precisely when the encounter is realized in positive law, its physical possibility disappears.

[43] As Lorenzo Pezzani explained in an interview in November 20, 2012, the lawsuit is being processed in the French legal system. According to a conversation I had with one of the activists involved, the strategy is to quickly "exhaust domestic remedies" and carry the case onto ECtHR.

hours later, they believed rescue was on its way. The helicopter "circled around us 4–5 times and came closer. It was making a lot of wind, and we almost lost our balance."[44] A photograph taken from the helicopter illustrates this close-up examination. "I think I saw them take our picture. I think I saw a photo camera or something like that," said one survivor, Abukurke Kabatto. The migrants made it abundantly clear that their *survival* was at stake: "The helicopter came very close to us down, we showed him our babies, we showed them we finished oil, we tell them 'Please help us'" [sic]. The helicopter left the area, but the migrants' "Captain" informed the passengers of anticipated rescue. He then tossed overboard his GPS, his satellite phone, and his compass, apparently to protect himself from criminal charges for smuggling or trafficking crimes.

After waiting in vain for rescue, the migrants decided to continue searching their way at sea. "When the fishermen saw the migrants' boat arriving . . . they drew in their nets and sailed away swiftly . . ." The same helicopter appeared again, this time lowering water and biscuits for the migrants before leaving. They finally ran out of fuel and started drifting. Left without food or water, they began drinking seawater and their own urine mixed with toothpaste. People started dying in increasing numbers. "During the night we would see the lights of other big boats in the distance, we could not see them but the reflection of their lights looked like a city in the distance," said Kabatto. After five to six days of drifting, a military ship approached the migrant boat. "At first the ship was far. Maybe 700 meters. They then circled around us, three times, until they came very close, 10 meters. We are watching them, they are watching us. We are showing them the dead bodies. We drank water from the sea to show them we were thirsty. The people on the boat took pictures, nothing else." Finally, the migrants drifted back to Libya.[45]

---

[44] Unless stated otherwise, all testimonies from the migrants are from Charles Heller, Lorenzo Pezzani, and Situ Studio, "Report on the 'Left to Die'" (Forensic Oceanography, Centre for Research Architecture, Goldsmiths, University of London, 2012) available at www.forensic-architecture.org/publications/report-on-the-left-to-die-boat/ (last accessed May 12, 2016) (hereinafter Heller et al., "Report on the 'Left to Die' ").

[45] Kabatto recounted these last parts of the journey. They were released from detention after humiliating treatment by the Libyan authorities:

> "The wind and the sea made us drift on Libyan land, to a small village area near Misrata. When we reached that place we didn't know it was Libya, we thought it was Italy! When we reached the land one girl died within the hour. The military took the ten of us to a pharmacy, not a hospital. They only gave us a bit of water and took us to prison in Zlitan. We spent three days there. Without food. One more of our brothers died there

On May 8, 2011, *The Guardian* exposed this chain of events to European readers: "Aircraft Carrier Left us to Die, Say Migrants." The MRCC distributed the distress call among seafarers. Under the law of the sea, such a distress call creates the obligation to assist. But the call was ignored. On October 3, 2011, NATO's spokesperson admitted to having received a warning sent from the Italian coast guard to all ships in the area. NATO explained that this warning did not call for assistance but only asked to notify sighting the boat. It admitted however that the closest NATO vessel was only 24 miles away. This "abdication of responsibility," said Eritrean priest Father Musie Zerrai, "constitutes a crime, and that crime cannot go unpunished just because the victims were African migrants and not tourists on a cruise liner."[46] Zerrai was the first to receive the distress call and he informed the Italian authorities about it.

The left-to-die boat was of course only one among many cases of drowning that the Mediterranean Sea has seen in ever growing numbers at least since 2011. Ongoing attempts to engage European courts in granting some form of redress to the drowned focus on individual responsibility. State agents and other seafarers who have failed to adhere to the duty of rescue should, according to this view, be held legally liable. Commentators have also suggested that the reasons for such lost lives are not rooted in individual responsibility, but rather in law. A salient example is that of seafarers who have suffered criminal law sanctions under people-smuggling provisions for having rendered assistance.[47] My own

> because of lack of food. When he died they took us to Homs hospital, all of us. But they still wouldn't give us anything and brought us back to Zlitan prison. The next day they took us to Tripoli prison, called Toyesha. We stayed there two days and told them we were very sick, that people were going to die, 'Please help us, take us to hospital'. But the policemen answered 'die die die!' After that my bother knew an Ethiopian boy in Tripoli, he knew his number. Using the phone of a Bangladeshi man we called him and Father Mussie. The man came to prison with drinks and food. He took us from Toyesha prison yesterday. He said 'I can take these people to my house', they said: 'Take them'. He rented a room and took us there in two taxi cars."

Some have since made their ways to Europe; others, to the best of my knowledge, are still languishing in North African camps.

[46] "Aircraft Carrier Left Us to Die, Say Migrants," *The Guardian*, Sunday May 8, 2011, available at www.theguardian.com/world/2011/may/08/nato-ship-libyan-migrants (last accessed May 12, 2016). Compare to the words by the Australian Able Seaman Bec Lynd, quoted in the previous chapter: "If that had been the Manly Ferry in Sydney Harbor we would have rushed over there and gotten everyone off as quickly as possible."

[47] Tugba Basaran, "The Saved and the Drowned: Governing Indifference in the Name of Security," *Security Dialogue*, April 16, 2015.

view is that the reasons are different. Attention to the left-to-die affair in particular is useful in illustrating the point. When the maritime space is subject to surveillance by multiple actors at the same time, the responsibility of no actor in particular is triggered. At issue, in other words, is a kind of collective action problem. Any actor may believe that others will act upon their obligations, and no one ends up bearing the costs of rescue. A call of distress, even by people that are within the distance of a photograph, is not experienced as an ethical and legal command binding upon the self. Any rescue operation that does occur becomes a matter of benevolent voluntarism and not a matter of fulfilling a duty. An intensely watched space becomes flattened and homogenized. Physical distances are shortened and become relatively unimportant. Such is the environment in which the human rights encounter may be eliminated.[48]

Restructuring the Encounter from Below

Like border-enforcement agencies, unauthorized migrants too use technology to reconstruct the conditions in which the human rights encounter appears. *Clandestinos,* as they have sometimes been called, often do not want to be detected. Thus, they may share with enforcement authorities an interest in eliminating the frequencies and potentials of encounter. Sometimes making a human rights claim is much less valuable than a furtive life beneath the radar of enforcement authorities. At other times, rather than pushing for the disappearance of encounter, migrants try to make it appear in ways that will allow their human rights claims to be seen and heard. In other words, they participate in constructing an encounter that will reach the relatively powerful party that may be able to help. Or they may even seek to create a spectacle that will reach a transnational audience of third-party observers.

Placing a call from a boat in distress is an intervention in the conditions of encounter. It allows whoever places the call to make the decision when to engage the relevant authorities.[49] Notice the role of

---

[48] The circumstances described in the later report by Lorenzo Pezzanni and Charles Heller are the direct continuation of the events described above. See *Death by Rescue: The Lethal Effects of the EU's Policies of Non-Assistance,* available at https://deathbyrescue.org/. See also Itamar Mann, *Killing by Omission,* www.ejiltalk.org/killing-by-omission/ (both last accessed May 12, 2016).

[49] This, of course, does not mean it will be lying: it might truly be exposed to danger, as were the passengers of the left-to-die boat, beyond all doubt.

the "smuggler" or "Captain" in the left-to-die affair. From the perspective of border enforcement, he may be suspected of a heinous crime. But from the perspective of migrants and refugees he has a more ambiguous position. Such professionals are motivated by monetary gain – sometimes charging extremely high fares. In various parts of the world, they have been horrifically cruel toward their clients. Nevertheless, within a limited set of options, they may still be perceived as helping to enforce human rights.[50] The smuggler-captain in the left-to-die case is interesting because he is actively engaged in restructuring the encounter. The phone may connect between smugglers and migrants or smugglers and other smugglers. But it can also connect the boat to a network that makes it possible to trigger rescue duties. The phone thus shortens maritime distances and allows its holder to step into visibility.

The role of the phone in structuring the human rights encounter is poignantly reflected in the decision to throw it overboard (same goes for GPS). Such action creates a setting in which even the most minimal measure of purposive action is no longer tenable for those on the migrant boat. When they start to drift directionless on the Mediterranean water, the boat passengers are reduced to bare life: "helpless leaves adrift in calm or stormy seas."[51] Any encounter will be severed from volition and agency. It will be reconstructed, as exclusively as possible, as a humanitarian emergency. But as argued in Chapter 2 above, survival and freedom are inextricably tied together. The recipients of humanitarian concern are never devoid of volition. Asking for humanitarian concern is often a way of realizing political aspirations.

One might compare a phoneless vessel today to what a "flagless vessel" was historically.[52] A flag is a conventional, agreed upon way to ascribe the responsibility for a particular vessel and its passengers to a state. If the vessel disrupts international legal order in any way, the flag state is answerable. Unlike the flag, the phone is not a signal of sovereignty or de jure status. Yet it is a factual clue as to where the vessel is coming from. As such it serves a similar function: it allows enforcement agencies to tie

---

[50] The grounds for that assumption have been systematically interrogated in Chapter 2. For this ambiguous relationship, see in the Australian context, Rebecca Puddy, "Asylum-Seeker Thanks Accused at People-Smuggling Trial for Saving His Family," *The Australian*, August 9, 2012, available at www.theaustralian.com.au/national-affairs/immigration/asylum-seeker-thanks-accused-in-people-smuggling-trial-for-saving-his-family/story-fn9hm1gu-1226446257324 (last accessed May 12, 2016).

[51] As one Vietnamese boatperson described his journey in Chapter 2.

[52] Compare with Fleur Johns, *Non-Legality in International Law: Unruly Law* (Cambridge: Cambridge University Press, 2013).

the boat back to authorities at its port of debarkation. The traces a mobile phone leaves will be relevant for border policing. They may make it easier for transnational law enforcement to fight smuggling networks. From the passengers' side – and it's important to try to suspend one's judgment regarding this decision – the strategy is to utilize mobile networks in a way that facilitates movement. It is just as important, however, to be able to deny such reliance, to cut one's own life-saving rope (which is the phone).

These forms of desperate action are only one way in which attempts to enforce human rights are attempts to *construct* a human rights encounter. The London-based group "Forensic Oceanography" offered another more elaborate technological reconstruction of the encounter. In April 2012, the group released an impressive report on the "left-to-die." The report integrates human testimony, satellite phone locations, satellite photographs of the Mediterranean, and an oceanographic drift analysis. Employing these data, the authors Charles Heller and Lorenzo Pezzani attempted to ascertain the positions of the vessels that sailed around the "left-to-die."

The report reiterates the word "encounter" numerous times. It is used only when the passengers meet other mariners face-to-face. It connects the dots between the first phone call to MRCC and the face-to-face encounters in which identifiable individuals came to believe that people before them would die without their help. It provides a measure of human rights enforcement by demonstrating individual guilt. Meticulously reconstructing the trajectory of the migrants' message loads it with normative consequence.

The maps in the report are visual representations of a criminal-law model of culpability. They are probative instruments in an effort to ascertain guilt or innocence and to hold an individual actor accountable. Thanks to the report, it literally becomes possible to see that by sending the communication out to the MRCC, legal duties were projected onto a considerable maritime space. While emphasizing the human rights imperative stemming from a face-to-face "encounter," the report also reflects that the encounter is not the result of happenstance or of God's will. It's the final link in a multi-nodal chain that can be traced back to both sovereign and transnational authorities. All the various links and connections in the chain are positioned in one expansive environment. This is where the reader of the report stands (becoming a kind of witness to the crime).

Surveillance technologies, which governments sometimes use to save migrants and at other times use to avoid the costs imposed by encounter, can be turned into tools for human rights enforcement.[53] This appropriation may generate encounters that would not otherwise have been perceptible, while deliberately concealing those unauthorized migrants that do not want to be seen.[54] But does the engagement of unauthorized migrants and their advocates in a reconstruction of place counter the forces by which the human rights encounter is eliminated?

The Place Where We Stand

Governmental and human rights networks may seem to be on the two opposite sides of one of our time's most contentious political issues: the regulation of borders. According to this picture, enforcement agencies tend to be primarily focused on border control. Their regard for the rights of all humans becomes lip service. For migrants and their advocates, the question of regulating the border is not only a question of European self-interest but also a question of survival and of freedom. When the court realizes the human rights encounter in its own positive jurisprudence, executive agencies push against it to eliminate the encounter. When the encounter fails to appear, migrants and activists may press it back into experience.

From a different perspective, however, all of these actors are engaged in a common enterprise. As one scholar has observed, "Sovereignty and human rights may seem like opposed political projects; most of the news items pit them against each other. Nevertheless, the two projects have together promoted . . . the reach of sovereignty into the sea."[55]

---

[53] See Nicola Perugini and Neve Gordon's discussion of "mirroring" in Nicola Perugini and Neve Gordon, *The Human Right to Dominate* (New York: Oxford University Press, 2015), 8–12, 129.

[54] As the Forensic Oceanography team explained, they chose to provide images in a level of pixilation that would not expose the smallest of boats. See Pezzani and Heller "A Disobedient Gaze," 293.

[55] Naor Ben-Yehoyada, "'Follow Me and I Will Make You Fishers of Men': The Moral and Political Scales of Migration in the Central Mediterranean," *Journal of the Royal Anthropological Institute* 22, no. 1 (2013): 188. See also: Katja Franko Aas and Helene O.I. Gundhus, "Policing Humanitarian Borderlands: Frontex, Human Rights and the Precariousness of Life," *British Journal of Criminology* 55, no. 1 (2015): 1–18, doi:10.1093/bjc/azu086.

One possible reaction to the way legal and surveillance technologies tend to dissolve the place of encounter is to challenge these policies (once again) in court. According to this view, decisions like *Hirsi* should not be expected to realize the rights of migrants or asylum seekers once and for all. At best, such judgments are small steps forward in a fight for global justice (and for the elimination of unacceptable violence at the border). Furthermore, the doctrine on issues such as personal jurisdiction evolves from decision to decision. With every new decision, the court can reconsider the threshold question of what forms of power constitute state jurisdiction, reviewing it at its appropriate locus. One might also add that the human rights encounter mustn't be a physical encounter at all. By discussing both de facto and de jure jurisdiction, the *Hirsi* Court in fact seems to invite such a challenge.

Suppose the boats involved in the November 2013 interception were indeed manned by a Maltese crew and acting under a Libyan flag. Assume also that Maltese or other European forces had detected the boat moving their way and alerted the Libyan forces. Assume that the latter responded as they were expected to do under a bilateral agreement (formal or informal): they intercepted the migrant boat and transferred the migrants to immigration detention in Libya. As the Court pointed out in *Hirsi*, from here the migrants could be sent back to countries they fled from. They could be exposed to torture, or other inhuman or degrading treatment "absolutely prohibited" under the European Convention on Human Rights and the Convention Against Torture. Would the Court find the Maltese forces responsible for human rights violations? Would it be able to review this operation under the 1951 Refugee Convention or ECHR?

A positive answer to this question would require a particularly expansive reading of de facto jurisdiction. Though such an expansive reading may theoretically be tenable, it is unlikely and – more importantly – probably unhelpful from the perspective of asylum seekers. It would require the Court to examine in detail the workings of a country not represented before it and beyond its jurisdiction. Practically, this would make it nearly impossible to obtain evidence of what the Libyan forces did. Theoretically, it would invite review of countless other activities of foreign governments, when supposedly acting to satisfy the interests of countries subject to ECtHR jurisdiction. Even if the appellants would succeed in showing that Libyans were merely acting as Maltese authorities instructed them, striking down any particular framework would suggest numerous alternative ways to restructure cooperation and surveillance. A finding of de facto jurisdiction would not dispose of the underlying concerns. Human rights violations may at times adhere to a kind of hydraulics: push their surface on one side of a system – and it will rise on another.[56]

The Court's decision in *Hirsi* was effective in deterring a country like Malta. Precisely for that reason Malta clarified that Libyan personnel were on board the intercepting boats. But this deterrence does not necessarily help migrants or refugees. Malta's compliance with positive human rights law does not bring them any closer to coupling human rights violations with a human rights remedy. In the same vein, one might also ask: would Moroccan security forces acting in the CLOSEYE framework be subject to ECtHR jurisdiction? The answer is almost surely negative.

The juxtaposition of *Hirsi* and the use of surveillance technologies by enforcement agencies reflect how the realization of rights and their erosion are tethered together. By demanding that Italian border-enforcement agents grant access to asylum, ECtHR has, like the technology industry, made border guards "think differently." At best, it made "traditional" border enforcement more costly for the Italian government. But this only opens other options for a disembodied enforcement in which an encounter will never take place. While imposing judicial review on border enforcement, ECtHR is in fact augmenting and entrenching a new structure of border enforcement.

This dialectic movement from enforcement to its violation is a structural set of constraints, resulting from the context of global asymmetries of power and wealth. It suggests that border enforcement requires decision makers in European and other developed countries to wield the kind of violence they supposedly find intolerable. Because unauthorized movement has become a form of human rights self-help, borders simply cannot be enforced without such violence. In some contexts, the motivation to migrate may be so powerful that it even becomes worth the risk of being subject to "absolutely prohibited" treatment, in order to have a chance to access host countries. If subjecting myself to the risk of "inhuman and degrading treatment" for a limited duration may allow me to alleviate the hunger my family or I suffer from that may be worth it. In this reality, relatively affluent countries use their economic and political clout to push other countries to carry out the necessary violence of border enforcement for

---

[56] Compare with Samuel Moyn, *The Last Utopia: Human Rights in History* (Cambridge: Harvard University Press), 88.

them.[57] The reality in which Libyan, Moroccan, and other non-European forces carried out border enforcement did not occur despite the ECtHR's enforcement of rights. It proceeded partially because of such enforcement.

For Hugo Grotius and other classical international lawyers who wrote about the law of the sea, the high seas modeled a kind of "state of nature."[58] As late as the mid-twentieth century, this is the world from which Weis's analogy of the flagless vessel appeared (in Chapter 1). By imposing the duty of rescue, the customary law of the sea made individual seafarers responsible for each other's survival. Though human rights law is not limited to maritime space, considering the law of the sea became useful in understanding the grounding of human rights law more generally. The sea figured as a crack between the territorial jurisdictions established by sovereignty. Through this crack it was possible to see the movement from a state of nature to citizenship in a transnational and historical context. This crack is the place where we stand in the human rights encounter.

The haphazard manipulations of the encounter, and the way they were struck down in *Hirsi*, reflect a world in which no such state of nature can exist. The governmental responses to the judgment demonstrate how that exterritorial space becomes managed and governed. The migrants' advocates' attempts to reconstruct the space of encounter following the left-to-die affair may end up doing the same thing. In the place these efforts construct, human rights duties are dispersed among a large number of potential addressees. It becomes increasingly implausible that any one of the addressees will experience the imperative corresponding to the universal boatperson's claim: "here I stand, I can do no other." Whether they intend to do so or not, all the actors reconstructing the place of encounter are now bringing about a condition in which the space of encounter is eliminated. Mutual obligations between persons may no longer have any purchase.[59]

---

[57] If, as I have argued in Chapter 3, the violence of border enforcement is constitutive violence, we see how such constitutive violence can also be transnational.

[58] Benedict Kingsbury and Benjamin Stausmann, "The State of Nature and Commercial Sociability in Early Modern International Legal Thought," *Grotania* 31 (2010): 22–43, 30 (quoting Grotius: "peoples in relation to the whole of mankind occupy the position of private individuals").

[59] Compare with Carl Schmitt's use of the term "sea-appropriations" for periods in which empires have imposed law on maritime spaces. Carl Scmitt, *The Nomos of the Earth* (Candor, NY: Telos Press Publishing, 2006), 44.

Pervasive conditions of surveillance distribute human rights duties on a large number of different authorities. In such conditions, who is and who is not implicated in this encounter?

The clearest illustrations of this wide distribution of authorities are the encounters in which the "left-to-die" were photographed but not offered a remedy. The camera supported the migrants' conclusion that they should have been saved; at the same time, it helped isolate the photographers from becoming addressees of human rights claims. Behind the camera, even those potentially able to assist end up occupying the position of a third-party spectator rather than that of an addressee. The constitutive event of encounter is at best diluted into a thin voluntarism organized around "coalitions of the willing."[60] Assistance to migrants becomes a form of activism, rather than an adherence to a duty. Rights and remedies can no longer be coupled. Human rights cease being law. Surveillance thus potentially has radical effects on human rights. It changes the ways in which persons are oriented in the world. We may no longer be oriented in a way that allows for duties toward non-citizens to appear. Surveillance allows for an endless diffusion of responsibility because the encounter never actually happens.

The disappearance of the place of encounter should not be read as a call to return to its original authenticity. Such a task would not only be impossible, it would probably also be meaningless. There is no imaginable point in time in which the encounter was not already constructed by technology. Just as we do not choose our most fundamental commitments, we do not choose the technology that makes us.[61] Perhaps the most ancient form of technology considered here has been the boat.[62] If human rights have any future at all, it does not depend on finding an authentic position outside of history. An "authentic" encounter that is binding upon the self can only be such for the self, which in turn is at least partially technologically

---

[60] On "coalitions of the willing", see David Singh Grewal, *Network Power* (New Haven: Yale University Press, 2009), 190.

[61] Paul Kahn, *Out of Eden* (Pinceton: Princton University Press, 2007) ("We inherit the forms of meaning as much as we inherit the forms of technology").

[62] Compare the neologism "boatperson" with Bruno Latour's famous discussion of the "gunman" in Bruno Latour, "A Collective of Humans and Nonhumans: Following Daedalus's Labyrinth" in *Readings in the Philosophy of Technology*, ed. David M. Kaplan (Lanham: Rowman and Littfield, 2009), 156.

constructed. It depends on our ability to account for and be cognizant of our place or orientation in the world. If there is no space between sovereign authorities in which our duties to one another can be exposed, is there any other position in which such duties are experienced as binding?

6

Imagination and the Human Rights Encounter

On September 9, 2015, President of the European Commission Jean-Claude Juncker delivered his State of the Union address. Entitled Time for Honesty, Unity, and Solidarity, the speech was pitched as a heroic intervention in a situation of crisis. At its center was an imagined encounter between Europe and destitute refugees clamoring at its doorstep.

Juncker spoke against the backdrop of a long and dramatic summer. The European Union (EU) was "witnessing perhaps the largest scale of immigration wave ever":[1] from January to the end of August, 300,000 refugees and migrants attempted the Mediterranean crossing, with approximately 200,000 of them landing in Greece and 110,000 in Italy.[2] Migrants and refugees were accompanied by a continuous flow of news and macabre images. While some families tried to make their way under barbed wire fences in the Balkans, others traveled as far as the Arctic Circle to enter Europe.[3] Countless migrant boats drowned off in Mediterranean waterways. A refrigerated truck abandoned outside of Vienna with seventy-one migrant bodies on board generated headlines globally. Perhaps the most iconic image was that of the body of a toddler, lying face down on a sandy beach on Turkey's Aegean coast.

This final chapter offers a critical analysis of Juncker's speech. Unlike previous chapters, it will not be organized around physical encounters between migrants at sea and border-enforcement agents or other sea-farers. As Chapter 5 explains, I doubt any such encounter can be severed from the political and economic environment in which it is constructed.

---

[1] "Integrated Actions and Humanitarian Aid Needed for the European Agenda on Migration," available at https://europa.eu/eyd2015/en/alda/posts/humanitarian-aid (last accessed February 16, 2016).

[2] "Crossings of Mediterranean Sea Exceed 300,000, Including 200,000 to Greece," UNHCR, available at www.unhcr.org/55e06a5b6.html (last accessed May 12, 2016).

[3] Patrick Kingsley, "Syrians fleeing war find new route to Europe – via the Arctic Circle," The Guardian, August 29 (2015), available at https://www.theguardian.com/world/2015/aug/29/syrian-refugees-europe-arctic-circle-russia-norway (last accessed June 16, 2016).

But this does not diminish the importance of the imagination of such an encounter for international legal theory. In previous chapters, I argued that the conception of the human rights encounter provides a useful interpretation of historical experience that constitutes human rights law: a non-positive set of imperatives both ethical and legal, independent of sovereignty and of state consent. In this chapter, I will emphasize that the human rights encounter is a fruit of the political imagination.[4] Understanding this, however, does not diminish its binding normative force.

The previous chapters present a phenomenological and descriptive effort to understand how human rights law, properly conceived, plays an essential part in international law. I have argued that being bound by human rights means being subject both to the positive law given by sovereign states and to non-positive human rights law, understood as the law of the human rights encounter. The possible tensions between these generate a kind of existential dilemma, which I characterized as *embarrassment*.[5] Once this is established, the human rights encounter also suggests a way in which particular kinds of prescriptions can be made. But how is this leap between a phenomenological description of experience and an essentially prescriptive discourse made possible? This chapter contains a modest proposal, cast in light of the current global migration and refugee crisis.

The imagination of an encounter can inform the way we decide to shape our laws and our institutions. Those of us who feel bound by human rights and are members of functioning social contracts should also act to ensure that our states expose themselves to the existential challenges of human rights. Human rights abiding states must to some degree remain open to the human rights claim of non-members. Sometimes, that will mean opening the social contract to new members.[6] It is morally desirable to experience the embarrassment characteristic of being bound both by positive law and by human rights. Certain political structures and institutions leave more space to that experience than others.

---

[4] On imagination in politics generally, see Benedict Anderson, *Imagined Communities: Reflections on the Origin and Spread of Nationalism*, Revised edition (London and New York: Verso, 2006); in the context of legal scholarship, see Paul W. Kahn, *The Cultural Study of Law: Reconstructing Legal Scholarship* (Chicago: University of Chicago Press, 2000).

[5] See Chapter 1 and Chapter 4 in particular.

[6] See also Chapters 2 and 3.

Migration Managerialism

In May 2015, the European Commission published its ambitious European Agenda on Migration.[7] The so-called European migration crisis had not yet reached the spectacular peak it would come to later that summer. But the drafting process was motivated by a sense of urgency. With large parts of the Middle East and North Africa in turmoil, and abject poverty in many parts of Africa, the presumption was that "migration pressures" would only increase. Policy solutions were demanded for an ever-growing policy problem. The published Agenda included four stated "pillars": (1) reducing incentives for unauthorized or "irregular" migration; (2) border management – understood both as border enforcement and as saving the lives of migrants at risk; (3) a "strong common asylum policy"; and (4) providing new avenues for legal migration.

This Agenda presents a self-conscious attempt to group together a rich and variegated set of policy questions. As the Commission parses the issues, they are, first of all, ethical problems: "The plight of thousands of migrants putting their lives in peril to cross the Mediterranean has shocked us all." But they are also – as importantly – economic problems, particularly in the areas of trade, labor, and development. The latter are closely linked to demographic problems stemming from an aging European population. Finally, they are legal problems, most centrally access to asylum and *non-refoulement*. The Agenda's largely pragmatic orientation toward policy allows treating these very different questions holistically. The agenda is thus intended to allow Europe to "build up a coherent and comprehensive approach to reap the benefits and address the challenges deriving from migration." The phenomenon of migration – both authorized and unauthorized – presents risks and opportunities. Good governance means seizing upon the former and avoiding the latter. And the framing of all of these problems as "European" creates an occasion to assert the vitality of European political integration. When conceived of together, the set of policy issues that migration raises demands deep coordination with "third countries" which migrants leave or transit from. Budgets are allocated and cooperation initiatives are aimed as close as Turkey and as far as the Horn of Africa. Multiple bilateral and multilateral frameworks are spawned to facilitate this cooperation, often based on treaties and soft-law instruments. The highest level of such cooperation, one that Turkey has constantly inched closer to and may

---

[7] Available at http://ec.europa.eu/lietuva/documents/power_pointai/communication_on_the_european_agenda_on_migration_en.pdf (last accessed May 12, 2016).

attain, is that of accession to membership in the European "ever closer Union."[8]

Inasmuch as Juncker's September speech includes any specific policy recommendations, it largely reiterates those of the May 2015 Agenda. Juncker does not go into these in any great detail. But he does push forward an expansion of policies already articulated in the Agenda. For example, he proposes to establish "an emergency Trust Fund, starting with €1.8 billion from our common EU financial means to address the crises in the Sahel and Lake Chad regions, the Horn of Africa, and the North of Africa." As the President of the Commission explains, "We want to help create lasting stability, for instance by creating employment opportunities in local communities, and thereby address the root causes of destabilisation, forced displacement and illegal migration." The emergency Fund is only one among multiple examples of the ways in which, in the speech too, development and migration are tethered together. (That stable employment in poverty-stricken regions may reduce the number of unauthorized migrants seeking to leave their homes seems relatively uncontroversial. Whether or not such a fund will indeed be successful in generating employment opportunities should remain an open question.)

Juncker echoes the Agenda's general orientation toward policy, best encapsulated by the idea of *migration management*.[9] Following the Agenda's cue, Juncker uses the verb "to manage," denoting a civilized, rational way of dealing with migrants. He says that "it is high time to manage the refugee crisis"; that "we must work together more closely to manage our external borders"; and that "migration must change from a problem to be tackled to a well-managed resource." Migration management is contrasted with instances of *refoulement* and of private xenophobic violence, particularly "pushing back boats from piers" and "setting fire to refugee camps." In short, managerialism is good; xenophobia is bad.

This managerial approach isn't novel. It has emerged as the dominant approach to border control among Western developed countries. Indeed,

---

[8] These are the famous words of the Treaty of Rome (1957).

[9] See, generally, Savitri Taylor, "From Border Control to Migration Management: The Case for a Paradigm Change in the Western Response to Transborder Population Movement," *Social Policy & Administration* 30, no. 6 (2005): 563–586; Philip L. Martin, Susan F. Martin, and Patrick Weil, *Managing Migration: The Promise of Cooperation* (Lanham, Rowman and Littlefield, 2006); Gregory Feldman, *The Migration Apparatus: Security, Labor, and Policymaking in the European Union* (Stanford: Stanford University Press, 2012).

it is yet another version of a transnational style of governance already explored in each of the chapters above. The European Agenda is merely the latest and most sophisticated version of previous arrangements. As this book has shown, these arrangements go at least as far back as the interwar period, and their emergence is closely linked with the emergence of the twentieth-century discipline of public international law.[10] This sophistication, however, comes with considerable difficulty. EU policymakers are well aware that they create incentives that will influence the behavior of migrants and would-be migrants. The emphasis on legal avenues for migration is intended to reduce the incentives for unauthorized and perilous migration through maritime routes. Looking closely at the Agenda, one finds that contradictory incentives are embedded in its institutional architecture. Aspects of the same policy militate toward different and often opposing outcomes. The Agenda, in this respect, is an attempt to square the circle of a commitment to asylum and a commitment to deterrence.

Frontex – an EU executive agency entrusted with border management – is the quintessential institutional example of such contradictory objectives.[11] Another good example of the contradictory objectives is the way the second pillar is formulated – tying the enforcement of borders to saving lives at sea. Frontex is tasked not only with helping to enforce borders but also with life-saving operations. Historically, saving lives at sea has sometimes been understood as an impediment to the reduction of migration.[12] Once people are saved they seek more than just protection from death. They submit asylum applications or otherwise strive to stay in the territory of the developed country that saved them. The aspirations

---

[10] Chapter 1 recounts the rise of international organizations for the control of migration in that period. See also Louise W. Holborn, "The Legal Status of Political Refugees, 1920–1938," *The American Journal of International Law* 32, no. 4 (1938): 680–703, doi:10.2307/219059; Louise W. Holborn, "The League of Nations and the Refugee Problem," *Annals of the American Academy of Political and Social Science* 203 (1939): 124–135.

[11] For a sustained analysis with regard to the European Border Surveillance System (EUROSUR) and Frontext, see Jorrit Rijpma and Mathias Vermeulen, "EUROSUR: Saving Lives or Building Borders?" *European Security* 24, no. 3 (2015): 454–472, doi:10.1080/09662839.2015.1028190. And compare: Katja Franko Aas and Helene O.I. Gundhus, "Policing Humanitarian Borderlands: Frontex, Human Rights and the Precariousness of Life," *British Journal of Criminology* 55, no. 1 (2015): 1–18. Itamar Mann, "Dialectic of Transnationalism: Unauthorized Migration and Human Rights, 1993–2013," *Harvard International Law Journal* 54, no. 2 (2013): 315.

[12] See, e.g., the US government's argument before the US Supreme Court in *Sale*, as explained in Chapter 3 above.

behind "reducing incentives" for unauthorized migration and ensuring access to asylum cancel each other out.

This, in a nutshell, is the risk the Agenda runs more generally: the effort to enforce Europe's border and at the same time open it to those who deserve international protection has the tendency to regenerate the dynamics it aims to solve. The answer to the question who should be entitled to international protection is never entirely pre-determined or given. It is never a matter of objective truth. The distinction requires judgment, and the need to judge invites would-be refugees to make ways to Europe and challenge the basic structure of positive international law: the structure whereby every state is considered to bear the duties that correspond to the rights of its own citizens.[13] From this perspective, whatever one's views about migration and immigration, addressing the policy questions they raise in the managerial mode seems like a sleight of hand. Managerialism might be an apt description of the policies Europe has been implementing. These policies do not, however, present any real "solution" to a problem.

The Agenda's managerialism, in other words, is an institutionalized attempt to elide deep normative commitments – and to elide the embarrassment characteristic of human rights commitments. The Agenda uses ethical language in its determination to put an end to deaths at sea. But the entailments of effectively doing so – making it much easier to enter Europe – are never fully admitted. The European Commission does not want to close Europe's external borders or take responsibility for the results this would entail for non-members of European member states. This option is presumably avoided; the lives of non-members are understood to be both morally and legally relevant. But the Commission does not want to take responsibility for an explicitly more open approach allowing vast numbers of asylum seekers in either. The latter option would be difficult to sell to domestic constituencies. The winter following the summer of 2015 has illustrated such unsurprising difficulties.

Migration managerialism appears as a politically safe middle ground between two perceived impossibilities: open or closed borders. But it is a particular way of capturing this middle ground while rendering the question whether incoming migrants are "refugees" or not secondary. The Commission employs a mode of governance that seemingly makes it

---

[13] As reflected clearly in Article 2(1) of the ICCPR: 1: "Each State Party to the present Covenant undertakes to respect and to ensure to all individuals within its territory and subject to its jurisdiction the rights recognized in the present Covenant."

possible to have the cake and eat it too. Different organs of the EU and of its member states will carry out varying tasks, some parts of which will have to do with keeping non-member populations at bay; others of which will grant international protection to those who have been determined to be bona fide asylum seekers. These tasks are distributed among various actors. On the member-state level, we find government agencies but also local and regional governments. On the EU level, the prominent actors are Frontex and EASO (the European Asylum Support Office).[14] While the former acts on the enforcement side, the latter acts on the protection side. Importantly, these two aspects of transnational executive action are bifurcated from one another and do not necessarily attach to a cohesive executive branch of any one state. More often than not, it has been the case that enforcement capacities are far quicker and more efficient than protection ones.[15]

This managerial mode of governance means that policy outcomes will be determined, in a context-specific way, by relationships between different governmental organs and by balances between them. Enforcement and protection competences are separated and flexibly reassembled in response to local and regional migration pressures. The ways in which they are reassembled may seem like a mere matter of implementation. But this implementation will determine the level of porousness of different frontiers. And it will decide whether any particular person will be able to access human rights remedies. The violence characteristic of border enforcement is thus shifted around and redistributed, often to states and agencies outside of the European space.[16] While historically the EU has been hailed as providing excellent human rights protections but criticized for its "democratic deficit," a kind of human rights deficit becomes apparent here. The story of the left-to-die boat (discussed in the previous chapter) is only one example of the kind of violence associated with this human rights deficit.

Managerialism is an attempt to detach law from the existential questions associated with what I have called the human rights encounter.

---

[14] I've explored this dynamic in some detail in Mann, "Dialectic of Transnationalism," 315–391.

[15] Human Rights Watch, "The EU's Dirty Hands: Frontex Involvement in Ill-Treatment of Migrant Detainees in Greece" (2011), available at www.hrw.org/report/2011/09/21/eus-dirty-hands/frontex-involvement-ill-treatment-migrant-detainees-greece (last accessed May12, 2016).

[16] See e.g., Jef Huysmans, *The Politics of Insecurity: Fear, Migration and Asylum in the EU* (Abingdon: Routledge, 2006), 95–96.

While embracing positive international legal obligations, migration management is a brand of bureaucratic rationality that prevents non-positive human rights questions from emerging. But whether or not it is successful ultimately depends, among other things, on its relationship with imagination. Imagination is the capacity of making present something that is absent. Even if a migrant boat is absent from my view because I'm not at sea, or the boat has drowned, or its passengers have somehow remained among the shadows of extra-legality, I still can render them present before me by the use of imagination. If the human rights encounter is not only a physical encounter but also an imaginary construct at the normative basis of legality, the question will become: should citizens of well-ordered states want such human rights questions to be raised? And if so, how should that possibility be safeguarded in political institutions?

A Short History of European Political Violence

Perhaps because he spoke after such a dramatic summer, Juncker seemed to go beyond the vocabulary of managerialism to advance his agenda. Unlike previous iterations of the same policies, Juncker couched European policies in a rhetoric that went beyond a consequentialist, cost–benefit calculus. Unauthorized migration involved a question about what it means to be European. It called upon Europeans to rearticulate the deepest commitments the EU stands for. Juncker expresses such commitments by integrating two narratives: one about the kinds of violence European polities have emerged out of; the other about the encounter of Europeans with the de facto stateless.

"This is not time to be afraid," says Juncker at the opening of his speech. Instead, Europe must uphold human dignity and its obligations under the 1951 Refugee Convention. However, rather than grounding Europe's obligations toward refugees upon the Convention, Juncker explains them through a reference to European history. Being committed to the protection of refugees is about the legacy of a particular history of displacement and about European identity. "We Europeans," he explains, "should remember well that Europe is a continent where nearly everyone has at one time been a refugee. Our common history is marked by millions of Europeans fleeing from religious or political persecution, from war, dictatorship, or oppression."[17] And Juncker spells out this

---

[17] As explained in Chapter 3, this reliance on historical experience is a constitutive aspect of the human rights commitment. But is Juncker really talking about human rights

trajectory. He draws a line starting from the Huguenots who fled France in the seventeenth century. The religiously persecuted minority found refuge in Germany. But with the 1789 Declaration of the Rights of Man and the Citizen, Protestants gained equal rights in the new Republic. Thus, the declaration embodied the promise that all humans could be protected by a social contract within a community of members.

The list of peoples Juncker includes and excludes from this narrative is interesting. After mentioning the Huguenots, he jumps to the twentieth century and talks of "Jews, Sinti, Roma and many others fleeing Germany during the Nazi horror of the 1930s and 1940s."[18] He mentions Spanish republicans fleeing to refugee camps in southern France at the end of the 1930s, after their defeat in the Civil War; "Hungarian revolutionaries fleeing to Austria after their uprising against communist rule was oppressed by Soviet tanks in 1956"; Czechs and Slovaks seeking exile after the oppression of the Prague Spring in 1968. These are all groups that are largely understood to have suffered religious, ethnic, racial, or political persecution.[19] After World War II, the parties to the Refugee Convention believed that their recent histories required them to grant elevated protections to members of groups who had suffered such fates. As such, mentioning them here may simply be a way of shedding light on the continued relevance of the Convention and its original purpose.

But Juncker does not stop here. In mentioning refugees from the former Yugoslavia, he acknowledges a challenge to refugee law, much discussed since the 1990s.[20] Unlike political, racial, or religious persecution, fleeing civil war is not recognized under the Refugee Convention. Precisely for this reason, the crisis in Yugoslavia came to be a formative one for refugee law. "Complementary protection" or "subsidiary protection" emerged as another form of duty toward noncitizens in danger of being returned to their countries. This status does

commitments, as they are explained there? Compare Patchen Markell, "Making Affect Safe for Democracy?: On 'Constitutional Patriotism'," *Political Theory* 28, no. 1 (2000): 38–63.

[18] Jews ended up establishing their own state. Romani groups are still largely discriminated against in Europe.

[19] Alongside "membership in a particular social group," these represent the group that the Refugee Convention has resolved to protect.

[20] See, e.g., Morten Kjaerum, "Temporary Protection in Europe in the 1990s," *International Journal of Refugee Law* 6 (1994): 444–456; Brian Gorlick, "The Convention and the Committee Against Torture: A Complementary Protection Regime for Refugees," *International Journal of Refugee Law* 11, no. 3 (2015): 479–495.

not grant its recipient the entire set of rights that the Refugee Convention recognizes.[21] It is a thinner but a very important protection from *non-refoulement*. In Juncker's speech, it is mentioned as one element within a longer list of historical precedents defining Europe's obligations toward non-Europeans.

Next come two several-century-long migrations: "Have we forgotten that there is a reason there are more McDonalds living in the U.S. than there are in Scotland? That there is a reason the number of O'Neills and Murphys in the U.S. exceeds by far those living in Ireland?" Irish and Scottish migration flows were steady movements westward during the nineteenth and early twentieth centuries. They were motivated not only by religious and political persecution but also by quests for subsistence. They were authorized by the United States – but nevertheless appear in the speech as pertinent for contemporary concerns related to unauthorized entries. An especially interesting historical example is the last one Juncker mentions: "20 million people of Polish ancestry." By mentioning Poland, the President presumably refers to a history of war associated with Poland's territorial dismemberment since Imperial times. But he also refers to the millions that due to Imperial subjugation had emigrated west over centuries: Catholics, members of the Greek Orthodox Church, and Jews. One might even read here an oblique reference to the wave of migration from Poland after its accession to the EU. Around 2006, the number of Polish labor migrants destined for Western Europe increased by over one million, representing probably the most intense migration in Polish history during peacetime.[22]

Juncker does not mention Arabic-speaking populations – Muslim, Christian, or Jewish – who moved into Europe during or after decolonization. Indeed, an entire history of colonization in which European settlers displaced, enslaved, and at times massacred populations around the globe is absent from his discourse. Implicit is a certain understanding of populations that are authentically "European."

Unlike the United States (discussed in Chapter 3), Europe is imagined neither as a "nation of refugees" nor as a "nation of immigrants."

---

[21] For a critical account of this difference, see Jane McAdam, "The European Union Qualification Directive: The Creation of a Subsidiary Protection Regime," *International Journal of Refugee Law* 17, no. 3 (2005): 461–516, doi:10.1093/ijrl/eei018.

[22] Marta Anacka and Marek Okólski, "Direct Demographic Consequences of Post-Accession Migration for Poland," in Richard Black, Godfried Engbersen, Marek Okólski, and Cristina Pantîru (eds.), *A Continent Moving West?: EU Enlargement and Labour Migration from Central and Eastern Europe* (Amersterdam: Amsterdam University Press, 2010), 141.

But there is something not entirely foreign to that ethos either. The history of Europe is charted as one of persecution, bloodshed, and hunger. The origins of these go further back than the postwar era, when Europe began to emerge as an integrated political entity. The continent and its political civilization are portrayed as the products of violence and of continuous expulsions. The literature about the emergence of the EU often repeats how the EU was designed as an economic union, but also that its institutions were put in place to quell the violence of interstate war. The idea in Juncker's speech is somewhat different: Europe is not made of autochthonous populations. Europe unites the uprooted, the displaced, the peripatetic. Reference to the Refugee Convention arrives only at the conclusion of this historical trajectory.

Looking back at the precedents Juncker mentions, it is striking that these are not all consonant with the underlying assumptions of the Refugee Convention. They are not all about well-founded fear of persecution. Indeed, the Convention's distinctions between various reasons for flight are less important than the exercise of naming various groups whose history is somehow entangled with displacement (and with European history). Once again, it is not that *every* group is mentioned in this line of precedents. Implicit is an act of choice, deliberate or not. One could easily think of excluded examples. This history however does clearly represent a divergence from the positive legal understanding of the term "refugee." Economic migration and journeys from civil war figure beside the Convention's narrower notion of "persecution." All these various kinds of displacement are in turn situated on a single plane. The basic element common to all of them is the violence that European peoples have suffered in the process of political self-determination.

Europe's Imaginary Encounter

By recounting the violence that European peoples purportedly emerged from, Juncker seeks to explain why Europe cannot seal its borders to refugees and asylum seekers. His explanation goes beyond cost and benefit and seemingly beyond the tenets of managerialism. It stakes a claim about European identity. But as explained above, another aspect of the speech is relevant here. Juncker concludes his words about the migration crisis by describing embodied encounters between refugees and European citizens. These encounters are worthy of some sustained attention. To understand the imagination at work here, consider the following passage: "Europe is the baker in Kos who gives away his bread to hungry and weary souls. Europe is the students in Munich and in Passau who bring clothes for the new arrivals at the train station. Europe is the policeman in Austria who welcomes exhausted refugees upon crossing the border. This is the Europe I want to live in."[23]

During the summer and fall of 2015, many Europeans displayed overwhelming solidarity with refugees and migrants. A week before Juncker's speech, locals stood at the train station in Munich, handing out provisions and basic toiletries. So many donations had been received that the police had to issue an appeal for people to stop.[24] Similar events unfolded at the German border town of Passau: "Maya Krug, 28, from Bavaria, hands out hot tea and blankets at her local train station, coming every day after work. Claudia Klöfkorn, a police officer, works 12-hour shifts managing the migrant flow at the border with humor and humanity."[25] For some, the actions had the magical consequence of momentarily suspending perceived distinctions between locals and immigrants: "The kebab vendors and cleaners who speak Pashto, Kurdish and Arabic have become ad hoc translators and mediators, explaining the world to fellow Germans who defer to their authority."[26] A twenty-one-year-old Turkish immigrant laughingly marveled at how – after growing up in an environment of suspicion toward police officers – he was now standing side by side with the police, welcoming refugees. These police officers do not get paid overtime, he said, but also do not stop their work when their shift is over.

The events Juncker referred to were widely celebrated in the media. These heroes of the summer drama embody the encounter Juncker imagines at the center of Europe's commitments toward migrants and refugees. But it should also be clear that Juncker is far from merely describing this encounter. His words actively and interpretively reconstruct it. Particularly notable is the image of Europe as the baker on the

[23] europa.eu/rapid/press-release_SPEECH-15-5614_en.htm (last accessed, May 12, 2016).

[24] "German Police Forced to Ask Public to Stop Bringing Donations for Refugees Arriving by Train," *The Independent*, available at www.independent.co.uk/news/world/europe/german-police-forced-to-ask-public-to-stop-bringing-donations-for-refugees-arriving-by-train-10481522.html (last accessed May 12, 2016).

[25] "Times Insider: Reporting Europe's Refugee Crisis," *New York Times*, November 12, 2015, available at www.nytimes.com/interactive/2015/11/11/insider/europe-refugees.html (last accessed May 12, 2016).

[26] "Times Insider."

island of Kos. Several of this image's elements are crucial in articulating the role of that image in a certain kind of political self-understanding. Juncker is referring to the seventy-six-year-old Dionysis Arvanitakis. Arvanitakis became a celebrity of sorts following reports showing how he distributed his oven's bread among the island's newcomers. Standing in a white apron, broken loaf in hand, his photos were enthusiastically disseminated not only by European news outlets but also in the United States. These reflect a longing for the self-sustaining life of small-business owners in intimate towns or villages – a life once common to many regions of the continent but growing extinct due to the forces of a globalized market.[27] I'll come back to that.

Even more importantly for the present purposes, the image of Arvanitakis is granted meaning within the context of Christian iconography. Providing bread for hungry and weary souls is a Biblical reference. In the book of Jeremiah, God promises that upon return from exile to the promised land, he will satiate his believers' hunger: "I will refresh the weary and satisfy the faint" (31:25).[28] The theme has been taken up and developed in the gospel. It is associated with the Last Supper and with the Eucharist. In the Bread of Life discourse, Jesus makes a universal promise of bread for the potential enjoyment of any destitute person (John 6: 22–59). Giving bread is understood as an act of hospitality, of grace, and of boundless love. This Christian tradition unmistakably informs Juncker's imagination of an encounter. Arvanitakis is cast in the role of a present-day Jesus. The migrants that receive his bread are not only symbolically invited to consume the body of Europe but also to transform into Europeans. Students, police officers, and the heroic Arvanitakis are all united at the forefront of the same very Christian

---

[27] For a beautiful description of this way of life, see John Berger, *Pig Earth*, 1st edition (New York: Vintage, 1992). The fact that Arvanitakis is Greek is surely also important. Juncker's address was about two crises, not one: after concluding his discourse about Europe's migration crisis, he discusses Greek debt. (Constructing an imagination of Europe using the image of an elderly Greek baker may supposedly help mend a still very deep fracture between Brussels and Athens.)

[28] By paraphrasing this passage Juncker is gesturing toward a story of deliverance, closely associated with migration. He is gesturing toward collective deliverance – political as well as spiritual – and toward a restoration of a glorious past that seems to have been destroyed: "Come, let us go up to Zion, to the Lord our God" (31:6). In the Old Testament, the food and drink that the weary soul is granted do not only quench a physical thirst and hunger. And it is not about the subsistence of any particular individual either. It is part of a utopian vision for a people that has been banished from its land and sought refuge in Babylon.

mise-en-scène. The refugees and migrants at Europe's doorsteps are imagined as the weary souls who are promised deliverance. Does this theologically informed notion of encounter allow Juncker to transcend the administrative and ultimately self-contradictory rationality of managerialism?

Encounter and the Violence of Politics

Thus, Juncker's speech includes not only the basic tenets of managerialism. It sketches an account of the foundational violence recurrent throughout European history, and one of an encounter between two parties with asymmetrical power. I introduced this coupling in Chapter 1, and have developed it in Chapter 3. In order to understand whether these latter two threads in Juncker's speech comport with his managerialism, I should first explain how they are woven together.

In the political imagination Juncker unfolds, no extra-political state of nature precedes the moment in which European political authority was established. Long before the line of treaties that created the EU – Maastricht, Schengen, Dublin, and Lisbon – European political authority goes back to the French Revolution. Remember that this is the event Arendt too returns to, when she discusses the sovereignty of the nation-state in *The Origins of Totalitarianism*.[29] But contrary to Arendt's analysis, the origin of commitments toward refugees is not to be found in revolutionary documents, such as The Declaration of the Rights of Man and the Citizen. Such commitments are prior to the foundation of a bounded political community in the form of the nation-state. Their origin lies in the darkness of an *ancien régime*.

Europe – in revolutionary times and in the preset – gains its legitimacy from rejecting the violence of a previous unjust rule. But this cannot only mean that European polities will protect their own members. Rejecting the violence of the pre-revolutionary moment entails a commitment to quell the violence inflicted upon those who remain unprotected by any social contract. These people are not understood as simply being exposed to the misery of a war of all against all; sometimes their plight is reminiscent of life under pre-revolutionary tyranny. This "tyranny" can take on multiple forms. What is important to emphasize, however, is that there is no moment that is conceived as pre-political, whether temporally

---

[29] Hannah Arendt, *The Origins of Totalitarianism*, New edition (New York: Harcourt, Brace, Jovanovich, 1973).

or analytically. For better or worse, there is no human life that is not already within politics.

This political imagination produces citizens with a dual set of commitments. Citizens with such commitments are tied to each other by a promise of mutual protection that is at the basis of democratic sovereignty. But they are also mindful of the violence that they had suffered under a (assumed) previous political rule. They are aware – explicitly or implicitly – of the possibility that closing borders may result in precisely the kind of violence that sovereignty was established to do away with. To account for such violence and grant it a role within the moral calculus of extant political institutions: this is the meaning of Juncker's concise history of European political violence. This too is what it means to exercise an imagination of the human rights encounter.[30]

Such histories of violence before the polity are by no means unique to European institutions.[31] Think of President Barack Obama's contention, during the 2015 celebration of Thanksgiving, that "Nearly four centuries after the Mayflower set sail, the world is still full of pilgrims – men and women who want nothing more than the chance for a safer, better future for themselves and their families ..."[32] Obama talked about Syrian refugees. The message here is that by closing its borders to European refugees, the United States would partake in the kind of violence the founding generation sought to leave behind.

Juncker's narrative begins from a moment in which a particular religious group suffered persecution. The narrative is not a timeless or a universal one. It is a story about when human rights were not enforced. It is a story about when human rights began *for the speaker*. This kind of story is based on a crisis that both the speaker and their addressees recognize as somehow their own. It is not because of their positive legal obligations that Europeans are committed to assist refugees. It is rather because of their histories, their identities, their ways of being in the world. It is, at least this is what Juncker wants his listeners to believe, part of who

---

[30] See also Chapter 3.

[31] Elsewhere, I have shown that they are operative in international criminal adjudication: Itamar Mann, "The Dual Foundation of Universal Jurisdiction: Towards a Jurisprudence for the 'Court of Critique'," *Transnational Legal Theory* 1, no. 4 (2015): 485–521.

[32] "Weekly Address: This Thanksgiving, Recognizing the Greatness of American Generosity," *whitehouse.gov*, November 25, 2015, available at www.whitehouse.gov/the-press-office/ 2015/11/26/weekly-address-thanksgiving-recognizing-greatness-american-generosity (last accessed May 12, 2016).

Europeans are. And as the invocation of bread demonstrates, it is about being Christian.

Indeed, the imagination of this violence is intimately tied to that of an encounter with non-members in dire need or risk. In Juncker's discourse, the latter is best represented by the image of Europe as the baker in Kos. The encounter offers a way of engaging with the problem of pre-revolutionary violence through a religious imagination. One is expected not to participate in actions by which her own polity propagates the violence she believes it was established to eliminate. The imagination of an encounter allows members of polities to operationalize that rule.

Reimagining the Encounter

But what exactly is the relationship, in Juncker's speech, between the EU's managerialism and the way he constructs the encounter? If the imagination of encounter has a *critical* role, it is in rethinking as vast an orientation toward policy as European migration managerialism.

One way to understand this relationship is to assume that managerialism can work only in "ordinary" circumstances (whatever those may be). Since the beginning of the twenty-first century, it has been clear to European policymakers that migration will remain an enduring and pressing policy concern. This problem, they realized, cannot be solved unilaterally. And so, transnational partnerships and cooperative policy programs were devised to shape a new ordinary that became known as "migration management."[33] The 2015 European Agenda on Migration is merely the latest iteration in a series of similar (former) initiatives. It is perhaps more sweeping, but it signals no underlying qualitative change. The outbreak of the "Arab Spring," the catastrophic war in Syria, and the rise of the Islamic State generated unprecedented ethical and border-enforcement challenges. They triggered a crisis of enormous magnitude in the Mediterranean, which "awakened" European constituencies. Juncker's imagination of an encounter, according to such an explanation, reflects the urgency of extraordinary events: migration can no longer simply be managed. It requires Europeans to go beyond the give and take of normal policy. When the problem of migration is no longer manageable, we must turn to our most basic

[33] Taylor, "From Border Control to Migration Management."

commitments. These, it turns out, are represented by an encounter. And this encounter is shaped by a Christian iconography. This interpretation is thus about a kind of spiritual awakening. A quasi-religious commitment temporarily displaces or supplants longstanding policy solutions (the latter are facilitated by positive law, domestic or international, "soft" or "hard").

There is some appeal to this way of thinking about the European migration and refugee crisis – and particularly about Juncker's intervention in its unfolding. It probably captures what many Europeans actually felt when they participated in solidaristic action aimed to support refugees. It is also true that European countries accepted a significant number of refugees, not anticipated in advance. Most dramatic, of course, was Germany's opening of its borders to around a million people (as I write these words).

But once the imagination of an encounter is established as a foundational category of the political imagination, one might also consider it from some conceptual remove. The relationships between the imagination of an encounter and that of a bounded political community are not unchanging. Juncker's discussion of migration and refugees in his State of the Union address reflects *one way* in which an imagination of encounter may find a place in a larger vision of politics. This imagination of encounter should not simply be accepted as reflecting human rights more generally.

How might we assess this particular invocation of the encounter, as opposed to other ways in which an encounter can be invoked, imagined, discursively employed? We must consider it within a wider project of managerialism. Two aspects of the way Juncker characterizes this encounter are particularly pertinent. One of them has to do with how he imagines the relatively powerless party to the encounter (and the human rights claim-as expounded upon in Chapter 2); the other has to do with how he imagines the relatively powerful party to the encounter (and the human rights commitment explained in Chapter 3).

When Juncker describes migrants and refugees as "hungry and weary souls," the imagination risks stripping them of their own agency. His construction of the encounter makes an objectionable (and by now very familiar) move: It is yet another example of the way in which policymakers invoke human rights precisely in order to ignore the political demands of those who seek remedies. It is easier to speak of grace and of boundless love than to recognize the unsettling and perilous aspects of welcoming refugees.[34] Ultimately, Juncker imagines the migrants not as bearers of claims but as destitute people who therefore cannot generate real challenges. His speech is one instance in a wider dynamic examined in Chapter 2 above: the powerless party to the encounter is reduced to bare life.

The way Juncker describes the polity in the name of which he is speaking – the EU – also raises fundamental questions. His examples of the students and of the baker Arvanitakis are evocative and even powerful. They represent photogenic moments worthy of some celebration. But they also assume an entirely *voluntary* decision to assist refugees and migrants. The images he paints are not of individuals acting according to a command of their conscience (or any other command). Such action would be required by a rule that – while not written – would be experienced as predetermined. But Juncker's is, instead, an image of benevolence. These are charitable decisions the beauty of which is precisely that they *could have not been taken* (while not violating any law – positive or other). They are images of private giving, above and beyond what the law requires. They do not capture – and indeed do not intend to capture – what it means to abide by law. This is, of course, not a problem in and of itself. It does, however, raise a real question of whether the encounter Juncker imagines can represent a response critical to managerialism.

It cannot. Juncker's imagination of an encounter is part and parcel of managerialism. Managerialism is a mode of governance that transforms rights and their corresponding duties into questions of pragmatic problem-solving. Correspondingly, the encounter Juncker imagines is one in which voluntarism occludes and displaces a notion of duty, at the basis of what I have called human rights law. It is here that we should take some distance from Juncker's description. It is quite a peculiar thing – and likely a misleading one – to imagine a supranational entity like the EU as acting out of private initiative. The EU and Mr. Arvanitakis – they are quite different entities.

An encounter constructed around a model of private initiative does not account for the experience of being bound by human rights. Such voluntarism may even figure as yet another way to eliminate the basic question of human rights. From the perspective I developed here,

---

[34] The closest Juncker comes to such an admission is when he says that this is not time to be afraid. Imagining an encounter in which migrants and refugees retain their agency is also imagining that, at times, there might be reason to be afraid. And it is insisting that even justified fear can be overcome in order to make a new space for refugees: those who have suffered the violence that one's own polity was established to overcome.

European citizens concerned about human rights should pay close attention to the way the human rights encounter is contextualized and constructed within a larger institutional environment.[35] There are profound
reasons to insist that one's polity will institutionalize certain *duties*
toward non-members – an insistence that a voluntaristic urge to give
does not satisfy.

As long as human rights are part of law, an imagination of an encounter in voluntaristic terms cannot entirely displace the experience of duty.
"We" as citizens of well-functioning sovereign states must find ways to
construct into our institutional arrangements the possibility of encounters in which non-members can trigger our duties. More than about
promoting philanthropy, human rights advocacy is about demanding
that one's polity remains institutionally exposed to the existential challenges of human rights. If one's polity does not institutionalize ways in
which it can be challenged from without, its positive law may lose its
binding force upon the self. This risk was described in Chapter 4 through
a personal account given by Able Seaman Bec Lynd. Human rights law,
properly understood, is non-positive law emanating from the command
of the conscience. But as the historical narrative above clarifies, this is not
just any conscience, grounded in disembodied, dislocated moral belief.
It also doesn't have to be the "conscience" that any organized religion
prescribes. I can be agnostic as to the metaphysical basis for the imperative that other human beings impose on me. But that imperative is not,
for that reason, more flexible or negotiable.

The voluntarism expressed in Juncker's imagination of encounter
ultimately sets it apart from human rights law. But his account of pre-
revolutionary violence is very useful in explaining the source of human
rights. Unlike purely moral prescription, the imperative emanating from
the memory of such violence isn't a universal one. It is *experienced* as
universally binding, in the following sense: when we experience it, we
typically also demand that all others do. But considering the obligations
that recognizing such violence weighs upon contemporary political institutions is the burden of those who enjoy membership in a functioning
social contract. What policy results do such obligations entail? Different
polities, and indeed different people, may answer differently. Inevitably,
imagination is involved in the interpretive task of answering this
question. Typically a distinction between members and non-members
will be preserved. The polity, of course, does not need to allow access to

[35] Chapter 5.

all non-members in order to abide by human rights law. But it cannot absolutely ignore their claims either.

Above and beyond the positive law definition of a "refugee," the question of who should enjoy the protections of *non-refoulement* is an open one.[36] One will answer it according to her understanding of pre-revolutionary violence and of the constitutive violence that establishing her own polity has inflicted upon others. Juncker's own interpretation of history is noteworthy: he implicitly suggests the violence that European polities should seek to rectify is not only the violence of persecution or even that of war. It is also a form of economic violence that now displaces populations perhaps more than ever – and that historically has displaced entire populations that are now recognized as European. If this is our imagination of pre-revolutionary violence, we must openly admit that wholly new categories of refugees may potentially be welcome instead of hiding behind "migration management" – that is, as long as this does not run against our basic commitments to other citizens. Rather than management or voluntarism, in order to respond to the tension between the two we need a phenomenology of *duty*. If I'm right, Arvanitakis's reenactment of the Eucharist is not about duty but about will. Communion is born out of free moral choice, not out of the experience of necessity characterized in the previous chapters as the human rights commitment. Thus, the image of Arvanitakis cannot ultimately be a symbol of human rights commitments.

Breaking Bread

Finally, does the image perhaps have yet another symbolic meaning? Rather than a God-given and potentially unlimited resource, bread comes to symbolize finite resources (as in the commonplace use of "dough" to represent money). Such resources must be generated through work and distributed among members of a community. It is here that human rights imperatives are in the clearest disjunction from those that emanate from the social contract. How will members of the social contract fulfill their obligations toward each other in the face of a seemingly infinite number of potential incoming refugees? Far from Juncker's intention, Arvanitakis's image raises the possibility that allowing refugees access to

---

[36] Hence, refugee law scholars often refer to the "protection gap." See, e.g., Tally Kritzman-Amir, "Looking Beyond the Protection Gap: The Moral Obligation of the State to Necessitous Immigrants," *University of Pennsylvania Journal of Law and Social Change* 13 (2009–2010): 47–89.

a polity will result in dearth at home. One important question is almost always asked in any discussion of duties toward refugees. We might give our bread, but in the wake of enormous migration flows, how much bread can we really give?[37] As an often-cited parable from the Jewish Halakha suggests, "the poor of your household have priority over the poor of your city, and the poor of your city have priority over the poor of another city."[38] The words seem to recommend considerable caution in spending public resources on newcomers to the community (let alone on creating an opening in the bounded social contract between citizens). God will not "rain down bread from the heavens."[39]

If states have duties toward non-members of the polity, they will be exposed to costs or risks that they would not otherwise be exposed to. Note that such a risk is not foreign to positive human rights law, at least not to its European version. The underlying imperative is reflected, for example, in the language of the European Convention on Human Rights. Article 15.1 allows state signatories to the convention to "derogate," or temporarily rescind, some human rights protections in times of emergency.[40] A core set of the convention's provisions is, however, not "derogable" even in circumstances "threatening the life of the nation."[41] The latter are roughly associated with *jus cogens* norms, which are understood as binding independently of state consent.[42] In other words, the Convention expects signatory governments to take on a measure of risk in order to protect non-citizens from certain egregious harms.

Unlike other areas of law such as national security, in the migration context it is seldom the case that life-threatening risks to citizens are involved. Since 9/11, and more so since the rise of the Islamic State, unauthorized migration and cross-border travel have also been perceived

---

[37] See Michael Walzer's seminal philosophical discussion of distribution among members in the context of the ethics of immigration in Michael Walzer, *Spheres of Justice: A Defense of Pluralism and Equality*, Reprint edition (New York: Basic Books, 1984), 31–34.

[38] I thank W. Michael Reisman for raising this as an objection during a discussion of Chapter 4.

[39] Exodus 16, 4.

[40] R. St. J. MacDonald, "Derogations under Article 15 of the European Convention on Human Rights," *Columbia Journal of Transnational Law* 36 (1998): 225.

[41] European Convention on Human Rights, Article 15.1.

[42] Scholars have debated the differences between "non-derogable" and *jus cogens* norms. See, e.g., Teraya Koji, "Emerging Hierarchy in International Human Rights and Beyond: From the Perspective of Non-derogable Rights," *European Journal of International Law* 12, no. 5 (2001): 917–941.

as security risks. But just as often, the real or perceived risks to members of the social contract are economic. Arvanitakis's image invites us to consider the possibility that regressive results toward fellow citizens may ensue from adherence to human rights imperatives. These seem to be particularly problematic precisely because of the uncompromising character of human rights as defined in this book.

This is yet another reflection of unresolved tensions constituting the identities of those committed both to their political communities' law and to human rights. Though surely not universally accepted, this dual commitment is prevalent among many of us, even if we have vastly disparate political orientations, cultural backgrounds, and religious beliefs. The migration context is a good place to explore these unresolved tensions because here they are familiar. The question is ordinarily framed more or less in the following terms: doesn't the admission of an unlimited number of newcomers risk the rights of citizens? Shouldn't the commitments of a state (or of a supranational entity like the EU) be first and foremost to members of the political community? The poor of one's city must take precedence.

In the migration and immigration debates, liberals often dismiss this argument in terms of self-interest. Migration, they insist, is good for the domestic economy and produces net benefits rather than costs for citizens; hence the temptation to "manage" – an enlightened alternative to sealing any border completely. There is no doubt much wisdom and value in this approach. It cuts against any automatic presumption that interests of would-be immigrants and local citizens necessarily compete. One of the latest policy innovations in the managerial vein takes this proposition even further. Recently, some have pushed toward a conception of refugees as entrepreneurs and innovators who can sustain themselves and advance the economies of receiving states. The question whether policies based on the mutual interests of host communities and refugees are successful or not depends on a host of circumstances. Perhaps the most often discussed are the skills refugees may bring with them.[43]

However, we must allow for at least the theoretical possibility that incoming populations may also present burdens on host societies. They may present competition to domestic workers, rendering their

[43] See, e.g., Anne Marie Slaughter, "New Refugee Homelands," *Project Syndicate*, November 27, 2015, available at www.project-syndicate.org/commentary/new-refugee-homelands-permanent-settlements-by-anne-marie-slaughter-2015-11?barrier=true (last accessed May 12, 2016).

livelihoods insecure. (For this reason, the immigration debate doesn't neatly fall in line with divisions between left and right.) Whatever one thinks of this debate, it is important to acknowledge that sometimes the acceptance of unauthorized migrants as refugees may compromise resources and opportunities otherwise reserved exclusively for citizens. An individual making a decision to save a single migrant and bring her home or a government exceptionally welcoming a vast number of asylum seekers may be caught in a complicated position: they may be violating their obligations under the social contract. Human rights obligations and positive legal obligations each rest on wholly different sets of commitments. To act in accordance with the law means to obey both.

This book did not present an argument for open borders. It presented, rather, an argument according to which there is an imperative that some cost is paid and some risk is taken in any interaction with all humans that come into contact with the state. Obligations under the social contract to fellow citizens cannot end up being death sentences for non-members of the social contract.[44] Though this may seem uncontroversial, one must always keep in mind the possibility that that's exactly what they are. The problem with the managerial approach, dominant not only in the EU but around the developed world, is that it conceals precisely that possibility. By citing the violence that modern European polities have sought to eradicate as well as the violence of their founding, Juncker seems to call attention to those whose lives are endangered by borders. But migration management has constantly sought to conceal such violence and export it to where it will not be seen.

Should states be permitted to deport persons they deem to be in dire risk when they believe the costs are too great for the domestic population to bear? And if so, under what circumstances? The approach I have chosen does not allow me to answer this question from an "objective" point of view. Each person must give their own answer, and in turn, each collective body of citizens must give its own answer.[45] Recall Arendt's insights that this book began from. One might agree with her that when

---

[44] Also, they cannot result in other treatments that we understand as "absolutely prohibited." See Ioannis Kalpouzos an Itamar Mann, "Banal Crimes Against Humanity: The Case of Asylum Seekers in Greece," *Melbourne Journal of International Law* 16, no. 1 (2015): 1.

[45] This explains some of the dynamics Moria Paz describes in Moria Paz, *Between the Kingdom and the Desert Sun: Human Rights, Immigration, and Border Walls*, SSRN Scholarly Paper (Rochester, NY: Social Science Research Network, November 17, 2014), available at http://papers.ssrn.com/abstract=2526521 (last accessed May 12, 2016).

faced with a decision between ensuring the survival of its own citizens and that of non-members, states are bound to choose the former. But one mustn't agree with her that when faced with the de facto stateless, states will tend to entirely disregard their claims. Positive law – however construed – will not give us a final answer to the question of how such claims should be responded to. And whatever answer we provide, it will not only be a moral determination. Clearly, the decision has a moral dimension. But this moral dimension is of a specific kind. It is one that emanates from a sense of duty, not from the more general question of what is the right thing to do. It is thus a legal choice.

~

Conclusion

The Dual Foundation of International Law

Physical movement has become a form of political action.[1] Refugees and migrants whose own states have become sources of danger rather than protection, or have otherwise disintegrated, are moving to seek a life worth living. Before they are in the clear jurisdiction of any other state, they meet individuals who must decide how to respond to them. Human rights law is triggered here – by the experience of obligation toward such people.[2] If no state carries out the duty that must be coupled with the right in order to make it enforceable, the duty falls upon individuals in instances of interpersonal encounter. Even if we do not actually experience in our lives such an interpersonal encounter, we need to answer the question: How should agents of our states respond? This question, I have argued, should become the basis for our understanding of human rights beyond the letter of the law.

Though in the late twentieth century international legal theorists sought to overcome sovereignty – or lamented its demise – sovereignty is firmly rooted as one of the bases of international law.[3] It is the basic category by which law recognizes collective political will. But alongside sovereignty, a second non-positive foundation exists. To paraphrase Andrea Bianchi, in contemporary international legal theory this second

[1] Compare with Hagar Kotef, *Movement and the Ordering of Freedom: On Liberal Governances of Mobility* (Durham and London: Duke University Press Books, 2015).

[2] The work of Emmanuel Lévinas has been at the background of my notion of experience. See, e.g., *Totality and Infinity: An Essay on Exteriority* (Pittsburgh: Duquesne University Press, 1969). On the constitutive role of emotion in law, see generally, Robin West, "Love, Rage, and Legal Theory," *Yale Journal of Law and Feminism* 1 (1989): 101–110; Robin West, *Caring for Justice* (New York: NYU Press, 1997). For a critique of the reliance on rationality as the basis for the social contract, see Paul Kahn, *Putting Liberalism in Its Place* (Princeton: Princeton University Press, 2008).

[3] Jose E. Alvarez, "State Sovereignty Is Not Withering Away: A Few Lessons for the Future," in Antonio Cassese (ed.), *Realizing Utopia: The Future of International Law* (Oxford: Oxford University Press, 2012). (Refuting arguments about the demise of sovereignty and emphasizing the continuum in the notion of sovereignty from the Treaty of Westphalia to the present.)

foundation has retained an "aura of mystery."[4] Far from being unique to migration or refugee law – or even especially central to this subfield – an appeal to non-positive sources is pervasive across international law. Of course, this appeal is not ordinarily thought of by reference to what I have called the human rights encounter. My experiential account of human rights is a corrective to a more traditional understanding of an unwritten foundation of international law.

In the tradition stemming from the writings of Hugo Grotius, often considered "the father of modern international law," international law had a dual foundation. On the one hand, there was natural law, also called the law of necessity or *jus naturale necessarium*. These rules were considered equally binding upon human and divine authority. They were part of a distinctly religious cosmology. On the other hand, there was voluntary law or *jus voluntarium*, freely authored by political rulers.[5] Allowing for some anachronism, we might call the latter positive law. Translated to contemporary terms, this second body of law would include both domestic sources such as statutes, case law, and regulations, and international sources such as treaties and customary international law.[6] The fiercest debates in twentieth-century jurisprudence were between natural lawyers and positivists, with each group claiming its own position to be an exclusively correct understanding of legality.[7] But for authors like Grotius, there was no need to choose between natural and positive law (or between *jus naturale necessarium* and *jus voluntarium*). Grotius embraced his own versions of both. They were complementary aspects of one normative universe.[8] Instead of staking one ultimate source for law, Grotius sought to define the respective spheres where each would be controlling. The vast majority of law was voluntary, but an important set of prescriptions was held as natural or necessary law.

---

[4] Andrea Bianchi, "Human Rights and the Magic of Jus Cogens," *European Journal of International Law* 19, no. 3 (2008): 491–508.

[5] Alfred Verdross, "Jus Dispositivum and Jus Cogens in International Law," *American Journal of International Law* 60 (1966): 56.

[6] See my own discussion in the context of the Eichmann trial in Itamar Mann, "The Dual Foundation of Universal Jurisdiction: Towards a Jurisprudence for the 'Court of Critique'," *Transnational Legal Theory* 1, no. 4 (2010): 485–521.

[7] The most famous of them between H.L.A. Hart and Lon Fuller. See, e.g., Nicola Lacey, "Philosophy, Political Morality, and History: Explaining the Enduring Resonance of the Hart-Fuller Debate," *New York University Law Review* 83 (2008): 1059–1087.

[8] See, generally, Benjamin Straumann, *Roman Law in the State of Nature: The Classical Foundations of Hugo Grotius' Natural Law* (Cambridge: Cambridge University Press, 2015).

Though admittedly anachronistic, this understanding of Grotius captures an important aspect of his legacy, which occasionally resurfaced in the language of international law centuries later.[9] Today, this dual foundation thesis is nearly forgotten.[10]

Even so, situations of crisis lead to the "return of the repressed."[11] Crises are central to international law.[12] The history of unauthorized maritime migration unfolded above should be understood, first and foremost, as a history of crises. Such crises have pushed states and individuals to actions and to a normative vocabulary beyond formal rules and processes – a vocabulary in which human rights are central, but in which the duties that correspond to them are not fastened securely to any particular actor.[13] These dynamics are often either untheorized or theorized very flimsily. But the experiences they emerge from are worth close attention, which I tried to grant in this book. As the figure of the universal boatperson illustrates, non-positive international legal vocabularies are often cast as a kind of fallback option. When all other law seems to fail, humanity is invoked as a last-resort normative commitment. This is the human rights commitment, properly understood.[14]

In the preceding chapters, such commitments appeared in the words of politicians. Think of Cyrus Vance, who explained to Congress why the United States should sponsor an enormous resettlement program for Vietnamese refugees (early in Chapter 3). A similar version of the same leap beyond positive authority appeared in Chapter 6, which analyzes Jean-Claude Juncker's words in his State of the Union address from September 2015. Other examples appeared in the more

---

[9] See, e.g., Benedict Kingsbury, "A Grotian Tradition of Theory and Practice: Grotius, Law, and Moral Skepticism in the Thought of Hedley Bull," *Quinnipiac Law Review* 17 (1997): 4 (providing bibliography of renewed interest in Grotius since the mid-nineteenth century); Hersch Lauterpacht, "The Grotian Tradition in International Law," *British Year Book of International Law* 23 (1946): 1.

[10] An exception is a book in progress, Oona Hathaway and Scott Shapiro, *The Worst Crime of All: The Paris Peace Pact and the Beginning of the End of War* (tentative title).

[11] The terminology is borrowed from Sigmund Freud. In the context of international law, see *The Juridical Unconscious: Trials and Traumas in the Twentieth Century* (Cambridge, MA: Harvard University Press, 2002), 57.

[12] Hilary Charlesworth, "International Law: A Discipline of Crisis," *The Modern Law Review* 65, no. 3 (2002): 377–392.

[13] On this correspondence, see generally, Wesley Newcomb Hohfeld, "Some Fundamental Legal Conceptions as Applied in Judicial Reasoning," *The Yale Law Journal* 23, no. 1 (1913): 16–59.

[14] See my discussion of the notion of a "court of last resort" in Mann, "The Dual Foundation of Universal Jurisdiction," 487–496.

professionalized terminologies of legal scholars such as Georg Schwarzenberger, a refugee who wrote about the postwar refugee crisis. The Australian lawyer David Johnson cited Schwarzenberger at the face of another similar crisis. As Chapter 2 recounts, Johnson considered how Australia should respond to Southeast Asian "boat people" after the Vietnam War in the terms of a very similar political imagination. There were certain options that were simply unavailable to Australian authorities when they confronted humans – even humans who seemed to be reduced to bare life. As I explained, the commitments underlying such limitations on policy are meaningless if they do not allow humans who need them to rely on them.

Far from these political and legal elites – but just as importantly – the actions and words of migrants and refugees have constantly pointed to a non-positive source of law as well. In Chapter 4, asylum seekers honed in on what seemed to be the last positive legal duty working in their favor: the duty of rescue at sea (which is enshrined both in treaty and in customary international law). But as I have argued, they sought to trigger a more robust set of non-positive commitments toward human presence. (From the perspective of the relatively powerless party to the encounters I have described, these were never merely about survival.) A central methodological claim I made across the book was that when it comes to human rights the professionalized language of lawyers shouldn't be given preference. The claims of migrants and refugees who seek human rights remedies were thus advanced at the forefront of this book's arguments. In order to understand what human rights are, we must always begin from the claims of those who demand: *You* must enforce *my* rights.

Sovereignty is still often thought of as the ultimate foundation of public international law, inasmuch as states have the capacity to consent to international law. As such, states are the authors of international law.[15] As a familiar story goes, sovereignty has been under the pressures of ever more networked interactions of, e.g., global markets, online communities, and terrorist organizations. These realities seemed to suggest a new world order.[16] International legal theorists have thus tirelessly

---

[15] See, e.g., Anthony Aust, *Handbook of International Law* (Cambridge and New York: Cambridge University Press, 2005), 4 (stating that international law "is based on the consent [express or implied] of states"); Duncan Hollis, "Why State Consent Still Matters – Non-State Actors, Treaties, and the Changing Sources of International Law," *Berkeley Journal of International Law* 23, no. 1 (2005): 137–174.

[16] Anne-Marie Slaughter, *A New World Order* (Princeton: Princeton University Press, 2005).

criticized the monopoly of states as the source of authority in international law, often claiming that sovereignty is an antiquated concept. Proposals for an alternative foundational account for international law are varied: Among the favorite candidates were democratic legitimacy, individual autonomy, and the pluralism of multiple non-hierarchical authorities.[17] Another characteristic response is reconceptualizing sovereignty as a notion involving global, universal, responsibility.[18]

But the recurring reference to "humanity" in the face of catastrophe suggests that these proposals are erroneous. Instead, a dual set of normative commitments endures. References to humanity have time and again been criticized as a moral rhetoric thinly masking the interests of the powerful. The point is surely accurate in some cases, especially those involving questions about military intervention.[19] But this focus is to some extent misleading: Even the staunchest supporters of such intervention rarely recognize it as a *duty*. But, as I have argued in this book, these references to humanity do entail some duties; and if we want to know something about rights, it is here that we must start.[20] International law – the law of international rights and duties – is founded neither solely on sovereignty, nor on its ever-growing parade of transnational and global-governance-based alternatives or reconcptualizations. The second basis for law – alongside sovereignty as the projection of collective political will, and the source of positive law – is a distinct and independent source: human rights.

---

[17] On democratic legitimacy, see, e.g., Thomas M. Franck, "The Emerging Right to Democratic Governance," *The American Journal of International Law* 86, no. 1 (1992): 46–91; Anne-Marie Slaughter, "International Law in a World of Liberal States," *European Journal of International Law* 6 (1995): 503; on individual autonomy, see Samantha Besson, "The Authority of International Law – Lifting the State Veil," *Sydney Law Review* 31 (2009): 343; on legal pluralism see Alec Stone Sweet, "Constitutionalism, Legal Pluralism, and International Regimes," *Indiana Journal of Global Legal Studies* 16, no. 2 (2009): 621–645; Armin von Bogdandy, "Pluralism, Direct Effect, and the Ultimate Say: On the Relationship between International and Domestic Constitutional Law," *International Journal of Constitutional Law* 6, nos. 3–4 (2008): 397–413; Ralf Michaels, "Global Legal Pluralism," *Annual Review of Law and Social Science* 5, no. 1 (2009): 243–262.

[18] Benvenisti.

[19] See, e.g., Anne Orford, *Reading Humanitarian Intervention: Human Rights and the Use of Force in International Law*, Reissue edition (Cambridge: Cambridge University Press, 2007); Anne Orford, *International Authority and the Responsibility to Protect* (Cambridge and New York: Cambridge University Press, 2011); Martti Koskenniemi, "'The Lady Doth Protest Too Much' Kosovo, and the Turn to Ethics in International Law," *The Modern Law Review* 65, no. 2 (2002): 159–175.

[20] Hohfeld, "Some Fundamental Legal Conceptions as Applied in Judicial Reasoning."

Unlike Grotius at his own time, today we can no longer say that this second basis is *natural*. The *experience* of the human rights encounter grants this second basis its content even without grounding it in an understanding of human nature. Instead of claims of religious or metaphysical truth, human rights commitments begin from an experience, whereby the actor experiencing the commitment remains, importantly, agnostic as to its basis in truth. To put it more starkly, the human rights commitment is such that it remains binding despite the fact we know it is *not* based in objective truth.[21] Precisely because we have no access to such truth, the individual exercising autonomous reason can also not be the basis for human rights. At the basis of sovereignty – understood in the social contract tradition – we have a collective constituent body. At the basis of human rights, we have a dyadic encounter. This, I believe, is the most fundamental insight from our contemporary condition of a global refugee or migration crisis; it is an insight that will remain important even as policymakers and lawyers will continue addressing burning structural problems such as global inequality and global warming.

All this may sound abstract or even speculative. Notice, however, that the appeal to non-positive norms recurs even in international law's more technical terms. In line with international lawyers' longstanding attempts to establish their discipline as truly *legal*, there has been an enduring attempt to codify such non-positive sources. This is a paradoxical and an ultimately unsuccessful exercise, the perplexities of which are visible in areas of law that pertain to exceptional situations of crisis or emergency. In the late nineteenth and twentieth centuries, these were paradigmatically situations of interstate or civil war.[22] But we are living through an era in which migration and refugee flows have exposed a crisis of comparable magnitude.

A famous example in which an appeal to non-positive law was "codified" in the context of war was that of the Martens Clause. The Martens Clause has been a part of the laws of armed conflict since its first appearance in the preamble to the 1899 Hague Convention. The Martens Clause provides that:

---

[21] Jacques Derrida, *Adieu to Emmanuel Levinas* (Stanford: Stanford University Press, 1999), 21–22.

[22] Perhaps the most iconic and influential account of war as crisis is Henry Dunant, *A Memory of Solferino* (Washington, DC: International Committee of the Red Cross, 1986).

Until a more complete code of the laws of war is issued, the High
Contracting Parties think it right to declare that in cases not included in
the Regulations adopted by them, populations and belligerents remain
under the protection and empire of the principles of international law, as
they result from the usages established between civilized nations, from the
laws of humanity and the requirements of the public conscience.[23]

The Martens Clause entered the Hague Convention against the background of disagreement between the parties to the Convention. The parties could not reach consensus on certain limitations to military power, and yet felt the need to assert that such limitations do exist. By making its way into the text, the Martens Clause *invited* inconsistent invocations and contestations over what a label like "public conscience" may demand.[24] Such contestations haven't ceased ever since.

The same dynamic is familiar around a category of "peremptory norms," or *jus cogens. Jus cogens* norms are considered binding upon all actors, even without consent. Historically, the category of *jus cogens* was often referred to as rules that bar practices that are repudiated by all "civilized" nations. The most commonly discussed examples are the prohibition of torture, wars of aggression, crimes against humanity, apartheid, and genocide. Perhaps the most authoritative body on the interpretation and development of international law is the International Law Commission. The Commission is a highly regarded group of international law experts convened under a UN mandate. But as the International Law Commission has found, the list of *jus cogens* norms is not a finite or closed list.[25] Enumerating such a finite list, the Commission recognizes, would not only be impossible but also mistaken. There may always be a possibility that a violation of international law be considered so heinous as to merit inclusion in this list of basic prohibitions. Thus, when tasked with explaining the precise scope of *jus cogens*, the Commission effectively reaches beyond the letter of the law. How might we know what other *jus cogens* prohibitions might appear? A second source of international law exists but remains ineffable, imperceptible, and – in mainstream

---

[23] See Rupert Ticehurst, "The Martens Clause and the Laws of Armed Conflict," *International Review of the Red Cross* 317, www.icrc.org/eng/resources/documents/misc/57jnhy.htm (last accessed May 13, 2016).

[24] Isabel V. Hull, *A Scrap of Paper: Breaking and Making International Law during the Great War*, 1st edition (Ithaca: Cornell University Press, 2014), 73–95.

[25] See document A/69/10, 281 (available at http://legal.un.org/ilc/reports/2014/english/annex.pdf) (last accessed May 13, 2016).

scholarship – untheorized.[26] It is as if we must first watch the world sink into new forms of terror, and only then will we know.

The Rome Statute, which established the International Criminal Court, reproduces the same problem. The Statute criminalizes a list of violations of *jus cogens* but leaves a residual category that, as it were, prepares lawyers who apply the statue for the unexpected: that of "other inhumane acts" (Article 7(1)(k)). This provision leaves the Statute open to the possibility that certain acts will be *criminalized* even though their prohibition is not spelled out in advance (in possible violation of the principle of legality). Tribunals and commentators have sought to minimize the difficulty here, mostly by emphasizing how narrowly this provision should be interpreted and how rarely it should be invoked.[27] However, the provision remains. And it reflects a larger aspect of the architecture of international law.

Importantly, peremptory norms (or *jus cogens*) are not considered binding only upon states but inasmuch as they are the basis of international criminal law, directly upon individuals.[28] This point is reflected, for example, in another doctrine of international criminal law: that of the "manifestly illegal order." No exemption from criminal liability can be given to those who perpetrate heinous acts as part of their military duty. There are certain acts that remain illegal no matter what positive law says. But as the subjects of international law we don't know, ex ante, what all those acts are. We must exercise our own judgment. This is not because those acts exist in some ideal sphere of truth that is independent of our judgment (though inaccessible as an epistemic matter). It is because judgment is necessary in establishing and constituting the category of absolutely prohibited acts.[29] Such a category simply does not exist if it does not exist as a matter of a person's judgment.

---

[26] Reliance on non-positive sources has often been considered the "original sin" of international criminal law. See discussion in Quincy Wright, "Legal Positivism and the Nuremberg Judgment," *The American Journal of International Law* 42, no. 2 (1948): 405–414.

[27] See Kenneth Gallant, *The Principle of Legality in International and Comparative Criminal Law* (Cambridge: Cambridge University Press, 2009), 336; Decision on the Confirmation of Charges Pursuant to Article 61(7)(a) and (b) of the Rome Statute, *Muthaura* (ICC-01/ 09–02/11), March 11, 2013, Pre-Trial Chamber [269].

[28] M. Cherif Bassiouni, "International Crimes: 'Jus Cogens' and 'Obligatio Erga Omnes'," *Law and Contemporary Problems* 59, no. 4 (1996): 63–74.

[29] See also Itamar Mann, "What Is a Manifestly Illegal Order? Law and Politics after Yoram Kaniuk's *Nevelot*," in *The Politics of Nihilism: From the Nineteenth Century to Contemporary Israel* (New York: Bloomsbury Publishing, 2014).

Shying away from any return to a "law of necessity," contemporary international lawyers typically make two moves to assert that international law is fully accountable in positivist terms. By doing so, scholars and practitioners seek to provide a quieting assurance that there is no inconsistency within the most fundamental principles of international law. First, the claim is that preemptory norms are supported by a *consensus* in the international community. This idea appears, for example, in the words of the International Law Commission, which found that "there is a number, albeit a small one, of international obligations which, by reason of the importance of their subject-matter for the international community as a whole, are – unlike the others – obligations in whose fulfillment all States have a legal *interest*" (emphasis added).[30] In other words, states essentially agree on what conduct should be considered as binding upon all of them. *Jus cogens* can therefore be squared within the realm of positive or *voluntary* law. Once that is established, a second move is made possible: because they are supported by a consensus, preemptory norms can play an integrative role, organizing the discipline of international law (otherwise often considered as fragmented).[31] *Jus cogens* thus helps alleviate a concern that has constantly cropped up in recent years, that of contradictions between the discipline's subfields.[32] Can tensions between the dictates of trade and environmental law be solved systematically? If the result of the application of one set of rules leads to the violation of *jus cogens*, the latter result is barred. A hierarchical order of international law is reestablished. The discipline is saved from the threat of lawlessness and reasserts its validity as a proper field of legal practice and inquiry. As a practical matter, of course, the fragmentation of international law may still generate quandaries or disputes. Clearly, only few of the apparent contradictions between subfields even implicate the "higher" law of *jus cogens*.

---

[30] *Yearbook of the International Law Commission* 2 (1975): 99. See also Theodor Meron, "On a Hierarchy of International Human Rights," *American Journal of International Law* 80 (1986): 1.

[31] Pierre-Marie Dupuy, "Some Reflections on Contemporary International Law and the Appeal to Universal Values: A Response to Martti Koskenniemi," *European Journal of International Law* 16, no. 1 (2005): 131–137.

[32] The notion of "fragmentation" has been subject of a copious amount of literature in recent years. See most importantly the International Law Commission report on the subject: Martti Koskenniemi, *Fragmentation of International Law: Difficulties Arising from the Diversification and Expansion of International Law*, General Assembly A/CN.4/L.682, April 13, 2006, available at http://legal.un.org/ilc/documentation/english/a_cn4_l682.pdf (last accessed May 13, 2016).

Yet, as a rhetorical and as a theoretical matter, such disputes are purportedly contained within an overall picture of order.

As others have argued, this reliance on consensus in the context of *jus cogens* couldn't be weaker. The lack of consensus that led to the drafting of the Martens Clause is indicative of the fate of the non-positive source of international law more generally. Far from being truly universal, these rules at best represent a faint semblance of universality. No agreement exists on the scope or definition of rules that are thought to be binding upon all. Given post-9/11 torture by US agents, with the tacit collusion of many governments around the world, it is hard to understand how consensus can even be contemplated in good faith.[33]

The text of the Martens Clause may serve as a proxy of the more general problem. "Until a more complete code of the laws of war is issued" reflects the hope that disagreement is temporary and that consensus can be achieved, if only we wait. The reference to an "empire of principles" reflects the thought that behind the rules there is a grand, determinable legal order.[34] The "usages established between civilized nations" calls attention to the fact that often "consensus" really means that not all nations are considered equally important. "The laws of humanity" reads as an oblique reference to human nature – a tacit bow to the natural law tradition. And lastly, "public conscience" – perhaps the most pertinent to the theory of the human rights encounter – implies that conscience is experienced as "public" (rather than private). More than a century after this text was first drafted, the underlying assumptions of many scholars and practitioners of public international law, human rights, international humanitarian law, and international criminal law, still comport with the basic elements of the text. But each and every one of these components is highly contestable. And if no consensus exists between states, the project of universal law collapses. This is a conceptual threat to human rights more generally; for even in standard accounts, human rights do not derive their universal authority from being enshrined in the text of their foundational treaties.

---

[33] This, of course, is not to say that consensus around certain basic rules, such as the rule against torture, wouldn't be desirable. Indeed, the realization that for some people torture is not only permitted but may be also legally required and may cause dismay or outrage. But one must admit: our own breath blows the dust of consensus away once we closely examine seemingly universal legal rules.

[34] My guess is that it aims somehow to mirror Immanuel Kant's famous notion of a "kingdom of ends."

Against the backdrop of these generalist public international law concerns, this book's inquiry into legal obligations toward refugees and
migrants upon the high seas may seem like a strange move.[35] Why an
analysis of a seemingly marginal case, to make such grand claims about
human rights? The basic point relates to one that has been made – in
a very different way – by scholars both on the right and on the left aiming
to demonstrate the primacy of politics over law. If in the exceptional case
the ultimate decisions are always political, these scholars claim, then
politics is the existential and defining category of public life.[36] In my
own analysis, the use of the exceptional case is different. Rather than
unmasking the politics behind law, I reveal non-positive human rights
law behind the surface of positive law. Human rights are defined by the
fact that in the exceptional case they cannot be suspended by an act of
sovereign will. Political rulers may try to do exactly that, and indeed
many have. But for those who feel bound by human rights, when they do
so, such rulers lose their own legitimacy. Ultimately, citizens might have
to choose to step out of the social contract and address their own country
as humans rather than as citizens. Political decision, I believe, is never
truly freed from law; it never occurs in a fully autonomous, self-
referential mode.[37]

Moreover, my focus on maritime migration put emphasis on one
particular aspect of refugee law: the duty of *non-refoulement*. While
this obligation has positive grounding in the Refugee Convention
(Article 33), it does not only accrue to those defined as refugees in
the Convention. And unlike the Convention, which relies on state
consent, the duty of *non-refoulement* retains an aura of universality.
Yet, even for those who believe that a core of consensus exists around
a list of *jus cogens* norms, *non-refoulement* is a controversial item in

---

[35] And yet, see Chantal Thomas's inquiry into the contemporary nature of sovereignty and
its relationship to the natural law tradition and with the social contract, in the context of
the challenge of global migration. Chantal Thomas, "What Does the Emerging
International Law of Migration Mean for Sovereignty?" *Melbourne Journal of
International Law*, 14 (2013): 409 ("[T]he rights of foreigners under natural law traditions
anticipate the rights of migrants emerging under contemporary international law").

[36] See, e.g., Carl Schmitt, *The Concept of the Political*, Enlarged edition (Chicago: University
of Chicago Press, 2007); Giorgio Agamben, *State of Exception*, 1st edition (Chicago:
University of Chicago Press, 2005); Paul W. Kahn, *Political Theology: Four New
Chapters on the Concept of Sovereignty*, Reprint edition (New York: Columbia
University Press, 2012).

[37] This argument has been made most forcefully and famously by Robert Cover.
Robert M. Cover, "Foreword: Nomos and Narrative," *Harvard Law Review* 97 (1983): 4.

the list. While some do claim that *non-refoulement* is a *jus cogens* norm, this obligation illustrates the paradoxical nature of the project of asserting consensus around certain universal norms. How can the prohibition of returning someone to where they will suffer inhuman or degrading treatment be considered as universal by some but not by others? This is not only the fate of *non-refoulement*. It is the fate of the entire list of *jus cogens* norms, whatever you choose to include in it. It is the fate of human rights.

If the seemingly universal norms do not really enjoy a stable consensus, choosing one that clearly does not enjoy consensus is the case in point. By doing so, I sought to illustrate that the universal validity of certain rules is not in fact about consensus at all. First – and this is a somewhat trite point that nevertheless has to be reiterated – no nation is more "civilized" than another.[38] If there is a law of humanity, it is not about emulating the determinations of any particular set of nations, whether they are good or not. It is not about human nature, nor is it about a public aspect of conscience that is already given regardless of our own active roles. It is a *demand* for universality that is at the heart of human rights law. Choosing *non-refoulement* and the plight of the universal boatperson allowed me to argue for this contemporary understanding of the dual foundation of international law.[39]

The positive law that we choose freely as members of our respective social contracts is by no means diminished or discarded by this account of a dual foundation. Neither are the treaties our states accede to, the dictates of customary international law, or any other positive source on the international or the domestic sphere. But for those of us who define ourselves through a commitment to human rights, another completely different kind of law exists, which emanates from a separate source. This is a law that *requires us to regard all human beings as if they enjoyed some necessary protections*, the duties corresponding to which can fall upon anyone's shoulders. It is important that we do so precisely because we know it is not in fact the case.[40] This is a law that consists of a conviction that there are certain terrible plights that no human should ever suffer

---

[38] Arnulf Becker Lorca has documented the demise of the standard of "civilization" in international law. See Arnulf Becker Lorca, *Mestizo International Law: A Global Intellectual History 1842–1933* (Cambridge: Cambridge University Press, 2015), 225–262.

[39] This, of course, does not mean a return to seventeenth-century doctrine, which would be a silly proposal.

[40] Compare with Jacques Rancière, "Who Is the Subject of the Rights of Man?" *The South Atlantic Quarterly* 103, no. 2 (2004): 297–310.

from. Thus, the second basis for law does not enjoy consensus. It cannot be squared with positive law. But it is also not given in the world regardless of our own convictions. This dependency of the law on our own conviction removes it from the realm of the "natural."[41]

This second basis of law is *necessary* not in some metaphysical sense, but rather in a personal, intimate, existential sense. We cannot violate it and remain true to ourselves. The phenomenology of embarrassment, which I introduce in Chapter 1 but which is then developed across the various chapters, is essentially the embarrassment of the subject of international law that experiences herself as bound by the two normative sources, which do not always point to the same results. This is not proposed as a *criticism* of international law, which would recommend somehow abandoning the international legal vocabulary, or employing it entirely instrumentally.[42] One can perhaps *foster* a way of experiencing the world (as I have suggested in Chapter 6); but one cannot simply *abandon* it. Thus, being bound by human rights means recognizing that such an embarrassment will remain in some profound way an important aspect of one's identity. Rather than criticism, one might propose the notion of *critique*, by which I mean the imperative to constantly be struggling with the dilemmas that this dual foundation imposes upon the self.[43] This imperative of critique does not mean being left passive or handicapped or not engaging with politics. But it does mean a constant engagement with the limitations of any form of collective identity or organizing, be it the state or be it some other group affiliation.

To be sure, moving away from the grounding of human rights in state consent, agreement, or consensus, invites an enormous risk.[44] One of the reasons why a basis in consensus has been such an important and enduring

---

[41] Here, I'm answering directly Samuel Moyn's critique of an early version of Chapter 1 of this book. See Samuel Moyn, "The Embarrassment of Human Rights," *Texas International Law Journal: The Forum* 50, no. 1 (2015), 2, available at www.tilj.org /content/forum/14%20MOYN%20PUBLICATION.pdf (last accessed May 13, 2016). Moyn described the chapter as "A New Natural Law" (while contesting that it is, in fact, new).

[42] This position is characteristic of a particular strain of critical international law scholarship, led by David Kennedy. See, e.g., David Kennedy, *The Dark Sides of Virtue: Reassessing International Humanitarianism* (Princeton: Princeton University Press, 2005).

[43] Compare Mann, "The Dual Foundation of Universal Jurisdiction" (on "the court of critique"); and Itamar Mann, "Dialectic of Transnationalism: Unauthorized Migration and Human Rights, 1993–2013," *Harvard International Law Journal* 54, no. 2 (2013): 315 (on the notion of "critical absolutism").

[44] See Moyn, "The Embarrassment of Human Rights."

aspect of international law is in order to espouse a kind of normative pluralism. Forgoing a basis in agreement, it would seem, would mean closing the space for the hard work of political negotiation and the establishment of bridges across vastly disparate groups. This reason is precisely why Martti Koskenniemi, for example, basically rejects the terminology of *jus cogens*.[45] Instead of pretending that agreement upon high values already exists, he contends, such agreement must be won through politics and through the active forging of alliances. The formal expressions of such hard-won agreements can, for example, be treaties. Treaties express their basis in will, rather than in any lofty discourse of existential necessity (always both moral and legal at the same time). In a slightly different vein of scholarship, authors analyzing documents such as the Universal Declaration of Human Rights have often emphasized the way in which representatives from drastically *different* cultures came to agree upon fundamental values.[46] Through such processes international law obtained an integrating and bridging role among cultures. And these values are in turn associated with benefits such as security and international stability. Claiming international legally binding force for a norm that clearly does not enjoy agreement – that would seem like a dangerously polarizing, disintegrating, and destabilizing move.

Surely, there is something to this point. Basing human rights on an independent, subjective judgment is in this sense proposed as a cautionary note. In order to embrace pluralism, we must abstain, as much as possible, from relying upon a human rights framework. More often than not, dominant actors have used such a framework in order to impose their own values and interests on far-away cultures. A related and slightly more nuanced point is that approaching foreign policy issues from a human rights perspective, dominant actors might impose on themselves unnecessary constraints. Such constraints might prevent them from reaching the kinds of flexibility and agreement that are needed in order to restore security and stability. My attempt to limit human rights to a very thin and very firm set of commitments is thus also an attempt to clear them *away* from a vast spectrum of foreign policy issues in which they may have occluded the political imagination.

Human rights impose on members of humanity who are also members of a functioning social contract the duty to enforce human rights.

---

[45] See Martti Koskenniemi, "International Law in Europe: Between Tradition and Renewal," *The European Journal of International Law* 16, no. 1 (2005): 122–123.

[46] See, e.g., Mary Ann Glendon, *A World Made New: Eleanor Roosevelt and the Universal Declaration of Human Rights* (New York: Random House, 2002).

Arendt's damning account of the fate of refugees in Europe in the interwar period repositions individuals in mutual responsibility to disallow such fate to recur. Individual people become the foremost addressees of human rights claims. This is not the often-reiterated, yet empty, idea of a responsibility of "the international community." As others have written, when a responsibility falls on everyone's shoulders, no one ends up carrying its burden. Within the realm of human rights, correctly understood, legality appears as a command of the conscience that all other humans can impose upon the self. Each dyad forming the human rights encounter creates a potential opportunity – small as it may be – to correct the horrors of collective political decisions. From the perspective of the relatively powerless party to the human rights encounter, this is an opportunity to expose that she has not been counted and assert herself as a potential *member*. From the perspective of the relatively powerful party to the encounter, this is an opportunity to exercise her own independent judgment against the determinations made by her state or by "the international community." A substantive condition that this judgment must meet in order to be the basis for a human rights commitment is that any human being who lacks effective membership can potentially trigger it.

Each individual's conscience is thus a potential counter-balance to "public conscience" – in the domestic or on the international spheres. When the result of the human rights encounter is that human rights are enforced, then "public conscience" has likely transformed. To paraphrase Arendt, a new "place in the world" is made for those who asserted a human rights claim. The category of being human becomes a stepping stone either toward establishing a new state (as was the case in Chapter 1) or toward acceptance in an existing one (as was the case in Chapter 2).

The imagination of a dyadic meeting as a conceptual starting point complementary to the social contract is not foreign to political thought. It has, however, been historically employed for quite different purposes. Take, for example, Jean-Jacques Rousseau's famous opening of his *Discourse on the Origins of Language*: "Upon encountering others, a savage man will first be afraid. His fright will make him see those men as taller and stronger than himself. He will give them the name *Giants*."[47] This asymmetry of power, Rousseau explains, will quickly prove illusory: "After many experiences he will recognize that as these supposed Giants are neither taller nor stronger than himself . . . He will therefore invent another name common to

---

[47] Jean Jacques Rousseau, *Essay on the Origin of Languages and Writings Related to Music* (Hanover and London: University Press of New England, 2009).

them and to him such as the name *man* for example . . ."[48] The story is a political coming-of-age: Once humans conceive of their own basic equality, they are ready to accede to the political pact of mutual interest and will give each other their own law.

The human rights encounter starts from a wholly different premise. From the perspective of a migrant or a refugee, the world may look like a Hobbesian state of nature. It certainly looked that way to many of the actors examined across this book, whether they were Jewish DPs, Vietnamese "boat people," Haitian migrants and refugees, or Iraqi and Afghan migrants seeking to reach Australia. It probably looks that way right now to Syrian refugees and to migrants and refugees from many other countries. But this omnipresent war is the product of politics and of history, rather than an external point for its departure. We experience ourselves as committed to human rights precisely *because* of the tolls history bears upon us and cannot be eliminated or diminished. The uprooting of populations by civil war, famine, or any other reason are all results of politics, rather than of its absence. Not original equality but stark political inequality is the condition we must start from in order to theorize human rights.

This inequality is anything but illusory. Parties to the human rights encounter are consequently not in the position to conclude a pact of mutual interest. From the perspective of the powerful party to the encounter, it isn't clear she has such an interest at all. Being bound by human rights means being subject to duties that correspond to the rights of non-members, which are in the first instance *beyond* any mutual interest. If such commitments are firm, Rousseau is right that recognition of mutual interests comes next.

---

[48] Rousseau, *Essay on the Origin of Languages and Writings Related to Music*, 294.

~

Postscript

Toward the end of the Book of Genesis, the Hebrews are described as guest workers in Egypt. They migrated after a drought caused a food shortage in Canaan, where they had previously resided. The Bible tells us they are initially hosted and tolerated, but at the outset of the Book of Exodus, Pharaoh realizes that they are multiplying uncontrollably. He is worried about the potential that the Hebrews may come to outnumber the Egyptians. He therefore perceives the demographic threat of multiplying foreigners as a security threat. He takes this threat as a license to employ exceptional measures against them: "Come, let us deal wisely with them, or else they will multiply and in the event of war, they will also join themselves to those who hate us."[1] The "wise" policies that Pharaoh devises are initially enslavement and then the systematized killing of the newborn males.[2]

The Exodus is of course one of the most important myths of political beginning, but its constitutive moment is not at Mount Sinai, as philosophical commentary has almost invariably assumed. Politics and the constitution of law start shortly after Moses is born.

Moses's mother, Jochebed, initially hides him from slavery and infanticide. At the age of three months, she sets her baby adrift in the Nile: "And when she could no longer hide him she took for him an ark of bulrushes, and daubed it with slime and with pitch, and put the child therein; and she laid it in the flags by the river's brink."[3] Miryam, Moses's sister, overlooked the river from afar, waiting to witness what would

---

[1] Exodus, Chapter 2:10. The recognition that the humiliation of the Hebrews may turn them from slaves to enemies is itself a tacit acknowledgment of their claim. Pharaoh's fear of the Hebrews is intimately tied with a kind of guilt. See Paul Kahn, *Out of Eden* (Princeton: Princeton University Press, 2007), 158–169. ("To acknowledge the possibility of a slave rebellion is implicitly to recognize the slave's humanity . . . Corresponding to the construction of the slave as the shame of nature is the construction of a master characterized by fear and guilt.")

[2] Pua and Shifra the midwives object.

[3] Exodus, 2:3.

become of the drifting baby.[4] The positioning illustrates that a risk is involved and that the baby's fate is yet unclear.

Jochebed's decision to expose her boy to danger is almost impossible to imagine outside of conditions of nightmarish persecution. Importantly, however, this danger is not justified in the context of sacrifice for something greater than life. To the contrary: while Jochebed's calculated risk is made in dire circumstances, it is ultimately meant to secure individual survival for her boy. Jochebed makes a decision after which she may suffer the most terrible form of loss. Even if it does not turn out to be a mistake, her son will still no longer be with her. The most optimistic hope she could have was that an Egyptian would find Moses and adopt him. Presumably, Jochebed intended her son neither to be the liberator of the Jewish people nor the leader of any other people. In the best imaginable scenario, Moses would integrate into Egyptian society, finding not only survival but also freedom as a member of a new polity.

Jochebed's action is not unlike a thread of similar actions throughout this book. Remember the British charge that the Zionists abducted young children and put them on a boat. Jochebed could have similarly been accused of neglecting her newborn. Remember aircraft carrier *Blue Ridge* and the Vietnamese woman that "stood up and held out her baby as if to say, 'At least take him.'" Vietnamese mothers who placed their babies in orphanages at the prospect of the United States' imminent retreat are another interesting analog. These mothers hoped their babies would be taken to the United States. Some were flown out of the country in "Operation Babylift."[5]

But perhaps the most pertinent comparison is with the testimony of the Iraqi Zainab Hassan in the context of the "Children Overboard" affair recounted in Chapter 4: "he was holding his child to tell them, look we have children, if you don't care about me care about my child." By placing her baby in the river, Jochebed told the Egyptian authorities, if you don't care about me care about my child. The African migrants described in Chapter 5 did the same thing.

Miryam's position as a spectator looking from afar is a way of constructing the encounter, actively manufacturing the space in which it will occur. One might even say she is using a measure of surveillance for her

---

[4] Exodus, 2:4.
[5] When they initiated legal battles to get babies back from foster families, mothers and other relatives had to explain their choices to American courts.

own needs. Rather than detached spectatorship, this gaze is meant to grant the boy a certain modicum of protection from afar.

By placing Moses in the river, his mother hoped to rid him of his ties to the persecuted group. In his famous essay about the story, *Moses and Monotheism*, Freud insists that "[t]he exposure in a casket is an unmistakable symbolic representation of birth: the casket is the womb and the water the amniotic fluid."[6] This may be consistent with his theory of psychoanalysis more generally. From the present perspective, however, the water is first of all a fluid *border* between Moses' early upbringing within the Hebrews and his insertion into the Egyptian polity. It delimits an area beyond sovereignty, from which it is still possible to partake in some form of politics. It thus prefigures the dried passage zone that will come later in the story when God will temporarily territorialize the Red Sea. In the floating basket Jochebed prepared, Moses would at least momentarily be detached from the grip of a group that the positive law of the time had deemed better dead than alive. The baby is in the position of bare life. Jochebed had no guarantee that her boy would be picked up if a stranger were to find him. But she did have reason to believe that the boy's presence – his face and his body – would have some binding normative force over that stranger.

The crucial encounter occurs when Pharaoh's daughter finds the baby Moses in the river when she goes down to bathe. Some interpreters have identified her as Bitya, a name that literally means that God, not Pharaoh, is her father (*bat-ya*). Other interpreters speculated that she must not have practiced Egyptian paganism. But these suggestions simply aim to bring her closer to the Jewish religion and are absent from the Biblical text. Taking our cue from Freud, we might safely assume she simply does not belong to the Hebrews.[7] This political myth of beginning indeed relies on the action of someone who is not a member of the Hebrew polity, as Freud argues. But unlike in Freud's argument, it turns out not to be Moses. Unlike every other turn in the story – and especially unlike the moment in which the Covenant is concluded – here God is distinctly *absent*. There is no one to rely on except a fellow human being. Let us therefore leave Pharaoh's daughter unnamed.

---

[6] Sigmund Freud, *Volume 13: The Origins of Religion* (London and New York: Pelican Books, 1985), 237–294.

[7] Freud famously argues that Moses was not a member of the tribe that later became known as the Jewish people. He compares Moses to the German poet Adelbert von Chamisso, French by birth; Napoleon Bonaparte, who was of Italian extraction; and to the British writer Benjamin Disraeli, an Italian Jew. Freud, *Volume 13*, 245.

Contrary to the absence of God in this founding myth, other *people* are decidedly present. Pharaoh's daughter is not alone when she decides to pick Moses up: "and when she saw the ark among the flags, she sent her maid to fetch it."[8] She is doubtlessly privileged, and one might imagine this may guard her from harsh punishment for violating Pharaoh's decree. Yet, we are told only a few lines later that members of the ancient Egyptian society inform on one another when they disobey.[9]

Like Jochebed, Pharaoh's daughter is taking a risk, but this is a risk of a different kind. Pharaoh's daughter engages in civil disobedience from within the insider group of citizens. Initially, she simply feels compassion. But she could not have disobeyed if she had not recognized the baby was Hebrew, a fact the Biblical author makes sure we don't miss: "And when she had opened it, she saw the child: and, behold, the babe wept. And she had compassion on him, and said, this is one of the Hebrews' children."[10] Pharaoh's daughter had to choose between two normative commitments. She decided to create an opening in her own social contract. Could she have seen the baby and simply let him drift downstream? Of course, as a *factual* matter she could. The crucial (and only) thing that would entail is the reader's reprimand.

When Pharaoh's daughter decides to disobey, Miryam appears and immediately offers to call a Hebrew nurse to breastfeed her baby brother. This is also prohibited under Pharaoh's law, but Pharaoh's daughter is no longer bound to that and accepts the offer. She ends up relying on help from the persecuted group in adopting Moses as *her own*. To be sure, this is only one particular baby. But the act already seems to imply an alternative rule according to which it is the right of *all* Jewish newborns to live. As Pharaoh knows all too well, allowing the Hebrews to live is also being exposed to their potential claims.

The constitutive moment in which human rights law originates – the moment of political beginning – is not the Covenant at Mount Sinai. It is the moment in which Pharaoh's daughter decides to lift the baby up from the river and adopt him. The entire political tradition stretching back at least to Spinoza may be correct in locating the original source of *rights given by sovereignty* at Mount Sinai. Spinoza aims to reduce the Covenant to a social contract.[11] But the sovereignty of the social contract does not

---

[8] Exodus, 2:5.
[9] Exodus, 2:14.
[10] Exodus, 2:6.
[11] Paul Kahn objects, much more recently, when he writes that "the authority of the legal decision is always located outside of the decision maker. To claim for the self an authority

preclude another aspect of the myth – this earlier event, which another kind of law rests upon. This first moment is distinguishable and independent from the Covenant. Being bound by an imperative that defines who she is, the self takes on both personal responsibility and personal risk. In doing that, a member of the polity chooses to respond to the proto-legal force that the presence of another human being who is not a member of her group imposes upon her.

The Biblical text invokes "compassion" – an emotion that Arendt banishes from politics as absolutely private. When compassion finds its expression in politics, Ardent thought, it becomes the seed of violence.[12] Not far from Arendt's position we find Edward Said. Without referring to Pharaoh's daughter, Said finds that Freud's reading of Moses as "non-European" may be a foundation for cosmopolitan politics – beyond the "palliative" of "compassion."[13] But in the Biblical text, compassion is operative within a particular context, in which it has a destabilizing and at the same time foundational potential.

For such a destabilizing effect to occur, there is need for more than just two parties in the encounter. The encounter with the universal boat-person always assumes and attempts to engage a third party, or a transnational audience. In this story too, Miryam's presence along with Pharaoh's daughter's maids transforms private compassion into a proto-political moment of foundation. Moses is found and saved within a group, which bridges not only class gaps within the Egyptian society. It is a group that crosses boundaries, in the sense that the Hebrew nurse belongs to a persecuted group of non-members. Across both hierarchies of class and nationality, the members of this constituent body are equalized, at least momentarily, through their actions. A group emerges as a primitive precursor for an alternative to the extant regime, in which Hebrews will be able to enforce their rights. The violence that comes later (with the shift to the paradigm of sovereignty) is not yet foreshadowed – although Arendt may have thought that compassion indeed foreshadows it. (Things might still have gone differently.) In any case, the imperative of human rights demands the urgency of a response here and now; it does not defer enforcement indefinitely in the expectation of the advent of an enlightened society. But the way freedom and survival are tied together

---

to make law is blasphemous. . . Apart from the sovereign source of law, everyone stands equally under the legal rules." Paul Kahn, *The Cultural Study of Law* (Chicago: University of Chicago Press, 1999), 47.

[12] Hannah Arendt, *On Revolution* (London: Penguin, 2006), 61–85.

[13] Edward Said, *Freud and the Non-European* (London: Verso, 2004): 54.

Figure 2   The finding of Moses, by Herbert J. Gute, Gouache on paper on board, 1933–1935 *(copy done during excavations at Dura Synagogue, Syria)*

nevertheless invokes a future society in which slaves are integrated as equals.

This public aspect of the daughter's choice is illustrated beautifully in a fresco from the third century, found in a synagog located in a Greek colony in Syria (Figure 2). Egyptian and Jewish women, nobility and slavery, are standing shoulder-to-shoulder; there is no hierarchical ordering between them. A dyadic, asymmetric encounter becomes a community of equals. This new arrangement is irreducible to mutual self-interest, benefit, or "rational choice."

In the context of unauthorized migration, promoting human rights institutionally means making space for judgment that is not reducible to either sentimentalism or rationalism. It is simultaneously a judgment about who I am and a judgment about the society to which I belong. Once a social contract can be opened, the global allocation of risks and protections is potentially changed for the benefit of the noncitizen who is suffering great harm. A human rights remedy outside one's community becomes *complementary* to a positive, constitutional remedy within the bounds of sovereignty. But unlike the complementarity sometimes offered by transnational institutions (for example by placing a stateless person under the authority of UNHCR), the terms of this remedy are not set by a predetermined administrative mandate. For better or worse, they assume a crack in bureaucratic mandates in which something else can appear.

American Churches have long engaged in civil disobedience in the context of unauthorized migration. As one commentator observed, "When Churches and their congregations confer 'sanctuary' they are interposing their bodies and lives between the government and these beleaguered individuals from overseas."[14] The important part of this statement is the emphasis on bodies and not words as the site of political action. But "interposing one's body" to save another does not demand the authorization of a church. This is precisely what Pharaoh's daughter did where there was no common God to speak of. Said's point is indispensable: the story of the Exodus does encapsulate a lesson about an irredeemable debt to people who are not members of one's own polity.

Moses started his life with a claim of survival, or literally, by *becoming* a claim of survival sent out as a message by his mother. Later he became the protagonist of one of the most momentous myths of political freedom. His ascent to this position is not to be understood as one that occurred *despite* his mother's preference for the preservation of life, but *because* of it. Jochebed's actions do not reflect a life of slavery and victimization that is totally reduced to causation. The aspiration for survival is, to the contrary, foundational to a politics of human rights. In that respect, hers is the first step not only toward survival but also toward freedom: toward exodus.

In this context, one might reinterpret the first and perhaps most important piece of evidence that Freud provides to substantiate that Moses was not a Hebrew. "We are told there," Freud observes, "that the Egyptian princess who rescued the infant boy from exposure in the Nile gave him that name, putting forward an etymological reason: 'because I drew him out of the water.'"[15] The word "Moses" (Mosheh) is, according to this argument, an inflection of the Hebrew verb "to draw." Freud responds with a grammatical analysis of the name (relying on a German source):

---

[14] Richard Falk, "Accountability, Asylum, and Sanctuary: Challenging Our Political and Legal Imagination," *Denver Journal of International Law and Policy* 16 (1987–1988): 199.

[15] Freud, *Volume 13*, 244.

> This explanation, however, is clearly inadequate. "The Biblical interpreta-
> tion of the name as 'he who was drawn from the water'", argues a writer in
> the *Jüdisches Lexicon*, is "popular etymology, with which, to begin with, it
> is impossible to harmonize the *active* form of the Hebrew word – for
> '*Mosheh*' can at most only mean 'he who draws out'."

This quip satisfies Freud, for "it is absurd to attribute to an Egyptian
princess a derivation of the name from the Hebrew ..." He quickly
proposes an alternative Egyptian etymology, no longer related to the
act of being drawn out of the water. But perhaps there is more to this
"popular etymology" than Freud's late scientism allows him to see. For
the substitution here from the passive moment of being pulled out of the
water to the arch-political modality of being "he who draws out" is
a critical aspect of the story. It encapsulates in a name the entire relationship between survival and freedom that Moses' figure comes to signify.
The infant has (the potential of) agency. The verb is inflected so as to lead
us from survival to freedom, implying that they have a common origin.
One of the most striking twentieth-century parallels of Moses' figure is
the poignant boy in the picture of "Boat Children's Lifestyle," at the end
of Chapter 2: *"Bui Quang Dung, four year old freedom fighter!
Liberation day, April 30, 1975 'freed' one arm ..."* For this boy and for
the Biblical Moses, activity and passivity are literally indistinguishable.

Two myths of political beginning animate "Western" political
thought.[16] One is the myth of the violent beginning, according to which
new political order arises out of original sin or rupture: "Romulus slew
Remus, Cain slew Abel."[17] According to this idea, law and politics are
founded upon violence. The other is the myth of the social contract, in
which politics begins from public deliberation and mutual promises.
The myth of violent beginning leads to an understanding of law as
a command backed by the threat of punishment. The myth of the social
contract leads to a democratic tradition, in which formally equal members
give themselves the law.

But these traditions are two aspects of one and the same conception of
law. The law *you and your community* give yourselves is, *for me*,
a command backed by brute force. This book set out to propose
a different idea of the most basic and fundamental law. Human rights
law emerges as global *grundnorm*. Unlike the myth of violent beginning,
political community was not imagined as a relationship between master

---

[16] Arendt, *On Revolution*.
[17] Arendt, *On Revolution*, 10.

and servant, or perpetrator and victim. Unlike the myth of social con-tract, it wasn't imagined in terms of the meeting of the minds of equals. Human rights begin in asymmetric encounter between a powerful party and a disempowered party, in which the terms of the relationship have not yet been determined.

INDEX

Printed in Great Britain
by Amazon

17065234R00153